THE PRESOCRATICS

THE
PRESOCRATICS

EDITED BY

Philip Wheelwright

Macmillan Publishing Company
New York
Collier Macmillan Publishers
London

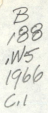

Copyright © 1966 by the Macmillan Publishing Company,
a division of Macmillan, Inc.
Printed in the United States of America
All rights reserved. No part of this book shall be reproduced or transmitted in any form or by any means, electronic or mechanical, including
photocopying, recording, or by any information or retrieval system, without written permission from the Publisher:

Macmillan Publishing Company
866 Third Avenue
New York, New York, 10022
Collier Macmillan Canada, Inc.

First Edition
Eighteenth Printing — 1988

Library of Congress Catalog Card Number: 66-12944
ISBN 0-02-426640-X

FOR TOBIN

(eventually)

PREFACE

THE PRESENT VOLUME offers in English translation a critically full collection of quotations from, and ancient testimonies about, early Greek philosophical writings, principally of the sixth and fifth centuries B.C. It is customary to speak of the philosophers of that period as "Presocratics," although in fact four of them—Democritus the atomist, Philolaus the Pythagorean, Gorgias the Sophist, and Hippocrates the physician—were roughly contemporary with Socrates. By "critically full" is meant that the editor's judgment has been exercised in attempting to include all such Fragments and Testimonia as are at once adequately authenticated and capable of throwing light on the doctrines in question.

The usual groups of philosophers contained in such a study are here supplemented by certain passages, chosen for their philosophical import, from Greek religious and medical writings, in the first and last chapters respectively. In addition to their lively intrinsic interest such materials are likely to be valuable in offering suggestive points of comparison with the more explicitly philosophical doctrines, particularly of Empedocles, the Pythagoreans, and (beyond the scope of the present volume) Plato.

My thanks for critical and corrective assistance in one way or another is offered particularly to Dr. Edward F. Little, who has put his historical scholarship at my disposal in our many discussions of what the various doctrines mean and imply; to the students in my graduate seminar on the Presocratics during the fall term of 1964-1965 at U.C.R.; and to my wife for her proof-reading and stylistic criticisms.

A very special debt of gratitude goes to Atheneum Publishers, New York, for allowing me to use the copyrighted arrangement and (with a few modifications) the translations of the Fragments published in the paperback edition of my *Heraclitus* (listed by them as No. 60 in the Atheneum series). Readers wanting fuller interpretation and discussion of those Fragments are referred to the Atheneum volume.

And now, as Parmenides wisely counsels in his third Fragment, let us "gaze steadfastly at things which, though far away, are yet present to the mind."

PHILIP WHEELWRIGHT

University of California, Riverside

CONTENTS

THE PRESOCRATICS

Introduction

THE EARLY PHILOSOPHERS of Greece, whose writings have survived
only in the form of fragments, which later Greek writers fortu-
nately considered worth quoting, are of unique value for anyone
interested in the intellectual history of mankind. The period of
less than two hundred years between Thales and Democritus
shows a development in the art of philosophical inquiry that is
quite unparalleled in world history. Nowhere else, not even in ancient India, is there shown so striking a combination of conceptual
imagination, attempted linguistic precision, and concern for intellectual consistency. Although the dialogues of Plato and the
vast intellectual explorations of Aristotle speak more comprehensively and pursue lines of thought more adequately, neither of
those achievements would have been possible without the two centuries of analysis and speculation that had gone before.

Philosophical thought is stirred to activity in the main by either
or both of two great human motives: the religious and the scientific. Man wants to feel at home in the universe; he also wants
to know what's what. Responsiveness on the one hand, observation and analysis on the other, give him respectively his goals and
his critical objectivity. Throughout man's intellectual history both
motives have been active, sometimes in happy equilibrium, sometimes with the one or the other predominating. In the earliest
period of Greek thought their interplay was various and mutually
profitable.

1

i. The Religious Factor

Religious thought, then as now and always, draws its meaning from man's sense of, or wonder about, the divine and his own relation to it. By the divine is meant that which, being greater and more excellent than man, enjoins upon him, as he comes to a recognition of it, the need to take stock of his own shortcomings and to enter into a new mode of being, wherein those shortcomings are somehow resolved or transcended. For worship is not a passive emotional state, but is a willing acquiescence in and self-commitment to what may be demanded or required by That which is worshipped. But the nature of the religious object, of its demands, and of the appropriate forms of response to it or them, differs widely in various ages, societies, and cults.

Man in his search for the divine tends to reach out imaginatively in one or more of three general directions—the upward, the downward, and the inward. That is to say, the divine (whether singular or plural) may be envisaged as residing primarily up above, in or beyond the sky; or as down here on earth and beneath the earth, especially manifesting itself in the creative forces of natural growth and reproduction; or as that which is to be sought not outside but in the purified mind and heart of the worshipper. The upward mode may be called the *ouranian* (from the Greek word *ouranos,* sky); the downward may be called the *chthonic* (from *chthôn,* earth). The third religious mode, the religion of inwardness, cannot rely upon such outward metaphors. Perhaps it may tentatively be described as *mystical,* provided we avoid the confused sentimentality which too often degrades that word, and employ it in the precise sense of the Hindu doctrine, *"Atman is Brahman"*—i.e., that the true inner self is ultimately identical with essential and selfless reality. In most religious cults and cultures it will be found that some two of these religious modes, and occasionally all three, get variously combined and interrelated. The Judaeo-Christian tradition in its more primitive stages, particularly in the Old Testament, was predominantly ouranian, worshipping a single god associated with the sky or the region above the sky; the ouranian influence remains strong in much of the New Testament also, although in certain of the letters of Paul the doctrine of the dying and arisen Christ as an event that is repeated in the soul of each reborn Christian is a mystical doctrine in the sense just defined; but while subsequent Christian thought shows much intermingling of the first and third modes of religious reference, Christianity has always rejected the second mode, doctrinally, although sometimes employing imagery derived from it.[1] The ancient Greeks, on the other hand, accepted all three modes, in various and changing combinations. It will be useful then, in approaching Greek philosophy, to take note of the main implications of each mode, considered by itself, for philosophical and ethical thought.

In ouranian religion man's natural and proper state involves subordination to a higher power or powers—higher at least in the sense of being "up there," and also in the metaphorical sense of being superior to man in power and knowledge. Man's typical form of wrongdoing from this point of view is *transgression*—i.e., overstepping, in some metaphorical way or other, the boundary between the human estate and the divine. Any endeavor to obtain or attain too much, or even the taking of too much for granted, is here tantamount to an act of *hybris* (arrogance, presumption) and of "overstepping the mark." [2] The likely result of such violation is *nemesis* (divine retribution) in one form or another. Human virtue as conceived in ouranian terms consists of one or both of two things: obedience (in those occasional situations where a divine command has been issued) but more generally, and for the ancient Greeks more characteristically, *moderation,* acceptance of one's human lot, and observance of the traditional maxim "Nothing too much."

But while man's eyes and mind may be turned toward the sky, his feet remain (or did in those days) upon the earth. His sustenance comes, directly or indirectly, from the earth, and it is to the dust of the earth that he will at length return. Man in chthonic perspective is a *zoön,* a living organism among other living organisms, and must share in the natural cycle of birth, growth, procreation, decay, and death. In that biologically conceived cycle a certain dominant value tends naturally to emerge—not life as against death, for the interplay of life and death is an inevitable routine of nature, but rather *health* as against sickness. From the pure biocentric standpoint it is health that is the primal good, sickness (including blight, famine, and related conditions) the primal evil. By metaphoric extension the chthonic idea develops a standard of values for the general human situation, conceiving the good of the community, as well as of the individual psyche, in terms of harmony, adjustment (*harmonia*), and spiritual health. It is no accident that Apollo was a god at once of medicine and of music. Consequently, human wrongdoing is that which destroys the natural harmony—as when the blood of a murdered man is spilled upon the ground. Such a crime as conceived from this standpoint is pollution; and when a murder is committed the blood of the victim as it seeps into the ground was regarded by the Greeks as a poison which would produce blight in the land and sickness among its inhabitants, as surely as an actual poison produces its deadly effects when injected into a human body.[3] Ritual cleansing and purification (*katharsis*) were the enjoined remedy; and even after men had lost their literal belief in the causal efficacy of such rites the idea of self-purification lingered on in their mental imagery and their linguistic symbols, even as we find it doing so today.

Now as a man's religion becomes more individual and reflective his thinking tends to dispense with the obvious metaphors of sky and earth, and to employ the subtler metaphor of inwardness, together with such associated images as the perfect circle with its central still point and its perpetual union of beginning and end. The ultimate metaphor which the way of inwardness takes as representing the final goal of its quest is that of the One—a metaphysical unity from which (so the usual doctrine goes) man by his self-will and craving for individuation has broken off, with the result that he must suffer a pervading sense of alienation and futility, against which the only remedy is self-subordination of one's private ego and assimilation to the impersonality of the All. Here the remedy for man's *hamartia* (fundamental wrongdoing) is neither forgiveness (as in ouranian perspective) nor return to health (as in chthonic) but full mystical reunion, complete transcendence of individual selfhood and of all particularity.

These three fundamental aspects of religious thought enter into early Greek philosophy in a rich variety of disguises and interrelationships. The Greek ethical stress upon temperance and the golden mean, for example, draws upon the first and second aspects together, for in the full meaning of temperance it involves both a prohibition against overstepping the boundary (an ouranian conception) and a respect for the organic balance and equilibrium that constitute health (chthonic). Again, in the sole surviving fragment of Anaximander there is the notion of things having to "do penance" for their injustice in maintaining for a while their distinctive thinghood—a thought-provoking combination of the first and third perspectives. And the metaphysical monism of Parmenides may be taken as an abstractly intellectual extension of the third mode. Other cases of such influence, singly or in combination, may suggest themselves as the utterances and doctrines of the Presocratic philosophers are reflected upon.

ii. The Scientific Factor

Man's interest in science is partly practical, partly conceptual and theoretical. What gives early Greek scientific thinking its peculiar character and high human value is the balanced and effective way in which these two complementary aspects are present in and contribute to the scientific enterprise. The point may be illustrated by a brief scrutiny of three typical areas of scientific interest during Presocratic times: terrestrial measurement, astronomy, and the analysis of physical matter.

Terrestrial measurement. As early man settled down to an agricultural way of living and developed his relationship with the land, with the result that serious attention had to be given to geographic boundaries and property divisions, he found himself impelled by the need to devise means of measurement. In order to measure there must be an established and relatively stable unit. For small household purposes the outer joint of the thumb offered such a unit; but for the larger needs of land measurement more workable units were found in the length of a man's foot and the length of his stride. Such units were not strictly unvarying, of course; but at first they were doubtless close enough for ordinary purposes, and in time a community might find it advantageous to standardize the foot-length and stride-length by setting up publicly an ideal foot-length and stride-length to be used as norms. Thereby from the thumb-joint, the foot, and the stride there eventually came to be the standardized lengths of the inch, the foot, and the yard.[4] The art of measuring, then, in its simplest form requires the acceptance of a standard unit; it requires also a technique of superimposing that unit repeatedly, without breaks or overlappings, upon the surface to be measured; and it requires a system of counting.

But the art of measurement in that simple sense is applicable only to things present, like the land that can be traversed on foot from boundary to boundary. What was early man to do in order to measure distances that could not be traversed—as when Thales was concerned to measure the height of pyramids and the distance of ships at sea? Thales solved the former problem, according to Diogenes Laertius (T 9 under "Thales"), by the simple expedient of waiting until that moment when a man's shadow was equal to his height and then quickly measuring the shadow of the pyramid. Diogenes reports the story as he had read it, and it may well be true that Thales made his first measurement in the manner described. It seems probable however, from the other evidences of his scientific imagination and ingenuity, that Thales would not have overlooked the question of how to employ the shadow method of measurement without waiting for a particular hour. It presumably would have occurred to his agile mind that when a man's shadow is just half or two-thirds of his height the pyramid's shadow will likewise be half or two-thirds of the pyramid's height. The concept of proportions, which was to become of fundamental importance for Pythagorean and subsequently for Euclidean mathematics, presumably took its rise out of problems of this type. In devising a means of measuring the distance of a ship at sea Thales' procedure was to construct a tower by the seaside and note the angle of deflection of the line of vision from the tower's top to the ship; the same angle of deflection could then be turned in the direction of level land, and the point at which it touched the land was concluded to be the same distance from the foot of the tower as the ship was. In reaching this conclusion Thales necessarily made use, perhaps implicitly, of the theorem that if two right-angled triangles are identical with respect to one side and its adjacent acute angle they are identical throughout.[5]

In Egypt, where the sense of geometrical design was strong, and where the river Nile annually overflowed its banks and washed away boundary lines, there had developed (no one knows how long ago) a practical way of erecting perpendiculars. The method was to join by knots three long ropes whose lengths were in the ratio 3, 4, 5: when the ropes were stretched out straight the result was a right-angled rope-triangle in which the two smaller lengths were perpendicular to each other. The story is that Pythagoras, having learnt about the rope-triangle during his visit to Egypt as a young man, began to speculate upon the general problem of the relation of lengths in any right-angled triangle, thus eventually giving birth to the so-called Pythagorean Theorem. However, while the practical ingenuity of Egyptian rope-measurers made a partial contribution to the Pythagorean Theorem, a purely intellectual discovery by Thales made another. For it was Thales, according to ancient testimony, who had discovered the geometrical truth that if the diagonal of a square is made the side of a second square, the second square will have twice the area of that of the first square.[6] Clearly Thales' theorem is a limited version of the later Pythagorean theorem, applying not to all right triangles but only to right triangles whose two perpendicular sides (the sides of the original square) are equal. Thus it appears that both practical and theoretical, both empirical and rational factors, contributed to Pythagoras' eventual discovery and proof of the theorem that bears his name.

Astronomy. The Greek word for astronomy was *astrologia,* "the science of the stars"; but except for some minor tendencies in Pythagoreanism there was virtually no astrology (as the word is now understood) in the philosophies here represented. The Greek word which is translated "stars" referred not only to the fixed stars but to the sun, moon, and known planets also; so perhaps "orb" is a more accurate English word, since all the bodies in question moved along some orbit or other. Various speculations about the nature and movements of those orbs and their relation to the vault along which they move will be found in the following pages. What mainly concerns us, however, is not cosmological opinions in themselves, but such discoveries and speculations as were significant for early philosophical thought.

One of the greatest innovations in ancient theoretical astronomy—as important in relation to its time as the later innovations of Copernicus and Einstein, which presupposed it, were to theirs— was the shift from the idea of a flat earth and an absolute up-down relation, to the idea of an earth situated at the center of a spherical universe. Later theories, from Philolaus onwards, which denied or questioned the earth's central position, would not have been possible except for the prior theory that the universe revolves about the earth as its center. The maker of that vast discovery was Thales' most original disciple, Anaximander. Nor was the difference confined to the question of cosmic shape; it involved a problem of causation as well—in essence a problem of what we now think of as gravitation. Thales, thinking still in terms of an up-down universe, was in the position of having to inquire what held the earth up, what kept it from falling, and he answered with his theory that the earth floats on water. But Anaximander, discarding the idea of an absolute up-down and hence the idea of a one-directional gravitation, propounded the revolutionary theory that the earth is poised at the center of the universe, held in place by the fact that the universe extends equally on all sides of it—that is to say, keeping its place because there is nothing to pull it in one direction rather than in another.[7] What has occurred here is no mere exchange of one theory for another, but a triumph of scientific and philosophical imagination in adopting an entirely new cosmological perspective. Thales, for all his brilliant discoveries and speculations, still thought in terms of a primitive cosmology—a nearly flat earth with the vaulting sky above and limitless water below. His notion of gravitation was accordingly limited to that which a child can discover for himself—viz., that things require a support or else they'll drop. Anaximander, in offering the novel idea that the earth, being in equipoise, needs no support, was taking the earliest known step toward a more sophisticated and more adequate idea of gravitation. But long after the spherical conception became well established the older way of thinking continued to influence men's habits of imagining and speaking. Thus when subsequent Greek philosophers spoke of the Way Up and the Way Down, intending the epithets at once descriptively and symbolically, it is clear that their inherited idea of up-down must have originated in a Thalean kind of universe. Overt cosmological doctrines were, then as now, often combined with habits of thought and idiom drawn from another source.

Analysis of physical matter. But man wants to know the character of the world around him in more specific terms than can be supplied by geometry and astronomy. He sees changes of various kinds going on, and to the curious observer the double question will insistently present itself: (1) "What is it, really?" and (2) "What makes it behave as it does?" This is the double question of the *what* and the *why.* Both questions have such a familiar look to a present-day reader that an effort may be required in order to realize the subtly different sense in which the questions of *what* and *why* were understood in Presocratic times.

The general ontological question of "What?" is never a pure question: it rests upon certain assumptions as to the kinds of answer that are possible or acceptable; and since the assumptions take different forms in different ages and different climates of opinion, the precise meaning of a question will vary accordingly. A question takes its rise within some human frame of reference, in which there is a natural expectation of certain alternative answers, or at any rate of certain general kinds of answer. Suppose that someone today, theorizing about the essential nature of things, were to propose the view that everything is ultimately electricity, or nuclear energy, or something of that sort: a listener, even if he were to reject the answer as too narrow, or even to dismiss the query as futile, would still regard the answer as making a kind of sense; but if the theorizer were to propose the answer that everything is ultimately water, or air, or an interplay of qualities like bright, dark, moist, dry, etc., he would generally be dismissed either as a fool or as a poet playing with fancies. An ancient Greek, on the other hand, had quite different explanatory expectations, and two of the principal sets of such expectations gave a distinctive character to his ontological queries and doctrines. For he tended to think, to a greater or lesser degree, in terms of opposing qualities and also in terms of the supposed four generic substances.

The meaning of qualitative opposites as a basic mode of thought can be illustrated by the following considerations. We today readily speak of "turning off the light," but to speak of "turning off the darkness" would sound very odd indeed; most of us would regard the former expression as literally descriptive, the latter as descriptive only by indirection, or perhaps as descriptive of subjective experience rather than of what was actually going on. To the Greek mind, on the other hand, light and darkness were both of them real states of being, opposed on equal terms. The same was true of the other main pairs of opposites: together with bright-dark there were dry-moist, rare-dense, and hot-cold— at least these were the pairs most widely emphasized. Instead of regarding cold as the mere absence of heat (in the manner of most of us) the ancient Greek took it to be equally true, as a child might, that heat is the absence of cold. Since both opposites of a pair are real and yet drive each other out, it was natural to regard them as mutually inimical—as engaged in a constant war for mastery, with the victory held temporarily now by the one, now by the other. Consequently to the Greeks, in a manner not possible to us, the question became acute as to how the change, or apparent change, from opposite to opposite was to be conceived as taking place.

The other main ontological presupposition of the early Greek thinkers was the assumption[8] of the four generic elements: earth, water, air, and fire. Each of the four bears a double reference:

it is at once concrete and abstract. Earth is at once the ground we walk on and the state of solidity in general; water is both what we drink and general liquidity; air is both what we breathe and more generally anything in a vaporous or gaseous state; fire is on the one hand what burns and illuminates while at the same time it represents universal change in its radical form of coming-to-be and perishing. The transformation from earth to water to air to fire constituted "the upward way" in the universe; the reverse process was "the downward way." The upward process (called *anathymiasis*) cannot be designated by any single English word; for today we regard as three distinct kinds of process what the Greeks regarded as phases of a single process—melting (earth to water), evaporating (water to air), and igniting (air to fire). The downward process consists of the three contrary transformations in reverse continuity—self-extinguishing (fire to air, but without the negative connotation of the English word), liquefying (air to water), and hardening or in some cases freezing (water to earth). A number of otherwise obscure passages in the following pages will become clearer if this set of concepts is understood.

Such, then, are three of the main ways in which the scientific motive worked in interrelation with the philosophical in early Greek thought. There were others too, and some of them will become evident in the following chapters—notably, musical harmonics (Chap. 7) and medicine (Chap. 9). Agriculture (the religious aspects of which were indicated in Section i above and will be somewhat in evidence in Chap. 1, Sec. ii) became eventually relevant to philosophy on the scientific side also, by providing models for the concepts of birth (coming-to-be), growth, maturity, decay, and death (ceasing-to-be); but the explicit utilization of those biological models did not take place to an appreciable extent until Aristotle built upon them, and hence they fall outside the scope of the present book.

iii. Phases of Presocratic Philosophy

Since Hegel it has been customary in histories of ancient philosophy to conceive the course of early Greek metaphysics as falling into four main stages, represented by the Milesians (Chap. 2), Heraclitus (Chap. 3), the Eleatics (Chap. 4), and the pluralistic naturalists (Chaps. 5, 6). There is, to be sure, a fairly plain logical development in this arrangement, so far as it goes. We can employ it profitably for the materials of Chapters 2 through 6, but not without a critical awareness of two limitations. For in the first place the classification applies not to the ethical but only to the metaphysical side of Presocratic philosophy, having primary reference to three fundamental and interrelated questions: the *ontological*, What is basically most real and why; the *cosmological*, How and in what sense, and perhaps by what agency, can change occur; and the *epistemological*, How can we validate our knowledge of anything. In the second place, even within these limits, the traditional structure ignores, as every structure must do, the rich variety of interests, inquiries, and opinions, and the individual tone which mark each philosopher when he is studied and responded to without insisting upon the structure. With these two qualifications the main direction of Presocratic metaphysical thought may be said to fall into the following fourfold schema.

(1) The three philosophers of Miletus (Thales, Anaximander, Anaximenes) sought a principle by which the nature of the world could be explained, and gradually they became more and more conscious of the question of *becoming*—of how the initial substance, whether water or air or an unlimited reservoir of potential qualities, could transform itself into existing things and qualities so numerous and various.

(2) Heraclitus carried the idea of becoming to the ultimate extreme, denying the existence of any unchanging substance, and declaring that everything without exception is subject to change—faster or slower, but in any case unremitting and inevitable.

(3) Parmenides (followed by Zeno and Melissus, the other principal members of the Eleatic school) opposed the doctrine of universal flux by going to the opposite extreme and dismissing all change as necessarily unreal and illusory, holding it to be rationally inconceivable that what was not should begin to be or that what was should cease to be. What truly is, he argued, must be what it is independently of time; hence only Being can exist and all becoming is illusory. The other two Eleatics differ from Parmenides only in approach and details.

(4) The metaphysical reconstructionists who followed Parmenides are Empedocles, Anaxagoras, and the atomists Leucippus and Democritus. Despite the large differences among them they share the same general attempt to reconcile Parmenides' principle, that reality must be one and changeless, with the obvious fact of plurality and ongoing change. This they do by postulating a plurality of unchanging basic entities, and hence explaining the changes that we see going on around us as changed relations among those primal entities.

Independent of the schema, and not assimilable to it without gross distortion, are the philosophical views and approaches represented by Chapters 1 (early Greek religious thought), 7 (Pythagoreanism), 8 (the Sophistic revolt against metaphysics), and 9 (medical philosophy). These four nonconformist types of philosophical expression raise somewhat different questions, establishing different perspectives of inquiry, from those represented by the central group. All such perspectives find a place, in one way or another, amid the wide-ranging inquiries and discussions of Plato's Dialogues, a study of which is the natural sequent of a study of the Presocratics.

iv. Problems of Translation

Where general ideas are in question accuracy of translation is always somewhat problematic. We cannot verify philosophical identities by pointing; therefore context and syntax take on added importance. The accepted ways of grouping semantic ingredients in Greek and in English are often different enough to make a Greek word appear, from an English-speaking standpoint, ambiguous. Thus the Greek *archê* wavers between the meanings "source" and "principle"; in a majority of cases the chosen translation is therefore "first-principle." The word *genesis* means "becoming" in the sense that carries a predicate ("the water becomes cool"); it also means absolute "coming-to-be," as when something begins to exist that did not formerly exist—a new-born baby, or a flame, or a sound of music. Throughout the persistent and varied tendency in Greek philosophy to distinguish between "is" and "becomes," one of an interpreter's difficulties is being unsure how far the two meanings of the latter word and its cognates are mingled and confused on a given occasion of its use. Again, the word *apeiron* is here sometimes translated "unlimited," particularly when it carries the secondary meaning "indefinite"; sometimes "infinite." The latter translation is reserved for passages, especially those as late as Zeno, where a more definite idea of infinite series appears to have been attained.

Sometimes an ambiguity takes the form of uncertainty as to how far a word and its normally attendant idea are to be taken literally, how far metaphorically. That "coalescence between concrete and abstract" which in the Atheneum *Heraclitus* (especially pp. 15-16) is discussed with reference to Heraclitus' central image-idea of fire, can be illustrated by the other three main elements also. How far Thales, for example, in speaking about water really meant water itself, how far liquids generally, and how far the vital cause of growth, cannot be precisely determined.

v. References and Abbreviations

In general the ancient materials are divided into Fragments and Testimonia. The former are direct quotations from the philospher under consideraton, the latter are ancient descriptions of and statements about the philosopher and his doctrine. An explanation of the documentary means by which the surviving Fragments and Testimonia have been preserved is offered in the Notes.

A Fragment is introduced by number only, a Testimonium by its number preceded by "T." References to them employ the designations "Fr." and "T" respectively. The parenthetical numbers which follow most of the Fragments represent the order of Fragments in Hermann Diels, *Fragmente der Vorsokratiker,* as revised by Walter Kranz.[9] The designation elsewhere for this standard collection of ancient philosophical texts is "DK". In each of its chapters the Fragments are located in the "B" section, the Testimonia in the "A" section; our references to DK will be to the "B" section unless specified otherwise. The source of any Fragment not followed by a DK number is given in the Notes.

Since abstract Greek words and the most nearly equivalent English words are never identical in meaning, and sometimes allow of quite different variations of meaning, it is occasionally needful for clarity's sake to supply the transliterated Greek word in parentheses after its English translation. In the transliteration of Greek words a circumflex accent is employed over "e" or "o" to distinguish the long vowels *êta* and *ômega* from the short vowels *epsilon* and *omikron.* Such transliterated words are collected in the Glossary at the end of the book, where each is followed by its spelling in Greek characters and by a definition or explanation of its meaning.

1

Early Religious Thought

IN SEEKING THE ROOTS of ancient Greek philosophy, as well as in interpreting many of its more mature manifestations, it is wise to begin with some understanding of those modes of thought and feeling which may be comprehensively, if somewhat vaguely, covered by the word religion. In an age such as ours, when to so many people the serious business of life is taken to be technological and secular, it is easy to misunderstand the role that religion formerly played, not only in the guidance of life (in which its success has always been far from complete) but also in the shaping of human thought and language even in fields which are not explicitly religious.

Even when we undertake to examine ancient religious phenomena as fairly and candidly as possible, we are likely to find our contemporary thought limited, and our judgment blunted, by an unconscious acceptance of certain religious presuppositions which permeate the thinking of those in a reputedly Christian society. Two thousand years of Christian thought and controversy have conditioned most of us to framing religious questions in prescribed terms; with the usual result that a certain pair of answers is seen as representing the reasonable alternatives, one of them to be accepted and the other to be rejected, while other possible answers are ignored or dismissed as idle fancies. This subtle and largely unconscious fallacy of the Stock Dilemma tends to show itself in virtually all branches of human thought; but our present focus of concern is upon the kind of thought that is distinctively religious—that is, the kind which is directed toward what transcends the human state, at once in quality of being, in power, and in moral authority.

Two examples of the Stock Dilemma are particularly important to recognize for anyone reared in the traditions of Christendom who would examine non-Christian religious phenomena thoughtfully and fairly. There is the problem of God, and there is the problem of survival after death. Within the framework of contemporary Christendom the familiar question "Does God exist?" is normally taken to offer the two alternatives: either say yes to the Christian conception of God which (regardless of minor variations) makes him single, omnipotent, omniscient, and utterly good, or else reject any belief in transcendent divinity altogether. (By "transcendent divinity" is meant divine nature, in some form or other, which has real and effective existence of its own, independently of human imagination and conception.) In the current climate of opinion it appears to make sense to say, "Yes, I believe in God" (with the implication of the four characteristics just mentioned), and it appears to make sense to say, "No, I disbelieve in, or I doubt, the existence of any kind of independently existing divinity." But when, rarely, some independent thinker dares to say, "I believe in a God who has good intentions but is limited in power" (John Stuart Mill, Renouvier, William James), or "I believe in a God who is limited in intelligence and not very competent to handle the problems of the universe," or "I believe in a God who enjoys human suffering and whose purposes are evil," or "I believe in a plurality of gods who work at cross-purposes to one another,"—anyone who were to think in such terms would probably be dismissed by most contemporaries, regardless of whether religious or secular at heart, as either an intellectual trifler or, by some, as psychically unbalanced.

Yet if we are to enter into the wider and more flexible intellectual horizons of the ancient world, we need to stretch our minds in order to reckon fairly with such heterodox possibilities.

The operation of a dilemmatic stereotype can be seen again with reference to immortality. "Is man immortal or not?" means, to such contemporaries as may pause to consider the question, "Will my personal existence somehow continue forever, or will it cease to exist at the time of that event which we call death?" But clearly the alternatives are not exhaustive, for there is also the logically intermediate alternative of survival after death for a limited time, and also in any of a variety of ways having nothing to do with moral deserts. Here, as in the former example, a habitual way of asking a question tends to blind us to possibilities which in many an earlier civilization were faced, explored, and sometimes feared, but which now are usually tossed outside the area of serious consideration.

The first thing to be aware of in attempting to understand ancient Greek religion, as indeed almost any religion outside the Judaeo-Christian area of influence, is the complementing importance of sky-religion and earth-religion, or, as they are commonly termed when referring to ancient Greece, Olympian or ouranian religion, and chthonic religion. Man's early expressions of religious concern—compounded of gratitude, wonder, fear, and hope, were naturally directed toward the two great obvious sources of bounty and bane—the light-giving, rain-giving sky and the food-giving earth. The interplay of these two directions of religious interest, and of their two associated modes of religious awareness, shows itself not only in the early stages of religion but also as contributing to the subsequent development of its more spiritual and more reflective forms.

The role of Olympian-ouranian religion in Greece has tended to be overemphasized in later Western literary and legendary tradition, thanks to the unequalled prestige of Homer. The Homeric gods are sky gods. In earlier times, it appears, they had lived on sacred Mount Olympus; later they dwelt in the more spacious but more vaguely located regions of the bright sky. Zeus, "father of gods and men," was their head; his name carries connotations of light, the upward skyey regions, and he was accepted as enjoying the possession of both powers and delights that far surpassed what was allotted to man. The Olympian-ouranian religion in general is an affair of bright space and clear boundaries. Homer recounts the legend that when Zeus, Poseidon, and Dis drew lots for shares of the universe, Zeus won the sky, Poseidon the sea, and Dis the underworld; whereupon they all swore by the River Styx (the most powerful and dreadful of oaths) to keep to the domain which chance had allotted and "not overstep the boundary." While it would be unwise to oversimplify so complicated a phenomenon as Greek religion, it can be suggested very tentatively that the Olympian mode of thought in religion had counterparts in the emphasis which the Greeks gave to such spatial ways of thinking as geometry, land-surveying, architecture, and the first steps of physical science. The Olympian influence shows itself, too, in Greek ethics—in the dominant emphasis that is put on moderation and the golden mean, which appears to have conceptual affinities with the primitive mythic command against overstepping territorial boundaries.

But it is impossible to understand Greek religious thought by reference to ouranian manifestations alone; for the chthonic was at least equally important. Man is as dependent upon the benefits of earth as upon those of sun and rain; the latter would be useless unless the earth were there to receive them. As Zeus or Sky tends naturally to be regarded in terms of fatherhood, so Earth is naturally the mother, for it is out of her broad womb that trees and vegetables, and hence indirectly beasts and men, have been born and are sustained. Mother Earth is compassionate, too, for she takes us back to her bosom again when we die. From the fact that corpses are buried in an earthy grave it was natural to think of the human self, the soul (*psychê*), of a dying man as journeying downward to a "hidden place" (*haidês*) below the earth's surface where, in one manner or another, departed spirits were believed to congregate.

As distinguished from ouranian religion which is so eminently spatial in its character and effects, chthonic religion is essentially a time religion. It is temporal not in the way of clocks and chronometers, for these are artificial products of human technology, but in the way of the major cosmic rhythms—night-day, death-life, and the procession of the seasons—which nature herself prescribes. A distinctive kind of ethics grows out of this way of regarding the world, an ethics drawn from the character of the rhythmic life-death sequence itself. What, from the standpoint of organic nature and without reference to any alien standard of judgment, is the criterion of good and ill? From the standpoint of naturalistic biology it is not true to say that death represents the evil side of things, because death, no less than life, is an inseparable part of the ongoing life-death rhythm. But it does appear to make sense chthonically to distinguish between a healthy, vigorous specimen of the birth-growth-death pattern and a specimen that is weak and sickly. Thus it is that health and disease tend to be, in biological perspective, the pair of contraries most essential in defining positive and negative values. Death is but an intermittent negative; its occurrence is periodic, and it carries the implicit assurance of new life potentially succeeding it. The normal cycle of life and death is a healthy cycle, and the purpose of the major seasonal festivals has traditionally been to celebrate joyfully the turning of the wheel of great creative nature.

From this basic chthonic valuation an important corollary follows. For what is health? All the known schools of Greek medicine were in agreement upon one basic truth in answering the question—that health is a right proportion of parts and functions in an organism, and that disease is an opposed disproportion. How then, it was naturally asked, can the disproportion be overcome and the right proportion restored? By a simple logic which appealed at a popular level to the Greek love of clarity the implicit argument ran: Disproportion means too much of something and too little of something else; it would seem therefore that disproportion in an organic body could be corrected by removing what is superfluous and thereby allowing the elements that remain to unite in (as Empedocles put it) health-giving love. From the viewpoint of medical science, of course, the logic is too simple to fit the facts; for in practice it is not usually true that good proportions can be reestablished in an organism by a simple act of removing superfluities. Nevertheless the idea of *katharsis* (purification as the washing away of unnatural and injurious superfluities), whatever its drawbacks and uncertainties in relation to effective medical practice, became in its metaphoric extensions a powerful and indeed an archetypal idea in the formation of religious imagery and myth.

In its religious and mythopoeic extensions the idea of katharsis took various symbolic forms, as Fragments 12 through 16 in Section ii will illustrate. The Chorus in Fr. 13 makes it amply clear that the reference is not to blood in its merely physical nature, but to blood that is spilt in an act of murder. Blood from a cut finger would not have any such dire effects. No, the blood to be abhorred is the blood of a murdered victim; and it is a tenet of chthonic thinking in its moral aspect that when such blood is spilt it infects and pollutes the ground, so that plants sicken and die, and animals are without healthful food. It is here that a symbolic act of katharsis is called for—not as a washing away of physical blood or any other physical superfluity, but as a symbolic and penitential removal of something that is morally evil.

The penitential character of katharsis, which thus involves ritualistic and spiritual absolution, becomes further developed, particularly in the Orphic tradition of ancient Greece, into a notion of the washing away of sin generally, the washing away of one's personal and tribal past or of some repugnant aspect of it. The higher forms of mystery religion, such as the Eleusinian cult, conceived of cult-initiation in this manner. The initiate renounced with proper ceremonies his old life and solemnly received admission into the inner active membership of the cult. And such initiation involves a further result of deepest importance. For as the religious initiate sheds the husk of his former life and enters fullheartedly into a shared life of the cult, he acquires not only a new *pathos* but a new *gnosis* as well: which is to say, he steps not only from a state of being which is evil and unhappy into one that is blessed and pure; he steps also, according to metachthonic doctrine, from the darkness of ignorance and confusion into the light of true and divinely revealed wisdom. The higher rites of religious initiation all involve in some way the assumption of a new gnosis opened up to the initiate by his conversion.

Spiritual religion, as distinguished from magical practices, from spasmodic emotions, and from merely habitual and perfunctory attitudes, involves essentially a conversion and self-purification in which one's own volition and self-commitment are genuine participants. In religious history such spirituality has been associated with ouranian and chthonic modes of worship alike. Nevertheless spiritual acts, although they may develop an autonomy of their own, can be understood and communicated only with some help from the imagination. As the forms of religious thought and expression develop it is interesting to observe the ways in which ouranian and chthonic tendencies have each contributed to religious imagery and formulations: from the chthonic source there grow such ideas as the washing away of sins, spiritual rebirth, and mystical oneness with Divinity; from the ouranian source such ideas as divine power and greatness, human smallness, and the moral need of submission to a remote but *awe*ful judge. These and other religious ideas get intermingled and confused, to be sure, and it would be distortive of religious actuality to think of them as always distinct and opposed. At any rate in one way or another the ouranian and the chthonic modes of sensitivity and belief are jointly contributive to the greatly varied ideas, forms, suppositions, and expectations in later and, for better or worse, more developed religions.

i. In Olympian Perspective

1.   *Thus spoke grey-eyed Athena and departed to Olympus, where, so they say, the abode of the gods is established forever. No winds shake it, no rain wets it, never does snow come near, but the bright air encompasses it without clouds, and white light floats over it. There the blessed gods live in joy for all eternity, and there it was that Athena went.*   (Homer *Odyssey* VI. 41)

2.   [Agamemnon, replying to Achilles' angry reproach:] *"Often have the Achaeans spoken thus to me, reproaching me for my conduct. But it is not I that am the cause; rather it is Zeus, and Destiny, and Erinys who walks in darkness,—it is they who put blind fury into my chest on that day in the assembly when I robbed Achilles of his rightful spoil. But what could I do? It is by some divine power that all things are brought about. The eldest daughter of Zeus is Atê, a power of evil who makes all men blind."*   (*Iliad* XIX. 85)

3.   *To the other gods seated in the halls of Olympian Zeus the father of gods and men began to speak; for he was thinking of noble Aegisthus, whom the son of Agamemnon, far-famed Orestes, slew. Thinking on him Zeus spoke among the immortals:*

"Alas, how vainly mortal men put blame upon the gods! For they complain that evil comes from us; but it is rather they,

in the blindness of their hearts, who make sorrows for themselves beyond what is ordained. A recent case is that of Aegisthus, who went beyond what is ordained in marrying the wedded wife of Agamemnon and slaying her lord on his return. He did this knowing that utter doom would be his recompense, for we had sent down keen-sighted Hermes to warn him that he should not kill Agamemnon or woo his wife; and we told him that he, son of Atreus, would be avenged by Orestes as soon as the latter should reach manhood and feel a desire for his native land. So Hermes told him, but his words did not touch the heart of Aegisthus, who now has paid for all his misdeeds in one all-embracing penalty." (*Odyssey* I. 26)

4. [Phoenix, an aged cavalry officer, addresses Achilles:] *"Subdue your proud spirit, Achilles; it is not seemly for you to have a ruthless heart. Why, even the gods can bend, despite their greater excellence, honor, and might. They are turned by men's prayers, especially when these are strengthened by incense, vows, drink-offerings and burnt-offerings, whenever anyone trespasses and sins. Prayers are the daughters of great Zeus; . . . they take care to follow in the track of dreadful Atê. But Atê, being strong and swift of foot, outruns them all; she speeds ahead of them over all the earth, deluding and disabling men's wills, and Prayers follow after her in order to heal the harm. When anyone shows reverence to these daughters of Zeus at their approach, they bless him and listen to his petitions; but when someone denies them and stubbornly refuses them, they return to the son of Cronus, Lord Zeus, and petition that Atê may pursue that man and delude him so that he will have to pay the penalty. Therefore take heed, Achilles, that you give to*

the daughters of Zeus the reverence that bends the minds of
all men of worth." (*Iliad* IX. 496)

5. *Hail, daughters of Zeus* [*Muses*]! *Grant me the gift*
of lovely song, by which to celebrate the holy race of the Im-
mortals, born of Earth and starry Heaven, as well as those born
of gloomy Night, and those whom the salt Sea nourished.

Surely the first of all things to exist was Chaos; then came
well-bosomed Earth, whose foundation is ever sure; and Tar-
tarus, lying deep below Earth's many paths; and Eros, who is
fairest among the Immortals and who loosens men's limbs, sub-
dues the mind and prudent counsel in gods and men alike.

From Chaos both Erebus and black Night were born; then
Night, joining with Erebus in sweet love-union, conceived and
bore Aether and Day. (Hesiod *Theogony* 104, 116)

6. *Zeus himself ordained law for mankind. As for fishes*
and beasts and winged fowls, they may feed on one another with-
out sin, for justice is unknown to them. But to man he gave
the law of justice. (Hesiod *Works and Days* 276-279)

7. *Lord Apollo, graciously hear their prayer, and mine too;*
for often have I approached thy altars with gifts from my rev-
erent hands. And now, O Lycean Apollo, I bow before thee
and with deep humility I beg and implore: aid our deliberations
by thy foresight, and reveal to us what is right and what is
wrong for men to do, and how we should deal with the gods.
(Sophocles *Electra*)

8. *Although the body of every mortal must give way to*
overmastering death, yet an image of life lives on, for it alone
comes from the gods. It sleeps while the limbs are alive, yet even

during sleep it gives to men in many a dream premonitions of happy and disastrous turning-points.   (Pindar *Threnodies* 131)

9.   *It is pleasant to learn how the Immortals have put before mankind many things which serve as outward signs of both miseries and blessings to come.*   (Ascribed to Musaeus)

ii. Chthonic Religion and Mystery Cults

10.   *The pure sky [Ouranos] desires to penetrate the earth, and the earth is filled with love so that she longs for blissful union with the sky. The rain falling from the beautiful sky impregnates the earth, so that she gives birth to plants and grain for beasts and men.*   (Aeschylus)

11.   *Parched earth loves the rain; and high heaven, rain-filled, loves to fall earthward.*   (Euripides)

12.   *There is blight on the growing plants of the earth;*
blight on the grazing cattle in the fields;
blight on our women, that they bear no children.
Ah, surely there is some god at work in this city,
spreading fire and dreadful pestilence.
                                        (Sophocles *Oedipus Tyrannus*)

13.   *When blood is shed and drunk by Mother Earth*
the vengeful gore congeals irremovably.
. . . Though stream on stream should pour
their swift-cleansing waters on the hand of blood,
the old stain shall not wash away.
                                        (Aeschylus *Choëphori*)

14.   *The holy blessed Delphian land,*
      throbbing with hymns, begins to dance
      when Thou thy holy shape revealest:
      poised upon Parnassus' slope,
      with reverent maidens attending.

                                    (Ode to Dionysus)

15.   *The whole earth bursts into joyous dance*
      when Bromios [Dionysus] leads his troop toward the hills,
      where the band of women await him, drawn
      from loom and shuttle in reverent ecstasy.

                                    (Euripides *Bacchae*)

16.   *Appear, appear, whatever thy shape or name,*
      O mountain Bull, Snake of a hundred names,
      Lion of the burning flame, God, Beast, Mystery, come!

                                    (*ibid.*)

17.   *Demeter, thou who feedeth all my thoughts, grant me worthiness to worship thee.*   (Aristophanes, *Frogs*)

18.   *Blessed is he upon earth who has seen these [Mysteries]. But he who is uninitiated and does not share in them will never enjoy the same good fortune after death; he must go down to the place of gloomy darkness.*   (*Homeric Hymn to Demeter*)

19.   *Thrice blessed are they who have beheld these Mysteries before going down to Hades. They alone will have life there; the others will suffer utter wretchedness.*   (Quoted by Sophocles)

20.   *Only those who have been courageous in keeping their souls pure may pass along the highways of Zeus into the palace*

of Cronus, where the sea breezes blow about the Isles of the Blessed.   (Pindar)

21.   *When your soul leaves the light of the sun, you will enter upon the right-hand path if you have kept all the laws well and faithfully. Rejoice in the utterly new experience of emerging from your human condition and becoming a god. You have fallen as a kid into its mother's milk. Hail, hail, as you travel on the right, through the holy meadows and groves of Persephone.* (Tomb inscription at Thurii)

iii. The Reflective Mood

22.   *Know thyself!*   (Inscription over the entrance to the Temple of Apollo at Delphi)

23.   *Nothing too much.*   (Greek maxim)

24.   *Taught by suffering. Drop by drop wisdom is distilled from pain.* (Aeschylus *Agamemnon*)

25.   *O Zeus, whoever he may be, by that name if it be acceptable I call on him.*   (*ibid.*)

26.   *To see into thy nature, O Zeus, is baffling to the mind. I have been praying to thee without knowing whether thou art necessity or nature or simply the intelligence of mortals.* (Euripides, *The Trojan Women*)

27.   *Dear Zeus, you baffle me. You are king of all; the highest honor and greatest power are yours, you discern what*

*goes on in each man's secret heart, and your lordship is su-
preme. Yet you make no distinction between the sinner and the
good man, between the man who devotes himself to temperate
and responsible acts and the man who commits deeds of hybris.
Tell me, son of Cronus, how can you deal such unfairness?*
(Theognis I. 373)

28.   *Count no mortal happy until he has reached the very
end of his life free from misfortune and pain.*   (Sophocles *Oedi-
pus Tyrannus*)

29.   *The best of all things is never to have been born on
earth, never to see the rays of the burning sun. And once a
man is born the best thing for him to do is to travel quickly
to the gates of Death and lie at rest under a close-fitted cover-
let of earth.*   (Theognis I. 425)

30.   *The Logos steers men and ever preserves them on the
right path. Men have the power of calculation, but there is
also the divine Logos. Human reasoning is born from the divine
Logos, which furnishes each man with the passageway both of
life and of nourishment. The divine Logos is present in all the
arts, ever teaching men what they must do to obtain good results. For it is not man, but God, who discovered the arts.*
(Epicharmus of Syracuse)

31.   *God holds the beginning and the end, as well as the
middle, of all that exists.*   (Ancient Orphic adage)

32.   *Men perish because they cannot join the beginning with
the end.*   (Alcmaeon of Crotona)

iv. Xenophanes

Xenophanes of Colophon was the first Greek thinker, so far as is known, to apply clear reasoning firmly and coherently to the central problem of religious theology, the problem of God's nature; and he answers his question emphatically declaring that God is one and unique, utterly unlike human beings in all respects but one. Thus he is the first known critical theologian in ancient Greece.

What is known about his life is scanty, and virtually all of it is to be found in what Diogenes Laertius chose to set down (T 4). It may be taken as true that he flourished in the middle of the sixth century B.C., that he lived to a very old age, that most of his adult life was spent in exile from his native city, and (T 1) that at one time he was teacher to Parmenides of Elea, the founder of metaphysical monism in the West. Because of this relationship many historians of philosophy have classified Xenophanes as an Eleatic. But Eleaticism (cf. Chap. 4) stands for a complete, unqualified metaphysical monism; Xenophanes, on the other hand, was not a monist but a monotheist, and the surviving Fragments of his utterance do not show any interest in metaphysical questions. He does not say that all being is one and that plurality is impossible, as the Eleatics were later to do; he confines himself to proclaiming the doctrine of God as single and transcendent. (For apparent counter-evidence see T 5.)

Xenophanes is very much a modern in his opposition to anthropomorphism (Frs. 1, 5-8), in his doctrine that investigation and discovery are more reliable than revelation (Fr. 9), and in his recognition of the relativity of sense-perception (Fr. 12). He recognizes, however, a problem which is often ignored by religious liberals who retain the concept of "God" while opposing all anthropomorphic ascriptions. For it is anthropomorphic, although limitedly so, to attribute thought and perceptual awareness to God. But if we deny these attributes to deity, then what are we talking about when we utter the name? For if God is divine and worthy of human worship, he must be superior and not inferior to man, and therefore in some sense he must know and be aware. Xenophanes, accepting this conclusion, stipulates (Frs. 2, 3) that at any rate God's knowledge and awareness are not intermittent and effortful as in the case of mortals, but are instantaneous, perpetual, and a property of his whole being rather than produced by parts and organs. Here, preserved for posterity in only two fragments, is a record of the first known case, in the West, of a clear grasp of the problem of divine knowledge. For the rest, Xenophanes' keen theological criticisms explain themselves with quite sufficient clarity. They may be usefully remembered when dealing in Chapter 3 with Heraclitus' paradoxical redefinition of God and in Chapter 4 with the extreme monism of Parmenides.

FRAGMENTS

CRITICAL AND SPECULATIVE

1. *God is one, supreme among gods and men, not at all like mortals in body or in mind.*   (23)

2. *It is the whole [of God] that sees, the whole that thinks, the whole that hears.*   (24)

3. *Without effort he sets everything in motion by the thought of his mind.*   (25)

4. *He always abides in the selfsame place, not moving at all; it is not appropriate to his nature to be in different places at different times.*   (26)

5. *But mortals suppose that the gods have been born, that they have voices and bodies and wear clothing like men.* (14)

6. *If oxen or lions had hands which enabled them to draw and paint pictures as men do, they would portray their gods as having bodies like their own: horses would portray them as horses, and oxen as oxen.* (15)

7. *Aethiopians have gods with snub noses and black hair, Thracians have gods with gray eyes and red hair.* (16)

8. *Homer and Hesiod attributed to the gods all sorts of actions which when done by men are disreputable and deserving of blame—such lawless deeds as theft, adultery, and mutual deception.* (11)

9. *Quite evidently the gods have not revealed everything to mortals at the outset; for mortals are obliged, in the slow course of time, to discover for themselves what is best.* (18)

10. *No man has existed, nor will exist, who has plain knowledge about the gods and the questions I discuss. For even if someone happened by chance to say what is true, he still would not know that he did so. Yet everybody thinks he knows.* (34)

11. *These things have seemed to me resemblances of what is true.* (35)

12. *If God had not created yellow honey, men would regard figs as sweeter than now.* (38)

13. *All things come from the earth, and they reach their end by returning to the earth at last.* (27)

14. *Whatever comes-to-be and grows is earth and water.* (29)

15. *We are all sprung from earth and water.* (33)

16. *What we see of the earth is its upper limit, where it is in contact with the air, but it goes downward "to infinity."* (28)

17. *The sea is the source of water and the source of wind. For blasts of wind could not come-to-be within the clouds and blow forth from them if it were not for the great sea; nor could there be rivers, nor any rain from the sky without it. The great sea is the begetter of clouds and winds and rivers.* (30)

18. *The sun moves along above the earth and gives it warmth.* (31)

19. *She whom men call Iris [rainbow] is a cloud of such a nature as to cause appearances of violet, red, and yellow-green.* (32)

ELEGIAC REFLECTIONS

20. *While sitting at the fireside in the winter, at ease on soft couches, well fed, sipping tasty wine and nibbling tidbits, it is then that a host may duly inquire of his guest: "Who are you among men, and whence do you come? How old are you, friend? How old were you at the time of the Mede invasion?"* (22)

21. *Now the floor is swept, hands and cups are washed clean. [An attendant] places woven garlands on our heads, another passes around a vase of fragrant ointment. The mixing bowl stands brimful of good cheer, and more wine in jars is at hand, delicious and with delicate aroma, never failing. Incense gives forth a sacred fragrance, and there is water, cold, refreshing, and pure. Golden-brown loaves are before us, with cheeses and rich honey, set out in abundance upon the princely*

*table. At the center is an altar decked with flowers on all sides.
Song and mirth fill the hall.*

*Men who are about to make merry should first honor the
gods with hymns composed of well-told tales and pure words.
After they have poured a libation and have prayed for the
power to do what is right—that, indeed, is the first business in
hand—then there is nothing wrong in drinking as much as a
man can hold without having to be taken home by a servant,
unless of course he is very old. The man to be praised is he
who, after drinking, can still express thoughts that are noble
and well arranged. But let him not repeat those old hackneyed
tales of Titans or Giants or Centaurs, nor those of violent civil
broils: there is nothing to be gained from all that. But it is
always good to give heedful reverence to the gods.* (1)

*22. If at Olympia, where the grove of Zeus lies by Pisa's
stream, a man were to win a victory by swiftness of foot or in
the pentathlon contest, or if he were victorious in wrestling, or
in painful boxing, or in the dreadful no-holds-barred contest:
such a man in the eyes of his townsfolk would be more glamorous
than his fellows; he would be awarded a front seat at as-
semblies and would be dined and entertained at the public expense, as well as receiving some gift of lasting value. So, too,
if he were to win a prize for the speed of his horses he would
get all these rewards.*

*Yet he would not deserve them as much as I deserve them;
for surely a man's wisdom is superior to strength and speed of
men or of horses. Popular opinion misjudges these matters; it
does wrong in prizing strength above wisdom. Suppose there
were to arise among the people some champion boxer or wrest-
ler, or a pentathlon winner, or, what they prize most of all,*

*one who excels in swiftness of foot, still the city would not be
any better governed on that account. It gives little joy to the
city that someone wins a victory on the Pisa's banks; for that
kind of thing brings no wealth into its treasure chambers.* (2)

23. *[The men of Colophon] had learned useless kinds of
luxury from the Lydians; and as long as they were free from
the tyrant's yoke they would stroll into the marketplace, perhaps a thousand of them, boastful, overdressed in purple gar-
ments, anointed with rare perfumes, and making a show of
their hairdresser's art.* (3)

24. *By now it is sixty-seven years that my thoughts have
been tossed restlessly up and down the land of Hellas; and
when that [period of wandering] began I was already twenty-
five years old, if I remember rightly such bygone details.* (8)

TESTIMONIA

FROM ARISTOTLE:

T 1. Xenophanes, who first upheld the doctrine of the one,
and whose pupil Parmenides is said to have been, produced no
definite doctrine, and does not seem to have grasped either of
these [types of causality], but contemplating the universe in
its entirety he declared that the oneness [of it] is God. (*Metaphysica* 986b 21)

T 2. Xenophanes declares that those who say the gods are
born are no less impious than those who say they die, since in
either case it is tantamount to saying that the gods do not
exist. (*Rhetorikê* 1399b 6)

T 3. When the citizens of Elea asked Xenophanes whether

or not they should sacrifice to [newly deceased] Leukothea and sing her a dirge, he advised them that if they believed her to be divine they should not sing her a dirge, and if they believed her human they should not sacrifice to her.   (*ibid*. 1400b 5)

FROM LATER GREEK SOURCES:

T 4.   Xenophanes of Colophon, son of Dexius or according to Apollodorus son of Orthomenes, is praised by Timon, who describes him as "a fairly modest man, who satirized Homer." Having been banished from his native city, he lived at Zancle in Sicily and for a while at Catana. Some say that he was no man's pupil, but others that he had been a pupil of Boton of Athens, or of Archelaus. Sotion says he was a contemporary of Anaximander. His writings are partly in epic [hexameter], partly in elegiac and iambic verse, and in them he denounces Homer and Hesiod for what they said about the gods. He used to recite his own verses. It is said that he criticized Thales and Pythagoras, too.

Xenophanes holds that God is spherical in substance, and that he is unlike man; for the whole of him sees, the whole of him hears, he does not breathe, he is totally mind and thought, and is eternal.

When Empedocles remarked to him that it is impossible to find a wise man, Xenophanes replied: "Naturally, for it takes a wise man to recognize a wise man."

He lived to a very great age, as he himself says somewhere: [Fr. 24]. He flourished about the sixtieth Olympiad [540-537 B.C.].   (Diogenes Laertius)

T 5.   Theophrastus says that Xenophanes of Colophon, teacher of Parmenides, declared that the first principle is One, and that What Is is one and all-embracing, that it is neither limited nor unlimited, and neither moving nor at rest. But Theophrastus admits that his opinions cannot be investigated by the same exact method that is applied to nature. (Simplicius *Commentaria*)

T 6.   Xenophanes assumes that what comes-to-be must come from what already is. Further he holds that God is supreme, by which he means most powerful and best. This goes against the customary opinion, which regards some gods as superior to others in various respects. (Pseudo-Aristotle *De Melisso, Xenophane, Gorgia* 977b 21)

T 7.   On the supposition that God is supreme over all things Xenophanes draws the conclusion that God is One. For if there were two or more gods, each of them would be supreme, and thus in effect none of them would be supreme and best. For the very meaning of God and of divine power involves supremacy over all else. So far as he is not superior he is not God. (*ibid.* 977a 23)

T 8.   Xenophanes was an eclectic philosopher who had sceptical doubts about everything except his own dogma that all things are one, and that this One is God, who is limited, rational, and immovable. (Galenus)

T 9.   Xenophanes of Colophon, going his own way and differing from all who preceded him, denied that there is any coming-to-be or perishing, declaring that the All is always the same. For if it had come-to-be it could not have existed before that moment when the coming-to-be occurred; but on the other hand not-being could not have come-to-be, because not-being has no power to bring anything about. Declaring that our senses are deceptive he even challenges the authority of reason itself.

He says that the earth is slowly but constantly sinking into the sea. And he says that the sun consists of a massing together of numerous fiery particles.

On the subject of the gods he denies that any one god could rule over other gods, for it is impious to suppose that any of

the gods could be ruled. The gods do not have need of anything, he argues, since it is the nature of godhood to hear and
see throughout the god's entire being, and not by any means
through particular organs.   (Pseudo-Plutarch *Stromata*)

T 10.   Xenophanes of Colophon was the first to declare that
nothing can be grasped with certainty, arguing: "Even if someone happened to chance to say what is true, he still could not
know [whether he was right or not]; yet all men have the
illusion of knowing" [Fr. 10]. He says that nothing comes-to-
be or perishes, that nothing is moved, and that the universe
is one and changeless. God is eternal and one, homogeneous
throughout, limited, spherical, and with the power of perception in all his parts.

The sun is formed anew each day out of small particles of
fire joined together. He declares the earth to be without limit
[downward], as against the view that it is entirely surrounded
by air or aether. An unlimited number of suns and moons exist,
and all things come out of earth.

He attributes the saltiness of the sea to the fact that so many
things flow together in it and form mixtures,—as opposed to
Metrodorus' view that the saltiness is the result of the sea's
having been filtered through the earth. The earth, he says, was
once mingled with the sea, but in course of time it got free from
moisture. As evidence he points to the shells found far inland
and among the mountains, to the fossils of fish that have been
found in the quarries of Syracuse, and to the imprints of various
sea-creatures at Paros deep down in the stone and at Melite
more faintly. These imprints, he believes, were made at a time
when everything was covered with mud, solidifying when the
mud dried. He says that at length the earth will sink into the
sea and become mud again, at which time mankind will be destroyed and afterwards a new race will begin to be. A similar
transformation he regards as taking place in all worlds.   (Hippolytus *Refutatio* I. 1)

2

The Scientist-Philosophers
of Miletus

ONE OF THE great significant steps in the development of human thought took place at the Ionian city of Miletus in the sixth century B.C. Miletus was then a thriving seaport on the lower shore of the Aegean Sea, in what is now southwestern Turkey, about midway between the Greek islands of Samos to the north and Cos to the south. Its location together with its harbor facilities made it an important center of maritime commerce in the ancient world, and as a natural consequence it enjoyed the benefits of much trading in ideas as well. An intelligent Milesian, being more or less constantly exposed to various tales and customs from abroad, would soon come to perceive the relative and therefore dubious nature of those tales of the gods and myths of cosmic beginnings on which he had been reared. Such challenges to traditional belief tend to stimulate fresh efforts of thought, provided there are thinkers capable of meeting the challenge. Miletus was fortunate in producing at least three such thinkers—Thales, his independent disciple Anaximander, and the last known member of the school Anaximenes.

These three ancient Milesian thinkers were philosophers and scientists at once. Fields of knowledge had not yet become compartmentalized, and any inquiry into the nature of things would normally express interests which today we would distinguish as philosophical, scientific, ethical, aesthetic, and religious. Thales' declaration that all things are full of gods (i, T 8), or that the gods are blended with all things (i, T 15), was not totally distinct from his explanation of things in terms of water; for water was to him a living substance with an aura of divine potentialities still clinging to the idea of it. Again, Anaximander's explanation of natural change with the help of the ethical and religious idea of doing penance (ii, Fr. 1) would not have appeared to him, as it would to us, a paradoxical combination of two diverse ideas, but a reasonable description of how the living world carries out its visible and teleologically oriented activities.

In what sense were these Milesian philosophers scientific? Not, to be sure, in the full sense of the word as accepted currently. The contemporary demands of maximum exactitude, of experimentally controlled verifications, and of intellectual economy, were unknown to them. Exactitude, by anything like modern standards, was by no means characteristic of ancient investigations of nature; nor could it possibly have been so, in view of the fact that scientific thinking in the ancient world was predominantly qualitative, and that the concept of identical units, on which quantitative analysis depends, was of little concern to them.

Nevertheless in a threefold sense they were naturalistic and to that extent scientific. In the first place, they tried systematically to explain nature in terms of nature, instead of referring to the supposed will or caprice of supernatural beings. While Thales' statements that the magnet "has soul" and that all things are full of gods may appear at first sight to run counter to this naturalistic commitment, yet if carefully interpreted they will serve to illustrate it. For neither the word "soul" (*psychê*) nor the word "god" (*theos*) is here intended to carry the older mythological implications. There is no suggestion of immortality when Thales speaks of soul, and little or no anthropomorphic attachment in his idea of god. He seems to be trying, in the absence of an adequate vocabulary, to point toward the notion which Aristotle was later to call "potentiality" or "potency" (*dynamis*). In both of his concretions of the idea Thales was expressing an awareness of the mystery of birth, growth, activity, and the unforeseen emergence of new qualities. Such ideas do break through the patterns of any naturalistic system and point to the unanswered questions that always extend indefinitely beyond the questions that get answered. But so far as our slim evidence can tell, they never tempted Thales to let his mind dwell upon the supernatural aspects; his focus and his emphasis kept their place and balance within, or just a little beyond, the world of nature as it can be experienced.

A second reason why the Milesian philosophers can be regarded as scientists is that they gave preference systematically, for perhaps the first time, to the kinds of observation that can be shared by virtually any interested and unprejudiced observer. The venerable prestige of inspired utterances by prophets and of privileged knowledge which could be imparted only after initiation into the secret mysteries of a religious cult was discarded. Heraclitus, writing quite independently at the nearby city of Ephesus, gave vivid expression, in his Fragment 15, to the principle of openly available knowledge, as that which is shared by men who are fully awake.

Thirdly, the Milesians began to make a practice of seeing the individual thing or event not as an isolated phenomenon of interest in itself alone, but as representative and symptomatic of a class. A solar eclipse was of interest to Thales not only as an event which changed the tide of battle between the Medes and the Lydians (T 2), but more significantly in relation to his hypothesis about the cause of eclipses (T 20) and to his intellectual faith that given the same conditions the same result would occur.

Thus it is not in their specific conclusions, not in their individual preferences for water or air or the Unlimited as the ultimate explanatory principle, that the Milesians are important. It is rather in their new method of procedure, manifested in their new way of asking questions. They were teaching themselves to ask "What?" instead of "Who?" and to ask "How?" instead of "With what intent and purpose?" These two revised modes of questioning took the more precise and metaphysical form: (1) "What is the primary stuff of which the world is constituted?" and (2) "How do the manifold and changing appearances come about?" The first question is of concern to all three of the Milesians; the second takes hold gradually. Basically the two questions are inseparable however, for to ask seriously what a thing *is* involves asking what it *does;* and their interplay, in one manner or another, may be seen as shaping the character of Greek metaphysics during at least the next two centuries.

In examining such proto-scientific inquiries, however, it is important to keep in mind certain characteristic differences of the early Greek intellectual perspective, particularly as represented by the two assumptions defined in the General Introduction—that of the four basic elements and that of the primacy of qualitative opposites. The former assumption finds expression in Thales' theory that water is the sole fundamental substance, all the various things and qualities of the world being mere transformations of it, as well as in Anaximenes' theory of the primacy of air. The latter assumption, on the other hand, finds expression in Anaximander's theory of the Boundless—i.e., of an infinite reservoir of all possible qualities, from which one and only one of each pair of opposites comes into existence at any given time. One of the chief tasks of subsequent Greek metaphysics then becomes to seek for principles of existence and change that are more fundamental than anything so contingent and perceptually familiar as the substances and qualities of everyday experience.

i. Thales

Thales, the founder of the Milesian school, "flourished" in 585 B.C. The high reputation which caused him to be named on virtually every list of the legendary Seven Sages in early Greece was by no means based on his theoretical exploits alone. He applied his knowledge to astronomy, drawing upon the long kept Babylonian tables of solar and lunar orbits, to predicting correctly the year (although not the month) of a solar eclipse which occurred during a battle between the Medes and the Lydians throwing both armies into confusion and rout (T 2). His practical business acumen is attested by Aristotle's account (T 4) of his success in cornering the olive market. Herodotus (T 3) indicates his competence as a military engineer. He wrote treatises for the use of mariners who might venture beyond the sight of land (cf. T 11). And, as remarked earlier, he devised means of measuring the height of pyramids and the distance of ships at sea (T 9, 10).

Although the main points of Thales' doctrines are securely known, there are no surviving quotations of his actual words. Consequently in his case there can be no section of Fragments, but in its place there is offered Aristotle's version of the four most important propositions which he affirmed. It is as close as we can get to the actuality of his thought and utterance.

MAIN PROPOSITIONS OF THALES AS STATED BY ARISTOTLE

1. *The first principle and basic nature of all things is water.* (T 6)
2. *The earth rests upon water.* (T 5, 6)

3.   *All things are full of gods.*   (T 8)

4.   *The magnetic stone has soul because it sets the iron in motion.*   (T 7)

TESTIMONIA

FROM HERODOTUS:

T 1.   Thales, a man of Miletus, was originally of Phoenician descent.   (*The Persian Wars* I. 170)

T 2.   In the sixth year of the war [between the Medes and the Lydians], neither side having gained much of an advantage, it suddenly happened in the midst of battle that the day turned into night. The shift from day to night had been foretold to the Ionians by Thales of Miletus, who set as its limit the year in which it actually occurred.   (I. 74)

T 3.   Once when [King] Croessus was at a loss how to take his army across a river where there was no bridge, it is said that Thales, who was then serving with the army, switched the course of the river, causing it to flow behind the army instead of altogether in front of them. Here is how he did it. Going upstream he dug a deep channel in the shape of a crescent, thereby dividing the river and partly diverting it to the rear of the army, letting it return to its original course after passing the camp. The result was that both parts of the river were now shallow enough to be forded.   (I. 75)

FROM ARISTOTLE:

T 4.   When people had been mocking him for his poverty, insinuating that his philosophy was of no practical use to him, he drew upon his knowledge of the heavenly bodies to predict a large olive crop, and collecting some money while it was still winter he bought up all the olive presses in Miletus and Chius, securing them by partial payments very cheaply because of the absence of competing bids. When the proper time arrived there was a sudden demand for olive presses, which he then rented out on his own terms, making large profits for himself. (*Politikê* 1259a 9)

T 5. As against those who say that the earth extends downward without limit there are those who say that the earth rests upon water. This is the oldest theory that has been preserved, and it is accredited to Thales of Miletus. The earth stays in place, he explained, because it floats like wood or some such substance of a nature to let it float upon water but not upon air. As if the same problem didn't logically arise for the water supporting the earth as for the earth itself! (*De Caelo* 294a 28)

T 6. Most of those who first engaged in philosophy supposed that the only principles of things were to be found as material elements. That of which all things consist, that from which they first arise and into which they finally vanish away, that of which the "basic being" (*ousia*) persists although the perceptible characteristics are changed,—this, they say, is the prime element and first-principle of things. Therein they hold that nothing either comes-to-be or is destroyed, since this kind of "basic nature" (*physis*) always persists.

As to the nature of what is fundamental, however, and even as to whether it is one or many, there was much disagreement. Thales, the founder of this type of philosophy, declared the first-principle to be water, and for that reason he also held that the earth rests upon water. Probably the idea was suggested to him by the fact that the nutriment of everything contains moisture, and that heat itself is generated out of moisture and is kept alive by it. For of course it is assumed that whatever something is generated out of must be its first-principle. He drew his notion also from the fact that the seeds of everything have a moist nature; and of course the first-principle of moist things is water.

There are some who think that men of olden times—those who, long before the present era, first began to speculate about the gods—held similar views about basic nature. For they represented Oceanus and Tethys as the parents of creation, and the gods as swearing their oaths by the River Styx, which is to say by water, the oldest and most honorable thing by which man swears. At any rate, while it is perhaps uncertain whether or not the view in question is really so ancient and venerable, it is generally accepted that Thales explained the primary cause in this way. (*Metaphysica* 983b 7)

T 7. From the stories that are told of him it would seem that Thales conceived of soul as somehow a motive power, since he said that the magnetic stone has soul in it because it sets a piece of iron in motion. (*De Anima* 405a 19)

T 8. Some say that soul is diffused throughout the universe; and perhaps that is what Thales meant in saying that all things are full of gods. (*ibid.* 411a 7)

FROM LATER GREEK SOURCES:

T 9. Thales was one of the seven sages, according to Plato. Moreover, Demetrius of Phalerum states in his *Catalogue of Archons* that Thales was the first man to be called a sage, the word then being applied to seven such men, and that this occurred at Athens when Damasias was archon [582 B.C.]. Although most writers speak of him as a native Milesian of distinguished family, it is held by some that he was admitted to citizenship at Miletus after having been exiled from Phoenicia.

Thales had no regular teacher, but went to Egypt and studied under the priests there. After an early period of political activity he became a student of natural science. He appears to have given excellent advice on political matters. For instance, when Croesus offered to Miletus certain terms of alliance it was Thales who thwarted the plan, and to this freedom from alliance the city later owed its salvation when Cyrus [of Persia] won the victory. On the other hand, Heraclides quotes Thales as declaring that he always lived in solitude as a private individual and kept himself aloof from state affairs.

Some say that he married and had a son Cybisthus. Others say that he adopted his sister's son, and that to those who asked why he had no children of his own he replied that it was because he loved children. It is reported that when his mother first urged him to marry he replied that the "right time" (*kairos*) had not yet come, and that when she urged him again at a later period of his life he replied that the right time had passed. Hermippus in his *Lives* attributes to Thales the statement of the three blessings for which he was most grateful to fortune: "first, that I was born a human being and not a beast; next, that I was born a man and not a woman; thirdly, that I was born a Greek and not a barbarian."

Thales was the first to predict eclipses and to determine the time of the solstices: so Eudoxus says in his treatise on astronomy. He determined the sun's course between one solstice and the next. According to some he was the first to declare that the size of the sun was a seven hundred and twentieth part of the solar orbit, and that the same ratio existed between the size of the moon and the lunar orbit. Pamphilê says that having studied geometry with the Egyptians he discovered for himself how to inscribe a right-angled triangle in a circle, whereupon in thanksgiving he sacrificed an ox. According to Hieronymus he measured the pyramids by their shadow, after noting the time of day at which the shadow of a man equalled his height. The basic principle of everything he identified as water; moreover he declared the universe to be ensouled and full of daemons. It was he, they say, who divided the year into four seasons and into

365 days, and it was he who first called the last day of the month "the thirtieth."

There is a story that on one occasion, while a woman servant was leading him through the fields by night in order that he might observe the stars, he stumbled into a ditch; whereupon the woman as she helped him out remarked, "How can you expect to know all about the heavens, Thales, when you can't know what lies right under your feet?"

He held that there was no difference between life and death. "Why, then, don't you kill yourself?" someone asked. "Because there is no difference," Thales replied. To the question what man is happiest he gave the answer, "He who enjoys a healthy body, a resourceful mind, and a calm disposition." When asked what is most difficult he replied, "To know oneself"; and when asked what is easiest he replied, "To give advice to others." (Diogenes Laertius I. 22-38)

T 10. Thales was the first to go into Egypt and bring back scientific knowledge into Greece. He discovered a number of propositions himself, and he explained to his successors the underlying principles of many others. In some cases he employed deduction from universals, in others his approach was empirical.

Eudemus in his treatise on geometry attributed to Thales this theorem [that triangles which are equal with respect to one side and its two adjacent angles are equal in all respects]; arguing that Thales must have employed the theorem in computing, as he is said to have done, the distance of ships at sea. (Proclus, *On Euclid*)

T 11. Thales is generally regarded as the first who taught the Greeks the investigation of nature. Although he had many predecessors, as Theophrastus has remarked, he surpassed them all to such a degree that they are forgotten. He is said by some to have left no writings except his so-called nautical star-guide. (Simplicius *Commentaria*)

T 12. Thales was the earliest thinker to say that water is the first-principle of things, all things having emerged from it and eventually returning to it. (Pseudo-Plutarch *Stromata*)

T 13. Of those who say that the first-principle is one and movable (i.e., those whom Aristotle has called *physikoi*) some consider it to be limited; this line is taken, for instance, by Thales of Miletus and, in an anti-religious vein, by Hippo. Both philosophers hold the first-principle to be water—a view to which they are led by certain perceptual evidences. For warmth lives in moisture. Moreover the seeds as well as the nourishment of things are moist; and it is natural that what gives birth to a thing should also be its means of nourishment. Since water is the first-principle of the moistness of anything, they declare it to be the first-principle of everything; hence they argue that the earth must rest upon water. (Theophrastus, *Physical Opinions*)

T 14. Thales declared that God is the same as mind in the universe, that the All is ensouled and full of spirits, and that a divine moving power pervades the elemental moisture. He was the first to declare that the soul by its very nature is always in motion, and indeed is self-moving. (Aëtius)

T 15. Thales says that gods are blended with all things—a strange doctrine! (Simplicius *Commentaria*)

T 16. It is said that Thales of Miletus, one of the seven wise men, was the first to undertake the study of natural philosophy. He declared water to be the beginning and the end of all things. As the water solidifies, things acquire firmness; as it melts, their individual existence is threatened. Such changes are the causes of earthquakes, whirlwinds, and the movements of the stars. (Hippolytus *Refutatio*)

T 17. Thales of Miletus, who mistakenly supposed "first-principle" to mean the same as "element," declared water to be both the element and the first-principle of things. All things, he held, come out of water and are resolved into water. His reasons for the belief were: first, that the first-principle of animals is their seed, which is moist; secondly, that plants bear fruit when they have moisture but wither away when they lack it; thirdly, that even the fire of the sun and stars is fed by exhalations that arise from the waters. (Aëtius)

T 18. Thales holds that the earth is one, and that it is spherical. (*ibid.*)

T 19. Thales and certain others agree with the astronomers of our day that the monthly phases of the moon indicate that it is lighted by the sun and travels in relation to it. Lunar eclipses he explained as caused by the earth's shadow, in that the earth cuts off the sun's light from the moon when it is directly between the two orbs. (*ibid.*)

T 20. And he says that eclipses of the sun occur when the moon passes directly in front of it; explaining that the moon is of an earthy nature, even though it gives the appearance of a disc laid across the disc of the sun. (*ibid.*)

FROM LATIN SOURCES:

T 21. Thales of Miletus, who was the first to study such matters, said that water is the first-principle of all things, and that "god" signifies the mind which forms all things out of water. (Cicero *De Natura Deorum* I. 25)

T 22. He discovered how to measure the height of pyramids, by waiting until that hour of the day when the shadow of a thing was equal to its body. (Pliny the Elder, *Natural History* XXXVI. 82)

T 23. Thales was distinguished as an investigator into the nature of things; and in order that he might have successors in his school he committed his dissertations to writing. What especially made him eminent, however, was his ability by astronomical calculations to predict eclipses of the sun and moon. He supposed water to be the first-principle of things, holding that all the elements of the world, the world itself, and whatever is generated in it, ultimately consist of water. In all his writings, however, so admirable in dealing with the world, he included nothing about the nature of the divine mind.   (Augustine *Civitas Dei* VIII. 2)

ii. Anaximander

Anaximander of Miletus, described by ancient writers as pupil and companion of Thales, is said to have been born in the second or third year of the forty-second Olympiad, which is to say in 611 or 610 B.C. His interests, like those of his eminent teacher, pointed mainly toward natural science, geometry, and astronomy; his one book that is generally mentioned by later ancient writers bore the title *On Nature*. In his own day he was particularly noted for having constructed, for the first time in Greece, a sundial, a map of the known world, and a celestial globe containing a chart of the stars.

Whereas Thales had continued to suppose that the earth must rest on a support of some kind, Anaximander with a bold leap of scientific imagination declared that it hangs in the middle of the sky, its stability assured by the fact that it is equally distant from what lies on all sides. To transcend the idea of an absolute up-vs.-down and to think in terms of the sphere as a basic cosmological form, represents a conceptual revolution of high importance for science and philosophy alike.

Another conceptual innovation, no less revolutionary, is to be found in Anaximander's theory of how physical change occurs. The question has to do with the changing qualities of things:

with the transformations which we perceive in everyday experience from bright to dark, from warm to cool, from moist to dry, and the reverse. What happens to the bright gleam when a torch is extinguished? What has become of the wintry cold when summer heat takes its place? Today, with a different set of intellectual demands imposed by a conspicuously different kind of civilization, we do not ask the questions in such terms; they probably sound to us naive and childish. That is equivalent to saying that since we have found the questions to be unanswerable in their older qualitative form, we have learned to give our attention to related questions of another order—to questions of molecular activity, of light-wave frequency, and such. But Anaximander was still addressing himself to questions of a pre-scientific kind and was undertaking to answer them by a first attempt at scientific method. Qualities, considered in themselves as qualities, come into existence and vanish away. Overhead the sky is now sparkling blue, but the hue will presently vanish and its place will be taken by cloudy gray or nocturnal black. The music will vanish when the lyre's string stops quivering: the string remains, but where is the sound? Evidently then there must be, Anaximander reasoned, a kind of storehouse or reservoir of qualities, from which the qualities that now confront us have "separated off" and into which, when their contraries come forth in turn, they will go back; the process being repeated in reverse, and so on in never-ending cycles.

What causes this alternation of qualities which, whether rapid or slow, goes on ceaselessly in the natural world? Anaximander gives his answer in the one substantial quotation of his own words that has been preserved. Each actually existing thing, he says in effect, is a usurper; for during the time that it exists it "commits injustice" by preventing its opposite from existing; accordingly it must eventually pay the penalty by yielding up its overt existence and returning to its submerged place in the great qualitative reservoir. That, he adds, is how time is ordered. The order is telic and basically moral, like the rise and fall of nations, the life and

death of organisms, the perpetual and complex alternation between good and evil, success and defeat.

The ontological storehouse is called by Anaximander the
Apeiron—that is, the Unlimited, or the Boundless. Probably the
most nearly accurate translation would be "the Qualitatively Unlimited"; the adjective should be present in thought, even if it
is not spoken. The word "infinite" has technical associations in
modern speech, which may render it misleading for so early a
mode of thought; the Greek word carries with it the secondary
meaning of "indeterminate." In any case the *Apeiron* must be
conceived as having unlimited potentialities since it has to account
for all the innumerable changes that make up the incessant on-
goingness of the world. And being qualitatively unlimited it is
logically superior to any and every kind of particularity.

FRAGMENT

*1. The Unlimited is the first-principle of things that are.
It is that from which the coming-to-be [of things and quali-
ties] takes place, and it is that into which they return when
they perish, by moral necessity, giving satisfaction to one another
and making reparation for their injustice, according to the order
of time.* (1)

TESTIMONIA

FROM ARISTOTLE:

T 1.   There is a second group [as distinguished from those
who explain in terms of a single element] who declare that
opposite qualities are contained in the One and emerge from
it by separation, as for instance Anaximander. (*Physica* 187a
20)

T 2. The Unlimited encompasses and governs all things. On this basis the Unlimited is equivalent to the Divine, since it is deathless and indestructable, as Anaximander says and as most physicists who employ the term will agree. (*ibid*. 203b 6)

T 3. If there were one simple unlimited corporeal principle, it would have to be either one of the elements or, as some maintain, something distinct from them. There are indeed some who have adopted the latter view, arguing that if the Unlimited were something specific like air or water, the other elements would be annihilated by it. For the different elements have contrariety with one another: air is cold, water warm, and fire hot. If one of them were unlimited the others would have ceased to exist by now. Such thinkers conclude, therefore, that the Unlimited is distinct from specific things of all kinds and is their source. (*ibid*. 204b 21)

T 4. There are some among the ancients, Anaximander for instance, who say that the earth keeps its place because of its spatial indifference. Movement upward, downward, or sidewards would be equally inappropriate, they argue, to what is situated at the very center equally distant from every extreme point; and therefore, since it is impossible to move in opposite directions at the same time, there is nothing for the earth to do but remain still. (*De Caelo* 295b 11)

FROM LATER GREEK SOURCES:

T 5. Anaximander, son of Praxiades, was a native of Miletus. He was the first inventor of the gnomon and, as Favorinus states in his *Miscellaneous History,* he set one up in Sparta for the purpose of determining the solstices and equinoxes. He also constructed instruments for marking the hours. He was the first to draw a map containing all the outlines of land and sea, and he constructed a global chart of the sky also. His exposition of his doctrine was made in the form of a summary which probably came into the hands of Apollodorus of Athens; that writer states in his *Chronology* that Anaximander was sixty-four years old in the second year of the fifty-eighth Olympiad [547-546 B.C.] and that he died soon after.

Anaximander held that while the parts undergo change the whole is unchangeable; that the earth, which is spherical, lies at the very center of things; and that the sun is as large as the earth and consists of purest fire. (Diogenes Laertius I. 1-2)

T 6.   Anaximander of Miletus, son of Praxiades, successor and disciple of Thales, said that the "ultimate source and first principle" (*archê*) as well as the primary substance (*stoicheion*) is the [qualitatively] Unlimited; he was the first to apply this name to the ultimate source. He maintained that it is neither water nor any other of the so-called elements, but is of an altogether different nature from them, in that it is unlimited [i.e., is not limited to being just this or that]. From it there arose the universe and all the worlds within it. (Simplicius *Commentaria,* followed by the quotation of Fr. 1)

T 7.   Evidently since he sees the four elements changing into one another he does not think it right to identify the underlying reality with any single one of them; it must be something distinct. Coming-to-be, he holds, does not involve any alteration of basic substance (*stoicheion*); it results from the separation of opposites which the eternal motion causes.   (*ibid.,* preceded by the quotation of Fr. 1)

T 8.   Anaximander's theory is that all change takes place by separation: that is to say, the opposites which are in the unlimited substratum are separated off from it. He was the first thinker to speak of the underlying reality as the "source and first principle" (*archê*). By the opposites he meant such [qualities] as hot and cold, dry and moist, etc.   (*ibid.*)

T 9. Those who believed in an unlimited number of worlds, as Anaximander and his associates did, regarded them as coming-to-be and passing away throughout unlimited time. There are always some worlds in process of coming to be, others in process of passing away, they hold; such motion being eternal. (*ibid.*)

T 10. Anaximander, an associate of Thales, said that the earth is cylindrical in shape, its depth being one-third its breadth. And he said that at the beginning of the world there separated itself out from the eternal a something capable of producing heat and cold. It took the form of a flame, surrounding the air that surrounds the earth, like the bark of a tree. This sphere became broken into parts, each of which was a different circle; which is how the sun, moon and stars were generated. (Pseudo-Plutarch *Stromata*)

T 11. Anaximander held that the Unlimited is the first-principle and is eternal, without age, and that it encompasses all the worlds; moreover that it is in perpetual activity, and that out of its activity the worlds have originated.

He held that the earth is a body suspended in the sky, not resting on anything else but keeping its position because it is the same distance away from all [extremities]; that it is in the shape of a cylinder like a stone column with a curved top surface; and that it has two faces, the one of them being the surface on which we walk, the other opposite to it.

He further held that each of the heavenly bodies is a wheel of fire, surrounded by air, which separates it from the fire at the extremities. The air has little breathing holes somewhat like the holes in a flute, and through them the orbs are seen. When the hole of the [solar or lunar] orb gets clogged an eclipse occurs. The moon goes through its phases as its breathing hole gets successively opened and stopped up. The sun's wheel is twenty-seven times as large as that of the moon, and is situated higher, while the wheel of the stars is lower. (Hippolytus *Refutatio* I. 6)

T 12.   Anaximander held that the stars are hoops of fire, compressed by air, and that they breathe out flames from little openings in the air. He said furthermore that the sun is as large as the earth, and that the wheel which carries it around and from which it breathes itself forth is twenty-seven times the size of the earth's wheel. When the sun is eclipsed, he said, it is because its breathing hole has gotten stopped up. (Aëtius)

T 13.   Some of the early philosophers of nature declared that the sea is a remnant of the primal moisture. The upper part of that original moisture, they explain, was evaporated by the sun; out of it there came-to-be the winds, as well as the revolutions of the sun and moon, the causes of their revolutions being the vapors and exhalations which exist there in abundance. A small part of the moisture got left in the hollow places on the earth's surface and became the sea, which goes on diminishing in quantity as it is evaporated by the sun, and will eventually be dried up altogether. Theophrastus says that Anaximander and Diogenes [of Apollonia] held this view. (Alexander of Aphrodisias *Commentaria*)

T 14.   Animals, according to Anaximander, came-to-be from vapors raised by the sun; and man came into being from an animal other than himself, namely the fish, which in early times he resembled. (Hippolytus, *loc. cit.*)

T 15.   He says, too, that in earliest times men were generated from various kinds of animals. For whereas the other animals can quickly get food for themselves, the human infant requires careful feeding for a long while after birth; so that if he had originated suddenly he could not have preserved his own existence. (Pseudo-Plutarch *Stromata*)

T 16.   Anaximander says that men were originally generated in the bodies of fishes; that after birth they were reared in the way that sharks are reared, until they became capable of protecting themselves; and that eventually they were cast ashore, so that they had to learn to live on dry land.   (Plutarch *Moralia* 730E)

T 17.   The first animals, according to Anaximander, were generated in moisture, and were covered with a prickly skin which, as they grew older, dried and broke off, whereupon they continued to live for a while without it.   (Aëtius)

FROM LATIN SOURCES:

T 18.   It was the opinion of Anaximander that the gods come into existence and perish, rising and setting at long intervals; and that there are countless worlds.   (Cicero *De Natura Deorum* I. 25)

T 19.   Thales was succeeded by his pupil Anaximander, who held a different opinion concerning the nature of things, beliving not like Thales that everything arose out of water as the only first-beginning of things, but rather that each thing arises from its own appropriate first-beginning. Such first-principles he held to be infinite in number. He believed that the worlds, too, are infinite in number, and that they contain everything that would grow upon them by nature. He held further that those worlds are subject to perpetual cycles of alternating dissolution and regeneration, each of them lasting for a longer or shorter time, according to the nature of the case. Nor did he, any more than Thales, attribute the cause of all this ceaseless activity to a divine mind.   (St. Augustine *Civitas Dei* VIII. 2)

iii. Anaximenes

The last of the three known Milesian philosophers, Anaximenes, is generally regarded as inferior to his two predecessors in philosophical stature. In going back to Thales' acceptance of a single element as the first-principle of physical nature he appears to have lacked both Thales' originality and Anaximander's abstractive acuteness. His main importance, however, lies not in his ontology but in his cosmology—not in his choice of air as the prototype of reality but in his dawning conception, so significant for later scientific thought and method, of serial order.

Anaximenes appears to have been the first to arrange the four elements explicitly in terms of what Heraclitus was describing as the upward and downward ways. Moreover he took a step toward overcoming the qualitative gaps between one element and the next, by indicating certain familiar kinds of matter as their intermediaries. Air, when it condenses, becomes successively wind, cloud, water, mud, earth, and finally stone; in rarefying it becomes aether (at once the buoyant and sparkling sky which we see above us and the inner brightness which may shoot through our minds and psyches in moments of inspiration and joy), then pure fire. The incipient notion of continuity and serial order which this otherwise primitive theory expresses must stand as Anaximenes' one real contribution to the development of scientific and philosophical thought.

FRAGMENT

1.   As our souls, being air, hold us together, so breath and air embrace the entire universe.   (2)

TESTIMONIA

FROM ARISTOTLE:

T 1. Anaximenes and Diogenes [of Apollonia] treat air as prior to water and as the most fundamental of all simple bodies. (*Metaphysica* 984a 5)

T 2. Anaximenes, Anaxagoras, and Democritus explain the immobility of the earth by its flatness, which lets the earth cover the air beneath like a lid without cutting it. The flatness of which they are speaking, as responsible for earth's immobility, is the flatness on the under side by which the earth is in contact with the air on which it rests. This air, having no room in which to change its position, thickens and becomes a mass pressing against the earth, like the water in a clepsydra. (*De Caelo* 294b 14)

T 3. Anaximenes says that when the earth changes from moist to dry or the reverse it cracks open, causing earthquakes and the toppling of hills. That is why earthquakes occur both in droughts and during rainy seasons. (*Meteorologica* 365b 7)

FROM LATER GREEK SOURCES:

T 4. Anaximenes, son of Eurystratus, a native of Miletus, was a disciple of Anaximander. He held that the first-principle is air, and that this is the unlimited. He denied that the stars pass under the earth, explaining that they travel around its periphery. He wrote in the Ionian dialect, in a plain style without affectation. Apollodorus says that he lived at the time of the taking of Sardis and died in the sixty-third Olympiad [528-525 B.C.]. (Diogenes Laertius II. 3)

T 5.   He says that all things, even gods and daemons, come-to-be as products of air.   (Hippolytus *Refutatio* I. 7)

T 6.   Anaximenes of Miletus, son of Eurystratus, was an associate of Anaximander and agreed with him that the essence of things is one and unlimited; on the other hand he declared that it is not indeterminate but that it has the specific nature of air, which differs in rarity and density according to the kind of things into which it forms itself. Rarefied it becomes fire; condensed it becomes wind, then cloud, and as the condensation increases it becomes successively water, earth, and then stones. Everything else gets made out of these.   (Simplicius *Commentaria*)

T 7.   Or should we, as Anaximenes of old maintained, accept neither hot nor cold as real things but regard them rather as epiphenomena and temporary states which occur in any material thing when it undergoes certain inner alterations? For he said that cold is a thing's contraction and condensation, and that heat is its distension and rarefaction.   (Plutarch *Moralia* 947f)

T 8.   He held that when the air is of most even consistency it is imperceptible to the eye; it becomes visible as a result of cold or heat or moisture or being stirred up. It is always in motion, for if it were not there would be no changes.   (Hippolytus, *loc. cit.*)

T 9.   Motion, according to Anaximenes, has existed forever. He adds that the earth came-to-be from a compression of the air; that it is very broad and rests on air. Sun, moon, and the other stars came-to-be as products of the earth.   (Pseudo-Plutarch *Stromata*)

T 10.   He says, too, that the stars are made of exhalations which arose from the earth and became attenuated into fire

as they ascended to the sky.   *   That the stars do not move
under the earth at night, as others had supposed, but travel
around its outer edge, as a cap is turned around on the head.
    *   That the rainbow is produced by the sun's rays falling
on compressed air.   (Hippolytus, *loc. cit.*)

T 11.   Anaximenes held that the world is perishable.   *
That it is shaped like the top of a table.   *   That the sky is
what revolves at greatest distance from the earth.   *   That the
stars are fixed like nails in the crystalline sky.   *   That the
stars shine by the light from the sun.   *   That the stars revolve because they are pushed by condensed air.   (Aëtius)

FROM LATIN SOURCES:

T 12.   After Anaximander his disciple Anaximenes posited
infinite air [as the first-principle] but held that the things which
originate from it are finite—earth, water, fire, and out of them
everything else.   (Cicero *Academica* II. 37)

T 13.   Anaximenes said that air is a god, that it is infinite
and always in motion. As if air could be a god, or as if it could
be an exception to the rule that everything must eventually
perish!   (Cicero *De Natura Deorum* I. 26)

T 14.   The successor to Anaximander was his disciple Anaximenes, who ascribed the causes of everything to infinite air.
He neither denied nor ignored the existence of the gods; but
instead of believing that the air had been created by them, he
held on the contrary that they themselves were products of the
air.   (St. Augustine *Civitas Dei* VIII. 2)

3

Heraclitus

HERACLITUS OF EPHESUS is reported to have flourished in the sixty-ninth Olympiad, 504 to 500 B.C., which is to say thirty-one years or more before the birth of Socrates. The city of Ephesus lay about thirty miles north of Miletus, the geographical scene of the preceding chapter. The patrician family into which Heraclitus was born held some kind of hereditary office, at once political and religious, which descended to the eldest son of each generation and required him among other things to supervise the city's official religious sacrifices. The task was not congenial to the philosopher, so he resigned in favor of a younger brother and went his own way. The banishment of his friend Hermadorus from Ephesus by the political party currently in power (we do not know on what charge, but see Frs. 95, 96) confirmed and increased Heraclitus' sharp opposition to the rule of "the many." Most of the rest of what Diogenes Laertius tells about his later years and the manner of his death is of doubtful credibility, except for the one plain fact that he died at the age of sixty, which would probably have been roughly between 490 and 480 B.C.

The traditional view of Heraclitus expressed by later ancient writers is that he was a pessimist and a snob, and that the latter trait caused him to write in deliberately obscure language in order to restrict his readers to such as were worthy and willing to make the required effort. Both of these charges need careful qualification.

Pessimism has more than one meaning. As a colloquial ascription it may describe a mood, or it may mean something like a refusal to indulge in wishful thinking. Philosophical pessimism, on the other hand, (as illustrated for instance by Schopenhauer) is centered in the doctrine that there is more evil in the world than good, or that the evil is somehow more fundamental than the good; and to this one-sided view of reality Heraclitus, on grounds of logic and taste alike, did not subscribe. His philosophy, ever dynamically serene, asserts that good and evil are two sides of the same coin, interpenetrating aspects of the one manifold and ever-changing reality (cf. Frs. 106, 108, etc.), and that the wise man looks at the ambivalence unflinchingly, seeing the bright and the dark, the ugly and the fair, with calm freedom of mind.

The accusation of deliberate concealment ("He was fond of concealing his metaphysics in the language of the Mysteries," Clement of Alexandria says of him) stems from a misunderstanding of his temperament and his style alike. His aristocratic pride made him indifferent or even hostile to the masses, granted; but for that very reason he would not have allowed a thought of them to alter the things he wished to say or his manner of saying them. Besides, whatever may have been the case with those parts of his writings which have been lost, a sensitive and reflective reader of the Fragments, even in translation, is not so likely to find them obscure as to find them terse, challenging, and stimulating to the imagination. New semantic tones, amounting sometimes to new dimensions of meaning, may emerge from reflecting on certain groups of the Fragments in interrelation. Try the experiment, for instance, of considering as a group Frs. 2, 11, 15, 16, last clause of 43, 58, 117, 120, all dealing somehow diversely with the problem of knowledge; or again Frs. 17, 18, 111, 116, 121; or again Frs. 19, 65, 67. Other combinations an alert reader will wish to discover and test for himself. Heraclitus' utterances, both singly

and in groups, are characteristically marked by paradox and pluri-
signation, and in that character lies their special appeal to an
active and mature mind. For there come stages in one's intellectual development when reality as actually encountered seems too
dark, too riddling, ambiguous and irreducibly many-sided to be
expressible in ordinary plain terms, and sometimes a well chosen
paradox comes closer to representing our experienced view of the
world than any logical tidiness can accomplish. Each reader must
of course judge for himself, comparing Heraclitus' brief semantic
vignettes with the testimonies of his own awareness, memory,
and imagination.

The most central paradox, which provides the fulcrum on
which Heraclitus' philosophy revolves, comes into focus when we
compare the strong valuation expressed in Fr. 46 with the indiffer-
entism of Fr. 108. Viewed with logical strictness the two Fragments clash; for how can the upward way be better than the
downward if it is true that the two ways are "one and the same"?
The paradox is a fundamental one, because the two opposing sides
of it both represent indispensable truth-claims when a person re-
flects on his relation to the world seriously and without clichés.
On the one hand we cannot live without some affirmation of
value, and for Heraclitus the foremost value consists in the mental clarity and self-honesty represented by dry light as against the
messy confusion of the downward way into sodden moisture, mud,
and at length into stony immobility. The large half-truth of that
valuation becomes evident when the direction of one's thought,
one's governing perspective, is set by an initial affirmation of one's
value as an individual endowed with the power of rational choice,
which involves the ethical power of distinguishing between better
and worse. But then comes the paradox. The same power of mind
which enables us to distinguish between good and evil and so to
make (occasionally) rational choices, proposes also another distinction, comprehensive and final—the metaphysical distinction
between the temporal and the eternal. *Sub specie aeternitatis*

man's ethical judgements, his strivings toward clarity and away from confusion, look very small indeed. Will it be of any consequence a million years from now that somewhere in our era a dedicated individual chose to accept poverty and pain rather than compromise his ideals and convictions, whereas someone else was content to drift along with the push of circumstance? "Even sleepers are workers and collaborators" without knowing it (Fr. 124): that is to say, they are an inevitable part of the universe no less than the awakened ones. And yet Fragments 14, 15, and 16 show plainly enough where Heraclitus' allegiance lies—not, certainly, on the side of those who sleep. Hence the inevitability of the paradox: neither side of it can be abandoned, because each side expresses an inescapable truth, and the two opposed insights cannot be fitted into a neat conceptual package without dismissing or distorting one or the other of them. The paradox is thus ontological; and that is where the distinctive character of Heraclitus' thought most eminently shows itself—in his unusual sensitivity to, and his arresting and varied expression of, the ontological paradox.

There may well be a connection, deeper than appears at first glance, between Heraclitus' acceptance of ontological paradox and the aristocratic pride which shows itself especially in the Fragments grouped under "Men among Men." For the aristocratism which Heraclitus' social aphorisms express is something sturdier and worthier than a mere attitude of disdain toward those whose souls are moist; the attitude is shaped by what Nietzsche has called a "passion of distance." By this phrase, which can serve as one of the main keys to the Nietzschean philosophy, Nietzsche means to include at once the "Dionysian" passionate yet self-controlled affirmation of one's own selfhood with its peculiar values and the "Apollinian" power of self-overcoming, of utter serenity in the midst of battle. The same double attitude marks Heraclitus—the pride of self-affirmation standing in balance with the wisdom of self-transcendence. Now every genuine and deep attitude (as opposed to attitudes that are imitative or self-advertised) creates its own epistemic, its own way of looking at the problems of being and value. The ambivalent attitude which gives life and shape to the aristocratic pride of the Heraclitean-Nietzschean sort of man generates a distinctive epistemic for him, a rooted perspective whereby to see and partly to understand the elements of experience, even the most hostile, without flinching. In that aristocratic outlook the ontological paradox shows and affirms itself. Aristocratic pride is thus the subjective correlative of the essential Heraclitean paradox which affirms with equal conviction the superiority of the upward way and the ultimate indifference of the ever-flowing universe to all human values of any and every kind.

But now let Heraclitus speak for himself; for no résumé or exposition can do him anything like justice. Seldom has a philosopher fashioned concepts of such power and flexibility combined. On first reading (for he needs to be read repeatedly, with meditation and excursion sandwiched between) let his terse remarks act on you as they will; some of them will speak more meaningfully than others. Then take the favored few, and with the memory of them in mind, including their meaning and tone and the suggestions they stir, read the body of Fragments a second time, and some that were at first obscure will now perhaps show gleams of intelligibility. By such oblique procedures must Heraclitus be approached, rather than by expository directness; for it is as true of his own utterances as he holds it to be of nature, that truth resides not in surface connections but in hidden depths.

FRAGMENTS*

THE WAY OF INQUIRY

1.   Although this Logos is eternally valid, yet men are unable to understand it—not only before hearing it, but even after they have heard it for the first time. That is to say, although all things come to pass in accordance with this Logos, men seem to be quite without any experience of it—at least if they are judged in the light of such words and deeds as I am here setting forth. My own method is to distinguish each thing according to its nature, and to specify how it behaves; other men, on the contrary, are as neglectful of what they do when awake as they are when asleep.   (1)

2.   We should let ourselves be guided by what is common to all. Yet, although the Logos is common to all, most men live as if each of them had a private intelligence of his own.   (2)

3.   Men who love wisdom should acquaint themselves with a great many particulars.   (35)

4.   Seekers after gold dig up much earth and find little.   (22)

5.   Let us not make arbitrary conjectures about the greatest matters.   (47)

6.   Much learning does not teach understanding, otherwise it would have taught Hesiod and Pythagoras, Xenophanes and Hectaeus.   (40)

---

* The present grouping and numbering of the Fragments, as well as the subtitles and most of the translations, are taken by permission of Athcneum Publishers from their paperback edition of the present editor's *Heraclitus*.

7. *Of those whose discourses I have heard there is not one who attains to the realization that wisdom stands apart from all else.* (108)

8. *I have searched myself.* (101)

9. *It pertains to all men to know themselves and to be temperate.* (116)

10. *To be temperate is the greatest virtue. Wisdom consists in speaking and acting the truth, giving heed to the nature of things.* (112)

11. *The things of which there can be sight, hearing, and learning—these are what I especially prize.* (55)

12. *Eyes are more accurate witnesses than ears.* (101a)

13. *Eyes and ears are bad witnesses to men having barbarian souls.* (107)

14. *One should not act or speak as if he were asleep.* (73)

15. *The waking have one world in common, whereas each sleeper turns away to a private world of his own.* (89)

16. *Whatever we see when awake is death; when asleep, dreams.* (21)

17. *Nature loves to hide.* (123)

18. *The lord whose oracle is at Delphi neither speaks nor conceals, but gives signs.* (93)

19. *Unless you expect the unexpected you will never find [truth], for it is hard to discover and hard to attain.* (18)

UNIVERSAL FLUX

20. *Everything flows and nothing abides; everything gives way and nothing stays fixed.* (—)

21. *You cannot step twice into the same river, for other waters and yet others go ever flowing on.* (91, 12)

22. *Cool things become warm, the warm grows cool; the moist dries, the parched becomes moist.* (126)

23. *It is in changing that things find repose.* (84a)

24. *Time is a child moving counters in a game; the royal power is a child's.* (52)

25. *War is both father and king of all; some he has shown forth as gods and others as men, some he has made slaves and others free.* (53)

26. *It should be understood that war is the common condition, that strife is justice, and that all things come to pass through the compulsion of strife.* (80)

27. *Homer was wrong in saying, "Would that strife might perish from amongst gods and men." For if that were to occur, then all things would cease to exist.* (—)

PROCESSES OF NATURE

28. *There is exchange of all things for fire and of fire for all things, as there is of wares for gold and of gold for wares.* (90)

29. *This universe, which is the same for all, has not been made by any god or man, but it always has been, is, and will be—an ever-living fire, kindling itself by regular measures and going out by regular measures.* (30)

30. *[The phases of fire are] craving and satiety.* (65)

31. *It throws apart and then brings together again; it advances and retires.* (91)

32.   The transformations of fire: first, sea; and of sea, half becomes earth and half the lightning-flash.   (31)

33.   When earth has melted into sea, the resultant amount is the same as there had been before sea became hardened into earth.   (31, ctd.)

34.   Fire lives in the death of earth, air in the death of fire, water in the death of air, and earth in the death of water.   (76)

35.   The thunderbolt pilots all things.   (64)

36.   The sun is new each day.   (6)

37.   The sun is the breadth of a man's foot.   (3)

38.   If there were no sun, the other stars would not suffice to prevent its being night.   (99)

39.   The boundary line of evening and morning is the Bear; and opposite the Bear is the boundary of bright Zeus.   (120)

40.   The fairest universe is but a heap of rubbish piled up at random.   (124)

41.   Every beast is driven to pasture by a blow.   (11)

HUMAN SOUL

42.   You could not discover the limits of soul, even if you traveled by every path in order to do so; such is the depth of its meaning.   (45)

43.   Soul is the vaporization out of which everything else is composed; moreover it is the least corporeal of things and is in ceaseless flux, for the moving world can only be known by what is in motion.   (—)

44.   Souls are vaporized from what is moist.   (12)

45.   Soul has its own inner law of growth.   (115)

46.   *A dry soul is wisest and best.* [Alternative version:] *The best and wisest soul is a dry beam of light.*   (118)

47.   *Souls take pleasure in becoming moist.*   (77)

48.   *A drunken man has to be led by a boy, whom he follows stumbling and not knowing whither he goes, for his soul is moist.*   (117)

49.   *It is death to souls to become water, and it is death to water to become earth. Conversely, water comes into existence out of earth, and souls out of water.*   (36)

50.   *Even the sacred barley drink separates when it is not stirred.*   (125)

51.   *It is hard to fight against impulsive desire; whatever it wants it will buy at the cost of the soul.*   (85)

52.   *It would not be better if things happened to men just as they wish.*   (110)

53.   *Although it is better to hide our ignorance, this is hard to do when we relax over wine.*   (95)

54.   *A foolish man is a-flutter at every word.*   (87)

55.   *Fools, although they hear, are like the deaf: to them the adage applies that when present they are absent.*   (34)

56.   *Bigotry is the sacred disease.*   (46)

57.   *Most people do not take heed of the things they encounter, nor do they grasp them even when they have learned about them, although they think they do.*   (17)

58.   *If all existing things were smoke, it is by smell that we would distinguish them.*   (7)

59.   *In Hades souls perceive by smelling.*   (98)

60.   *Corpses are more fit to be thrown out than dung.*   (96)

IN RELIGIOUS PERSPECTIVE

61. *Human nature has no real understanding; only the divine nature has it.* (78)

62. *Man is not rational; there is intelligence only in what encompasses him.* (—)

63. *What is divine escapes men's notice because of their incredulity.* (86)

64. *Although intimately connected with the Logos, men keep setting themselves against it.* (72)

65. *As in the nighttime a man kindles for himself* (haptetai) *a light, so when a living man lies down in death with his vision extinguished he attaches himself* (haptetai) *to the state of death; even as one who has been awake lies down with his vision extinguished and attaches himself to the state of sleep.* (26)

66. *Immortals become mortals, mortals become immortals; they live in each other's death and die in each other's life.* (62)

67. *There await men after death such things as they neither expect nor have any conception of.* (27)

68. *They arise into wakefulness and become guardians of the living and the dead.* (63)

69. *A man's character is his guardian divinity.* (119)

70. *Greater dooms win greater destinies.* (25)

71. *Justice will overtake fabricators of lies and false witnesses.* (28)

72. *Fire in its advance will catch all things by surprise and judge them.* (66)

73. *How can anyone hide from that which never sets?* (16)

74. [When visitors unexpectedly found Heraclitus warming himself by the cooking fire:] *Here, too, are gods.* (—)

75. *They pray to images, much as if they were to talk to houses; for they do not know what gods and heroes are.* (5)

76. *Night-walkers, magicians, bacchantes, revellers, and participants in the mysteries! What are regarded as mysteries among men are unholy rituals.* (14)

77. *Their processions and their phallic hymns would be disgraceful exhibitions were it not that they are done in honor of Dionysus. But Dionysus, in whose honor they rave and hold revels, is the same as Hades.* (15)

78. *When defiled they purify themselves with blood, as though one who had stepped into filth were to wash himself with filth. If any of his fellowmen should perceive him acting in such a way, they would regard him as mad.* (5, ctd.)

79. *The Sibyl with raving mouth utters solemn, unadorned, unlovely words, but she reaches out over a thousand years with her voice because of the god within her.* (92)

MAN AMONG MEN

80. *Thinking is common to all.* (113)

81. *Men should speak with rational awareness and thereby hold on strongly to that which is shared in common—as a city holds on to its law, and even more strongly. For all human laws are nourished by the one divine law, which prevails as far as it wishes, suffices for all things, and yet is something more than they.* (114)

82. *The people should fight for their law as for their city wall.* (44)

83. *Law involves obeying the counsel of one.* (33)

84. *To me one man is worth ten thousand if he is first-rate.* (49)

85. *The best of men choose one thing in preference to all else, immortal glory in preference to mortal good; whereas the masses simply glut themselves like cattle.* (29)

86. *Gods and men honor those slain in battle.* (24)

87. *Even those who are most in repute know and maintain only what is reputed.* (28)

88. *To extinguish hybris is more needful than to extinguish a fire.* (43)

89. *It is weariness to keep toiling at the same things so that one becomes ruled by them.* (84b)

90. *Dogs bark at a person whom they do not know.* (97)

91. *What sort of mind or intelligence have they? They believe popular folktales and follow the crowd as their teachers, ignoring the adage that the many are bad, the good are few.* (104)

92. *Men are deceived in their knowledge of things that are manifest, even as Homer was who was the wisest of all the Greeks. For he was even deceived by boys killing lice when they said to him: "What we have seen and grasped, these we leave behind; whereas what we have not seen and grasped, these we carry away."* (56)

93. *Homer deserves to be thrown out of the contests and flogged, and Archilochus too.* (42)

94. *Hesiod distinguishes good days and evil days, not knowing that every day is like every other.* (106)

95. *The Ephesians had better go hang themselves, every man of them, and leave their city to be governed by youngsters, for they have banished Hermadorus, the finest man among them, declaring: "Let us not have anyone among us who excels the rest; if there should be such a one, let him go and live elsewhere."* (121)

96. *May you have plenty of wealth, you men of Ephesus, in order that you may be punished for your evil ways!* (125a)

97. *After birth men have the wish to live and to accept their dooms; then they leave behind them children to become dooms in their turn.* (20)

RELATIVITY AND PARADOX

98. *Opposition brings concord. Out of discord comes the fairest harmony.* (8)

99. *It is by disease that health is pleasant, by evil that good is pleasant, by hunger satiety, by weariness rest.* (111)

100. *Men would not have known the name of justice if these things had not occurred.* (23)

101. *Sea water is at once very pure and very foul: it is drinkable and healthful for fishes, but undrinkable and deadly for men.* (61)

102. *Donkeys would prefer hay to gold.* (9)

103. *Pigs wash in mud, and domestic fowls in dust or ashes.* (37)

104. *The handsomest ape is ugly compared with humankind; the wisest man appears as an ape when compared with a god—in wisdom, in beauty, and in all other ways.* (82, 83)

105.   A man is regarded as childish by a spirit (daemon),
just as a boy is by a man. (79)

*106.   To God all things are beautiful, good, and right; men,
on the other hand, deem some things right and others wrong.*
(102)

*107.   Doctors cut, burn, and torture the sick, and then de-
mand of them an undeserved fee for such services.* (58)

108.   The way up and the way down are one and the same.
(60)

*109.   In the circumference of the circle the beginning and
the end are common.* (103)

110.   Into the same rivers we step and do not step. (49a)

*111.   For wool-carders the straight and the winding way are
one and the same.* (59)

*112.   The bones connected by joints are at once a unitary
whole and not a unitary whole. To be in agreement is to differ;
the concordant is the discordant. From out of all the many
particulars comes oneness, and out of oneness come all the many
particulars.* (10)

*113.   It is one and the same thing to be living and dead,
awake or asleep, young or old. The former aspect in each case
becomes the latter, and the latter becomes the former, by sudden unexpected reversal.* (88)

*114.   Hesiod, whom so many accept as their wise teacher,
did not even understand the nature of day and night; for they
are one.* (57)

115.   The name of the bow is life, but its work is death.
(48)

THE HIDDEN HARMONY

116.   The hidden harmony is better than the obvious.   (54)

117.   People do not understand how that which is at variance with itself agrees with itself. There is a harmony in the bending back, as in the cases of the bow and the lyre.   (51)

118.   Listening not to me but to the Logos, it is wise to acknowledge that all things are one.   (50)

119.   Wisdom is one and unique; it is unwilling and yet willing to be called by the name of Zeus.   (32)

120.   Wisdom is one—to know the intelligence by which all things are steered through all things.   (41)

*121.   God is day and night, winter and summer, war and peace, satiety and want. But he undergoes transformations, just as * * * * * when mixed with a fragrance is named according to the particular aroma which it gives off.*   (67)

122.   The sun will not overstep his measures; if he were to do so, the Erinyes, handmaids of justice, would seek him out [for punishment].   (94)

123.   All things come in their due season.   (100)

124.   Even sleepers are workers and collaborators in what goes on in the universe.   (75)

TESTIMONIA

FROM PLATO:

T 1.   There are those who incline to the opinion of Heraclitus that all things move and nothing abides. . . . Heraclitus says, you know, that all things flow and nothing abides, and he likens the things that exist to the current of a river, saying that one cannot step into the same river twice. (*Cratylus* 401E, 402A)

T 2.   There are wise men who tell us that all things are continually flowing both upwards and downwards. (*Philebus* 43A)

FROM ARISTOTLE:

T 3.   All things are in motion, as Heraclitus says. (*Topica* 104b 21)

T 4.   Hippasus of Metapontum and Heraclitus of Ephesus declare that fire is the first-principle. (*Metaphysica* 984a 7)

T 5.   Heraclitus says that all things at some time become fire. (*Physica* 205a 3)

T 6.   Some, such as Empedocles of Akragas and Heraclitus of Ephesus, say that there is alternation in the destructive process, which goes on now in this way, now in that, continuing without end. (*De Caelo* 279b 16)

T 7.   It is logically impossible to suppose that the same thing is and is not, as some think Heraclitus said. (*Metaphysica* 1005b 24)

T 8.   Supporters of the theory of Forms were led to it by means of Heraclitus' argument concerning truth, in which he holds that whatever is perceived by the senses is in a state of flux. [Accepting that much of his argument these philosophers go on to argue] that if there is to be science or knowledge of anything there must be other entities in nature besides those perceived by the senses, inasmuch as there can be no science of what is in a state of flux. (*ibid.* 1078b 12)

T 9.   Whereas some think of the like as a friend and the opposite as an enemy, . . . others think of opposites as friends, and Heraclitus blames the poet who wrote, "Would that strife might perish from among gods and men," arguing that there could be no harmony without both low and high notes, and no living things without the pair of opposites male and female. (*Ethica Eudemia* 125a 20, 25)

T 10.   To punctuate Heraclitus is difficult because it is [often] unclear whether a given word should go with what follows or with what precedes it. When, for instance, at the beginning of his treatise he says, "Although this Logos exists always men are unaware [of it]," it is unclear whether "always" belongs with "exists" or with "are unaware."   (*Rhetorikê* 1407b 13)

FROM LATER GREEK SOURCES:

T 11.   Heraclitus, son of Blosson, was a native of Ephesus and flourished in the sixty-ninth Olympiad [504-500 B.C.]. He was lofty-minded to an unusual degree, but haughty and overbearing. When the Ephesians requested him to draw up a set of laws for the city, he refused because he considered the city's constitution to be hopelessly bad. He would retire to the temple of Artemis where he would play knuckle-bones with boys. To the Ephesians who stood around watching he burst out: "Why do you look surprised, you scoundrels? Isn't this a better pastime than taking part in your politics?" Eventually, becoming a hater of mankind, he retired into the mountains and stayed there nourishing himself on grass and roots—a mode of life that made him ill of dropsy. He died at the age of sixty.

He was nobody's pupil; he said that he sought to know himself and that he learned everything by his own efforts. Some declare, however, according to Sotion, that he had been a pupil of Xenophanes. Antisthenes, in his *Succession of the Philoso-*

phers, speaks of Heraclitus' magnanimity in renouncing his claim to the hereditary governorship [of Ephesus] in favor of his brother.

The book of which he was author is called *On Nature,* a continuous treatise divided into three parts—one on the universe, one on politics, and one on theology. Theophrastus thinks it is because of his melancholy that some parts of the work are unfinished while other parts are queerly put together. He dedicated the book in the temple of Artemis. Some say that he wrote it obscurely on purpose, in order to ensure that those who might read it would be worthy and that none should undertake it lightly. Sometimes, however, he writes with penetrating clarity, so that even the dullest can grasp his meaning and feel themselves stirred and challenged by it. For pithy profundity his exposition has no equal. (Diogenes Laertius, IX. 1, 5-7)

T 12. Heraclitus' main tenets are these. Fire is the basic element. All things are interchangeable with fire, and they come-to-be by rarefaction and condensation, but how this occurs he has not clearly explained. All things come-to-be by conflict between opposites, and the universe in its entirety flows like a river. The All is limited, constituting a single world, which is alternately born from fire and dissolved into fire, and the succession of this endless cycle of alternating periods is fixed by Destiny. That phase of the cycle which involves a coming-to-be of things is called war and strife, while that which involves destruction by fire is called concord and peace. He refers to change as the road up-down, by which the cosmos comes-to-be.

Fire by compression becomes moist, by further compression it turns into water, and then the water as it stiffens is transformed into stone. This process he calls the downward road. Then the reverse process takes place, starting with earth, which changes into water, and so on through the other phases [of the continuous process of liquefying, evaporating, and finally bursting into flame]. This process is the upward road.

Most of the phenomena [along the upward way] he explains by reference to exhalations from the sea. But there are exhalations from the earth also; those from the sea are bright and pure, while those from the earth are dark. Fire is nourished and increased by the bright exhalations, moisture by the dark ones.

Although he does not explain clearly the nature of the surrounding medium, he does say that it contains bowls with their hollow side turned toward us, and that bright exhalations collect in these concavities, where they are vaporized into flame. The resultant phenomena are the stars. The sun's flame is the brightest and hottest of these; the other stars are farther away from the earth, which is why we receive less light and heat from them. The moon is nearer to the earth, but it has to travel in a region that is impure. The sun, on the other hand, moves in a region that is transparent and unmixed, which is why it gives us more heat and light. Eclipses of the sun and moon occur when the bowls are turned upwards. The monthly phases of the moon take place as its bowl is gradually overturned. Day and night, months, and seasons of the year are due to different exhalations. Bright exhalations, when they have been vaporized into flame in the hollow orb of the sun, produce day; when dark exhalations win mastery there is night. The former cause an increase of warmth and summer; the latter, an increase of moisture and winter. His explanations of other natural phenomena are along much the same lines. (Diogenes Laertius, IX. 8-11)

T 13.   To cite the testimony of poets and mythographers regarding matters of which we are ignorant is to take, as Heraclitus says, untrustworthy and disputable claims for facts. (Polybius, *Histories* IV. xl. 3)

T 14. When I consider the propositions "Socrates is healthy" and "Socrates is sick," I must necessarily confine my acceptance to a single one only. . . . Those philosophers think otherwise, however, who posit pairs of opposites as the first-principles—notably the Heracliteans, who argue that if one term of an opposition were to cease-to-be all things would dissolve and perish. (Simplicius *Commentaria*)

T 15. Hippasus of Metapontum and Heraclitus of Ephesus declare that reality is one and in motion and limited. Taking fire as the first-principle they explain all things as derived from fire and resolved again into fire through the complementary processes of condensation and rarefaction; for fire, they assert, is the one essential nature that underlies appearances. Whatever occurs, Heraclitus declares, is a transformation of fire; and in what occurs he finds a certain order and definite time, determined by fated necessity. (Theophrastus, *Physical Opinions*)

T 16. Heraclitus and Hippasus say that the first-principle of all things is fire, and that all things both come-to-be from fire and complete their existence by turning into fire again. As the fire gets extinguished things take shape and arrange themselves into an orderly universe. First by compression the dense earth is formed; then earth, being relaxed by fire, transforms itself into water; which in turn, by rarefying, becomes air. At another time the universe and all the bodies that compose it are consumed by fire in the Conflagration. (Aëtius)

T 17. Heraclitus says that the periodic fire is eternal, and that the Logos, which is Destiny, is the craftsman who has produced all things. (*ibid.*)

T 18. Heraclitus says that war and Zeus are the same thing. (Chrysippus)

T 19.   In designating fire as the basic element of all other things Heraclitus does not identify fire with the pyramid. (Simplicius *Commentaria*)

T 20.   Whereas Parmenides, Empedocles, and Plato explain sense-perception by similarity [between sense-object and sense-organ], Anaxagoras and Heraclitus explain it in terms of contrast. . . . On the assumption that sense-perception takes place as a result of some alteration they argue that the like is not affected by the like but only by what is contrasted and thus opposite to it. On this reasoning their theory of knowledge is based. Further evidence, they think, is given by the phenomenon of touch, inasmuch as we get no sensation when the heat or cold of what touches us is the same as that of our flesh. (Theophrastus *De Sensu* I. 2)

T 21.   From the fact that honey appears bitter to some and sweet to others Democritus declared that it is neither sweet nor bitter, whereas Heraclitus said it is both. (Sextus Empiricus, *Outline of Pyrrhonism* II. 63)

T 22.   Whereas the sceptics say that things appear to have contradictory qualities, Heraclitus says that they really do have them. (*ibid.* I. 210)

T 23.   As for the first-principle and basic element of everything . . . Heraclitus, according to some, declared it to be air. (Sextus Empiricus, *Against the Physicists* I. 360)

T 24.   In distinguishing the two instruments by which men seek to obtain a knowledge of truth—namely, sense and reason—Heraclitus holds that the findings of sense-experience are untrustworthy, and he sets up reason as the criterion. He expresses his criticisms of sense-experience in the statement [Fr. 13]; by which he means to say that to trust the non-rational appearances of sense is to be a barbarian soul. He declares that reason (*logos*) is the judge of truth—not just any kind of reason, but such as is sharable and divine. The meaning of this must be briefly explained.

One of his favorite tenets as a "philosopher of nature" (*physikos*) is that what encompasses us is rational and intelligent. . . . According to Heraclitus it is by inbreathing the divine Reason that we become intelligent. During sleep the pores of our senses are closed, so that the mind in us is shut off from what is akin to it in the surrounding world, and its connection with other things is then preserved only at the vegetative level through the pores of the skin. Being thus cut off it loses its formative power of memory. But when we wake up again it peers out through the pores of the senses, which serve as little windows, and by thus entering into relation with what surrounds us it regains its power of reason. Just as coals when brought close to the fire undergo a change which renders them incandescent, while if moved away they become extinguished; so likewise that portion of the surrounding milieu which is making a sojourn in the body, in losing contact with its source, therein loses its rational character by the separation, inasmuch as its only communion with the outer universe now takes place through the body's very numerous pores.

Heraclitus asserts, then, that the sharable and divine Reason (*logos*), by participating in which we become rational, is the criterion of truth. Hence that which appears to all men as a shared experience is trustworthy, inasmuch as it is perceived by the sharable and divine Reason; but what affects only a single individual is, on the contrary, untrustworthy. Thus in beginning his discourse on Nature the writer of whom I am speaking points, in effect, to the enveloping reality when he declares [Fr. 1]. Then having in these words expressly stated that we do and think everything through participation in the divine Reason, he goes on to say after a short space [Fr. 2]. This is nothing else but an explanation of how things are ordered in the All. Therefore, in so far as we share in the memory of It we say what is true, but when we utter our own private thoughts we speak false.

In this passage and in these words, then, he most explicitly declares that the sharable Reason is the criterion: i.e., that appearances are trustworthy when they are shared in common and are judged by the sharable Reason, whereas appearances which are private to a single individual are false. (Sextus Empiricus, *Against the Logicians* I. 126-134)

T 25.   Heraclitus says that both life and death exist in our state of life and in our state of death alike; that during life our souls are dead and buried within us, and that when we die our souls revive and live. (Sextus Empiricus, *Outlines of Pyrrhonism* III. 230)

T 26.   Heraclitus' language is close to that of Empedocles when he says that strife and love are the first-principles of everything, that God is intelligent fire, and that everything shares in the universal movement of things so that nothing stands still. Moreover he agrees with Empedocles' expressed view that the entire region occupied by man, from the earth's surface up to the level of the moon, is full of evils, the regions beyond the moon being much purer. (Hippolytus *Refutatio* Bk. I, Chap. 4)

T 27.   Heraclitus says that souls when set free from the body pass into the soul of the All, which is akin to them in nature and essence. (Aëtius)

T 28.   Heraclitus says that all things happen according to Destiny, and that Destiny itself is necessary, for he uses the expression, "It is absolutely determined." He says furthermore that reason, which pervades the All to its very essence, is one with Destiny. It has the form of aetherial matter, it is the seed from which all things are generated, and it is the measure of allotted time. (*ibid.*)

T 29.   The universe, he says, is generated not according to time but according to thought.   (*ibid.*)

T 30.   The sun, he says, is an intelligent burning mass, which has arisen [and daily renews itself] from the sea.   (*ibid.*)

T 31.   He says that the sun and moon are bowl-shaped; that they receive bright rays from the moist vaporizations [from the sea], and thus produce their visible light. The sun's appearance is brighter because it moves through purer air; whereas the moon, moving through thicker air, shines more dimly. (*ibid.*)

T 32.   Even wise old Heraclitus was unable to dissuade the Ephesians from washing away mud with mud.   (*Letters of Apollonius of Tyana* 27)

T 33.   Heraclitus describes these [religious mysteries] as "cures," on the ground that they heal our sufferings and release our souls from the conditions which beset them at birth. (Iamblichus *De Mysteriis* I. 11)

T 34.   Heraclitus says that men's conjectures are like children's toys.   (Iamblichus *De Anima*)

T 35.   Sacrifices are of two kinds. There are those, as Heraclitus says, in which only one or a very few engage after they have undergone full purification; the rest are merely material. (Iamblichus *De Mysteriis* V. 15)

FROM LATIN SOURCES:

T 36.   As for those who have believed that fire is the basic substance of everything and that the universe is composed of fire alone, it is evident that they have fallen far away from true reasoning. Their leader, the first to enter the fray, was Heraclitus, of bright repute because of his dark sayings. . . .

But what I want to know is, how can things be so various if they are made of fire purely? It does no good to explain that hot fire becomes densified and rarified, since the particles of fire still have the same nature as fire itself, and how could the existing variety of things be produced by variations of density and rarity of fire alone? (Lucretius *De Rerum Natura* I. 635-654)

T 37.   In tracing all things back to a primal fiery force, Balbus, you seem to be following Heraclitus; however, not all are agreed as to how he should be interpreted, for he did not want to make his meaning clear. . . . At any rate, why should fire rather than air (*anima*) be regarded as that from which the mind (*animus*) of living beings is derived? (Cicero *De Natura Deorum* III. 35-36)

T 38.   Heraclitus the philosopher says that the soul is a spark of starry essence. (Macrobius, *Commentary on the Dream of Scipio* I. 14)

T 39.   Heraclitus says that if happiness consisted in bodily pleasures we would have to describe cattle as happy when they are eating fodder. (Albertus Magnus)

4

The Eleatic School

THE SCHOOL OF ELEA is of unique historical importance. It represents the first all-out attempt in the western world to establish
pure reason, with its demands of logical consistency and related-
ness, as the sole criterion of truth. The main Eleatic position,
established by Parmenides, reaffirmed and developed with individual approaches and twists by Zeno and Melissus, can be sum-
marized in the two propositions, (1) *Being is one* and (2) *Being
is unchanging.* These are formidably abstract avowals, and they
bring us to the very limits of what can be said and asked; some
would complain, indeed, that they take us quite beyond those
limits. At any rate the challenge which the two Eleatic propositions have presented to subsequent philosophers—notably to the
critical pluralists who are the subject of the next two chapters
and to Plato—was both forceful and pervasive, and a student of
Greek philosophy cannot avoid coming to terms with them.
Granted the dubious nature of the questions, or purported questions, "Is ultimate reality one or many?" and "Does ultimate reality change or remain always the same?" (questions which, more
than any others, have brought metaphysics into disrepute in certain quarters), we should nevertheless agree that a school of
powerful and serious thinkers, such as the surviving arguments
of the Eleatics show them unmistakably to be, is not likely to
dedicate its mental energies for two or more generations to ques-

tions that mean nothing at all. The meanings may be partisan and one-sided, sometimes quaintly so, and perhaps no one would care to uphold them today as offering a suitable procedure for philosophical inquiry. Nevertheless the very limitations of Eleaticism serve to delineate its monistic perspective the more clearly; and monism has long been, whatever its guises and combinations, one of the dominant ideas, even to its opponents, in the range of human thought.

i. Parmenides

The founder of the philosophy in question was Parmenides of Elea, by the name of which city the philosophy came to be designated. Even if, as an ancient tradition asserts, Parmenides may have studied in his younger days under Xenophanes, the temperaments of the two men are vastly different, as will be evident to anyone who compares their respective groups of utterances, and the alleged connection between the lively religious monotheism of the one and the abstract metaphysical monism of the other is too tenuous to be of any service in suggesting a view as to their relations.

In trying to date Parmenides we are pulled in one direction by Diogenes Laertius' report that he flourished in the sixty-ninth Olympiad, which is to say 504 to 500 B.C., and in the contrary direction by Plato's statement that Parmenides had visited Athens while Socrates was a very young man (T 1, 2). Since we know, by deduction from Socrates' own statement in the *Apologia,* that he himself was born about 469 B.C., and since he could hardly have been less than eighteen or nineteen at the time of the philosophical encounter which Plato elaborates in his dialogue the *Parmenides,* we must suppose that Parmenides' visit to Athens occurred close to 450 B.C. Although in T 2 Plato speaks loosely of Parmenides as "very old" at that time, in T 1 he calls him

"elderly" and gives his age as sixty-five. It seems unlikely that
Plato would have specified the exact age of so eminent a man
unless it were known to be true; and the vaguer remark which in
the *Theaetetus* he attributes to Socrates (T 2) is doubtless meant
to suggest the impression made upon a nineteen-year-old youth
by so venerable a man. Proceeding on the evidence of T 1, then,
we must estimate that Parmenides was born close to 515 B.C.;
which would knock out, of course, the statement (T 15) that he
flourished between 504 and 500. But considering Plato's strong interest in the Eleatic philosophy and the occasional participation
by Eleatic visitors in the Socratic discussions (cf. T 5) it seems
reasonable to accept Plato's dates as the more probable ones. As
a result we may take it as likely that Parmenides' poem *On Nature*
was completed at some time after 480 and probably between 470
and 460 B.C.

The poem, composed in the epic meter of dactylic hexameters,
begins with a symbolic description of what was presumably a
unique and central experience in Parmenides' life—the passage out
of darkness into light, away from illusion and into the presence of
the Goddess of Truth. It is she who speaks forth the doctrines of
the poem. That is not to say, however, that Parmenides is a passive hearer; he, too, is the speaker of the divinely received words,
and he utters them on the authority of "true belief"—at once
the rational intuition of his own mind and the yielding of his
individual mind to the impersonal demands of rational self-
evidence. The Goddess is a symbol, yes, but as with all deeply
felt symbols there is continuity and interplay between image and
meaning, between what is described and what is meant. Any
attempt to sever the two aspects would at once reduce the description to triviality and subtly shift the focus of the doctrine. The
passage from illusion to truth is not a trick to be mastered, nor a
task for the conscious mind alone; it is, when genuine, a conversion of the whole self away from the trivial and toward the newly
found point of ultimate concern. Plato in his parable of the cave

in *The Republic* and Dante at the outset of *The Divine Comedy* offer two of the most familiar symbolic accounts of this kind; Parmenides, hampered by the limitations of a more primitive language and with a less practiced literary skill, attempts in his opening lines to say much the same thing. But of course no two such experiences are ever the same, and it is never certain when and how far a particular symbolic description will speak inwardly to a particular reader.

After graciously welcoming the newly arrived postulant and assuring him of the divine nature of the forces that have guided his conversion, the Goddess makes her opening statement of the two "ways"—the two modes of consciousness between which man is capable of choosing: the way of strict rational coherence ("well-rounded truth") and the way of popular opinion, of custom, of yielding uncritically to familiar belief. The way of truth is rigorous; the fullest formulation of it is contained in the long passage (Fr. 7) which has been preserved for us by the ever admirable labors of Simplicius. The core of its meaning is put into a single word: *Esti*, "Is." Greek syntax permits, as English normally does not, the use of the verb without an expressed subject; our English linguistic habits make us want to say "It is," and then the purity of the utterance is spoiled, for the "it" appears to raise a question. Any such question is illegitimate, however, a mere by-product of our modern syntax, distorting the precarious meaning of the Greek. The truth which the Goddess is declaring lies in the simple verb "is," and to the Greek mind this word tends to stand in natural contrast to the word "becomes." Now as pointed out in the General Introduction, the verb "becomes," no less than the verb "is," tends in Greek to blend two usages—the absolute and the copulative. "Becomes" (*genetai*) taken absolutely means "comes-to-be"; taken copulatively it means "turns into," as when we might say of the sky at sunset "the blue becomes red." The meanings, as shown earlier, are never entirely separable, for when blue changes into red there is a coming-to-be of red. What the Goddess declares is

that in neither of its aspects can the word "become" describe
what is real; that it expresses only popular prejudice, something
like what Bacon calls an idol of the tribe, and that in reality
there is no becoming—i.e., there is no changing from this to that,
and there is no coming-to-be.

In attempting to utter so imposingly abstract a doctrine Parmenides is obliged to use metaphors; for in passing from simple
and concrete affairs to complex and remote ones our preëxisting
language is never adequate, and we have to stretch familiar words
and images to new demanding uses. Consider, for example, in
Sections A and C of Fragment 7, the metaphoric use of the ideas
of Justice (*Dikê*), Necessity (*Anangkê*), and Natural Law (*Themis*), and read what the Glossary has to say about the independent
meaning of these words. Other functional uses of metaphor can
be discovered with a little exploration.

But it is not enough for a man to know the way of truth, the
Goddess warns; it is needful also to learn about "the opinions of
mortals which lack true belief"—in order to be able to appraise
them judiciously and not be taken in by them. Sound advice no
doubt, and a welcome antidote to the uncompromising strictness of
the True Way. But now we meet with a difficulty. Men have established the habit, we are told, of "naming two thought-forms,"
described as fire and earth, or the bright and the dark (Fr. 9),
light and night (Fr. 10), but *one* of these "ought not to be named."
Does this mean that the fiery bright belongs to the way of truth
while its contrary the dense dark belongs to the way of opinion?
Is it the latter alone that "ought not to be named"? Taking the
qualities symbolically we might find such an interpretation plausible, for it has long been the practice of man to connect the sun
and the visible brightness of the upper sky (the *aether*) with the
intellectual ideas of truth and wisdom. But if we consider the antithesis in its logical import, we clearly cannot affirm one member
of the pair while denying the other. The opposites light and dark
belong equally to the world of becoming; if the reality of that

world is denied, then light and darkness together (not just one of them) must fall into the shadowland of opinion. It does not seem that the difficulty is sufficiently resolved in the surviving Fragments.

FRAGMENTS

THE JOURNEY

1. The steeds that draw my chariot were conducting me to the farthermost reach of my desire, bringing me at length on to the resounding road of the Goddess, along which he who knows is borne through all cities. Along this road I was carried— yes, the wise horses drew me in my chariot while maidens led the way. The axle, urged round and round by the whirling wheels on either side, glowed in the sockets and gave forth a singing hum. The handmaidens of the sun, who had left the realms of night and had thrown back their veils from their faces, were driving the chariot speedily toward the light.

We came to the gates of day and night, which are fitted between a lintel above and a stone threshold below. Although the gates are of aetherial substance they have the strength of mighty doors when closed, and retributive Justice secures them with bolts that both punish and reward. But the maidens cajoled her with gentle words and soon managed to persuade her to pull back the bolts from the gates. When these gates were flung back on their hinges, which were nailed to bronze posts on either side, a wide expanse was revealed through the open doorway: it showed a broad avenue, along which the maidens steered my horses and chariot. The Goddess greeted me kindly, and taking my hand in hers she spoke these words:

*"Welcome, my son, you who come to our abode with im-
mortal charioteers at the reins! It is no evil fate that has set you
on this road, but Right and Justice have brought you here,
far away from the beaten paths of men. It is needful that you
learn of all matters—both the unshaken heart of well-rounded
truth and the opinions of mortals which lack true belief. For it
is needful that by passing everything under review you should
learn this also—how to judge of mere seeming."*   (1)

THE WAY OF TRUTH

2.   [The Goddess speaks further:] *"Never shall it be proven
that not-being is. From that path of inquiry restrain your mind.
Do not let custom, born of everyday experience, tempt your
eyes to be aimless, your ear and tongue to be echoes. Let reason
be your judge when you consider this much disputed question.
The heart when left to itself misses the road."*   (7)

3.   *"Gaze steadfastly at things which, though far away, are
yet present to the mind. For you cannot cut off being from being: it does not scatter itself into a universe and then reunify."*
(4)

4.   *"It is indifferent to me at what point I begin, for in
any case I must return again to that from which I set out."*   (5)

5.   *"Come, then, listen to my word and take heed of it: I
will tell you of the two roads of inquiry which offer themselves
to the mind. The one way, that It Is and cannot not-be, is the
way of credibility based on truth. The other way, that It Is Not
and that not-being must be, cannot be grasped by the mind;
for you cannot know not-being and cannot express it."*   (2)

6. *"It is necessary both to say and to think that being is. For to be is possible and not-to-be is impossible. I bid you consider this, and I warn you against another path, along which mortals wander ignorantly, with divided minds and scattered thoughts, so befuddled and helpless as to resemble the deaf and blind. There are crowds of them, without discernment, maintaining that to be and not to be are the same and not the same, and that everything is in a state of movement and counter-movement."* (6)

7. *(A) "There remains, then, but one word by which to express the [true] road: Is. And on this road there are many signs that What Is has no beginning and never will be destroyed: it is whole, still, and without end. It neither was nor will be, it simply is—now, altogether, one, continuous. How could you go about investigating its birth? How and whence could it have grown? I shall not allow you to say or think of it as coming from not-being, for it is impossible to say or think that not-being is. Besides, what could have stirred up activity so that it should arise from not-being later rather than earlier?*

Necessarily therefore, either it simply Is or it simply Is Not. Strong conviction will not let us think that anything springs from Being except itself. Justice does not loosen her fetters to let Being be born or destroyed, but holds them fast. Thus our decision must be made in these terms: Is or Is Not. Surely by now we agree that it is necessary to reject the unthinkable unsayable path as untrue and to affirm the alternative as the path of reality and truth. (8: 1-18)

(B) "How could What Is be something of the future? How could it come-to-be? For if it were coming-to-be, or if it

were going to be in the future, in either case there would be a time when it is not. Thus coming-to-be is quenched, and [by similar reasoning] destruction is unthinkable.   (8: 19-25)

(C)   *"Moreover it is immovable, held so in mighty bonds. And it is without beginning and end, because both creation and destruction have been driven away by true belief. Remaining always the same and in the same place by itself, it stays fixed where it is. For strong Necessity holds it in bonds of limit, which constrain it on all sides; Natural Law forbids that Being should be other than perfectly complete. It stands in need of nothing; for if it needed anything at all it would need everything.*   (8: 26-33)

(D)   *"Thinking and the object of thought are the same. For you will not find thought apart from being, nor either of them apart from utterance. Indeed, there is not anything at all apart from being, because Fate has bound it together so as to be whole and immovable. Accordingly, all the usual notions that mortals accept and rely on as if true—coming-to-be and perishing, being and not-being, change of place and variegated shades of color—these are nothing more than names.*   (8: 34-41)

(E)   *"Since there has to be limit, Being is complete on every side, like the mass of a well-rounded sphere, equally balanced in every direction from the center. Clearly it cannot be greater in any direction than in any other, inasmuch as there is no not-being to prevent it from reaching out equally, nor is it the nature of Being to be more here and less there. The All is inviolable. Since it is equal to itself in all directions, it must be homogeneous within the limits."*   (8: 42-49)

8.   *Thought and being are the same.*   (3)

THE WAY OF OPINION

9.   [The Goddess continues:] *"Here I bring to a close my trustworthy rational discourse concerning truth. Learn next about the opinions of men, as you listen to the deceptive ordering of my words. For men have established the habit of naming two thought-forms; therein they have erred, because one of the forms ought not to be named. They have distinguished the thought-forms as opposed in character and as having properties which set them apart from each other. On the one hand there is the fire of the upper sky, gentle, rarefied, and everywhere identical with itself; on the other hand there lies opposed to it utter darkness, dense and heavy. I shall tell you about this supposed arrangement as men understand it, in order that your knowledge of such matters may not be inferior to theirs."*   (8: 50-61)

10.   *"When all things have been named light and night [according to the distinction that is supposed to exist between them] then everything must be full of light and of obscure darkness at once, and of both equally, since neither of them has anything in common with the other."*   (9)

11.   *"You shall come to know the nature of the sky, and the signs of the sky, and the unseen works of the pure bright torch of the sun and how they came into being. You shall learn the nature of the round-faced moon and its wandering works. You shall know also the encompassing empyrean, whence it arose, and how Necessity grasped and chained it so as to fix the limits of the stars."*   (10)

12. *"[You shall learn] how earth and sun and moon and the sky that is common to all, how the Milky Way and outermost Olympus and all the burning power of the stars arose."* (11)

13. *The smaller orbits are filled with unmixed fire; those next to them are filled with darkness, although an allotted measure of light accompanies them. In their midst is the divinity who steers everything; she it is who rules over love-unions and painful births everywhere, prompting female to join with male and male with female.* (12)

14. *First of all the gods she devised Eros.* (13)

15. *[The moon], as she wanders around the earth, shines at night with a light that is not her own. . . . She is always gazing towards the rays of the sun.* (14, 15)

16. *When woman and man mix the seeds of love together, the power that results from the mingling of different bloods, if it preserve harmony, fashions a well-formed body. But if there is hostility between the seeds that intermingle, so that they do not produce a unity in the newly formed body, then the growing embryo will be badly disturbed by the conflict of the seeds.* (18)

17. *On the right boys, on the left girls.* (17)

18. *The mind of man is constituted according to the blending of the very complex bodily parts in each instance. In all men and on all occasions it is the same: thinking consists in the composition of bodily parts. For it is an excess in the body that constitutes thought.* (16)

19. *Thus according to common opinion things came into being, thus they are now, and thus at length after they have reached maturity they will perish. To each kind of thing men have assigned a distinctive name.* (19)

TESTIMONIA

FROM PLATO:

T 1.   Antiphon said Pythadorus had told him that Zeno and Parmenides once came to Athens for the great Panathenaea. At that time Parmenides was already elderly, about sixty-five years of age, with white hair and a handsome and noble countenance, while Zeno was about forty, tall and good-looking. It is said that they had at one time been lovers. On that visit they were lodging at the house of Pythadorus outside the wall; and Socrates and a number of others came there, mainly in order to hear Zeno's writings, which the visitors had brought with them to Athens for the first time. Socrates was then a very young man.   (*Parmenides* 127B-C)

T 2.   *Socrates:* Parmenides seems to me, in the words of Homer, a man toward whom one feels reverence tinged with awe. When I was but a youth and he was a very old man I conversed with him, and he struck me as having a wonderful depth of mind. I fear that perhaps we fail to understand what he said, and even more to understand his reasons for saying it. (*Theaetetus* 183B)

T 3.   *Socrates:* When you want to clarify a point do you like to begin with a long explanation of your own or do you prefer to proceed by raising questions? I was present once when Parmenides used the latter method, and the discussion that he elicited was really admirable. I was a young man at that time, and he was very old.   (*Sophist* 217C)

T 4.   *Socrates:* There are some who teach the very opposite of the doctrine [of perpetual change] and who declare: "It is immovable and its name is the All." This and other such dissenting doctrines are taught by Melissus, Parmenides, and their associates: they maintain that everything is one and stationary and entirely self-contained, since there is no empty place into which to move. (*Theaetetus* 180a)

T 5. *An unnamed visitor from Elea:* The Eleatic group in our part of the world, starting with Xenophanes or even earlier, says that all things, although many in name, are really one. (*Sophist* 242d)

FROM ARISTOTLE:

T 6. If there is only one first-principle in the universe and it is changeless, as Parmenides and Melissus say . . . (*Physica* 184b 16)

T 7. All these thinkers set up as first-principles some pair of opposites, despite the fact that they declare the All to be unchanging; for even Parmenides sets up hot and cold as first-principles, calling them fire and water. (*ibid*. 188a 19)

T 8. Whereas Melissus speaks of the Whole as unlimited, Parmenides offers a more acceptable view in declaring that the Whole is limited and extends equally in every direction from the center. (*ibid*. 207a 16)

T 9. Parmenides seems to have conceived of reality as one by definition, whereas Melissus conceived of it as one materially; therefore the former takes it as limited, the latter as unlimited. (*Metaphysica* 986b 19)

T 10. On the ground that not-being, as contrasted with being, is nothing at all, Parmenides is forced to conclude that Being is one and that there is nothing else. But again, like the others, he posits two basic principles, the hot and the cold, or, as he calls them, fire and earth; and of these he puts the hot on the side of Being, the cold on the side of Not-Being. (*ibid*. 986b 29)

T 11. None of those who have affirmed that the All is a unity have grasped clearly the meaning of that kind of causal explanation, except perhaps Parmenides, and he in so far as he virtually postulates not a single cause but two. (*ibid.* 984b 2)

T 12.   That which is other than Being is not; hence, by Parmenides' argument, it must follow that all things are Being, and hence one. (*ibid.* 1001a 32)

T 13.   When dealing with apparent coming-to-be Parmenides described the being and not-being which it involves as fire and earth. (*De Generatione et Corruptione* 318b 17)

T 14.   Certain earlier thinkers maintained that What Is must necessarily be one and immovable: they argue that since the void does not exist What Is cannot be moved, and that there cannot be a plurality of things because there is no void to keep them apart. (*ibid.* 325a 3)

FROM LATER GREEK SOURCES:

T 15.   Parmenides, son of Pyres and a native of Elea, was a pupil of Xenophanes. But although he listened to Xenophanes' teachings Parmenides was no follower of his. According to Sotion's account he also associated with Ameinias the Pythagorean, who although poor was a most worthy man. After the death of Ameinias, whose teachings were more to his taste, Parmenides, who was of good family and quite wealthy, built him a shrine. It was Ameinias and not Xenophanes who led him to adopt the peaceful life of a student.

Parmenides was the first to declare that the earth is spherical and is situated at the center. He maintained that there are two elements, fire and earth, the one playing the role of craftsman, the other of material. The coming-to-be of man he explained as originating from the sun. Heat and cold he regarded as more basic than the sun, and indeed as the basic constituents of everything. Soul and mind he held to be identical. He divided philosophy into two parts, the one dealing with truth, the other with opinion.

He flourished in the sixty-ninth Olympiad [504-500 B.C.].
It is said that he was the first to discover the identity of Hesperus
and Phosphorus [the evening and morning appearances of the
planet Venus]: at least so Favorinus says in the fifth book of
his *Memorabilia,* although some others attribute the discovery
to Pythagoras. On the authority of Speusippus in his treatise
On Philosophers it is said that Parmenides held a legislative
office in his native city. According to Favorinus in his *Miscellaneous History* Parmenides was the first to use the "Achilles
and the Tortoise" argument. (Diogenes Laertius IX. 3)

T 16.   Declaring that the All is eternal and yet undertaking
to explain the coming-to-be of things, Parmenides tries to work
out his views in a double manner. From the standpoint of truth
he postulates that the All is one, ungenerated, and in the form
of a sphere; while in terms of popular opinion he explains the
generation of phenomena by two first-principles, fire and earth,
the latter being identified with matter, the former with cause
and agent. (Theophrastus, *Physical Opinions*)

T 17.   In the first book of his *Physical Opinions* Theophrastus summarizes Parmenides' view as follows: Whatever is other
than being is not-being; not-being is nothing whatever; therefore
being is one. (Simplicius *Commentaria*)

T 18.   Parmenides holds that the All is one and eternal,
without beginning, and spherical in shape. However, he does
not escape the opinion of the many, for he speaks of fire and
earth as first-principles, earth being the material and fire the
active cause. He declares that the world will come to an end,
but he does not say how. The All is eternal, he says, without
beginning, spherical, homogeneous, independent of place, unchanging, and limited. (Hippolytus *Refutatio*)

T 19.   Parmenides taught that there are "crowns," or con-
centric orbits,—one of rarefied matter, another of dense, and
others containing various mixtures of light [rare] and dark

[dense]. A solid wall, he said, forms the periphery, and under it is a crown of fire; the innermost center of all the crowns is solid, and is immediately surrounded by a ring of fire. Of the mixed crowns the one that is nearest the center is the source of motion and generation; this is what he has described as "the goddess who steers and who holds the keys"; he characterizes her as Justice and as Necessity.   (Aëtius)

T 20.   On the whole Parmenides has said nothing definite about sensation, except that rational awareness exists according as one or other of the two basic elements is in excess. For according as the hot or the cold predominates so does the understanding come-to-be [and diminish]. A better and purer understanding is derived from the hot; but it, too, requires a certain proportion. [Fr. 18 is quoted.]

Since he holds that thinking and perceiving are the same, it follows that remembering and forgetting also come about as a result of the mixture. He does not explain, however, what happens if the elements [the hot and the cold] enter into the mixture in equal amounts—i.e., whether or not thinking will then occur, and what its disposition will then be.   (Theophrastus *De Sensu* I. 3)

T 21.   He says it is owing to its complete lack of fire that a corpse does not perceive light, heat, and sound; that it does, however, perceive cold and silence and similar qualities. In general, he holds, all being involves a certain degree of knowing. (*ibid*. I. 4)

FROM A LATIN SOURCE:

T 22.   Parmenides devised the theory that there is a sort of contrivance like a "crown," as he called it,—an orb of light with continuous heat, arching the sky. He spoke of this as a god. . . . Moreover he raised war, discord, desire, and other such transient things to the status of gods.   (Cicero *De Natura Deorum* I. 28)

ii. Zeno

Zeno of Elea, the most eminent disciple of Parmenides, flourished about the middle of the fifth century B.C. Evidently he was a man who combined cleverness and fortitude to an unusual degree; the one virtue being shown by the skill of his arguments, the other by the well attested tale of his accepting death by torture rather than reveal the names of the friends who had conspired with him unsuccessfully to overthrow a local tyrant. He was about twenty-five years younger than Parmenides, according to Plato, and devoted himself largely to devising arguments to confute opponents of the doctrine of the One.

Zeno's method of counter-attack consisted in undertaking to prove that the thesis of pluralism, the not unusual assumption that a plurality of things does really exist, runs into even greater absurdities than Parmenides' own doctrine. In order to do so he employed, and some say he first invented, the method of *reductio ad absurdum*—the form of argument which then or soon afterwards came to be called the *epicheirêma*. Aristotle, in Book VII of his *Topica*, defines an *epicheirêma* as "a dialectical syllogism"; that is to say, a connected piece of reasoning which takes as its initial premise not an independently chosen proposition, but something which an opponent has affirmed and which the disputant undertakes to break down. Zeno is said to have devised forty different *epicheirêmata* in support of one or another aspect of Parmenides' monism. He carried his destructive method of argument so far and so effectively as to draw from Seneca a few centuries later the remark: "If I accede to Parmenides there is nothing left but the One; if I accede to Zeno, not even the One is left."

Unfortunately not much is available that can be accepted as direct quotation of Zeno's actual words. The ever resourceful

Simplicius, in his commentary on Aristotle's *Physica,* has quoted the three passages which constitute the Fragments that follow. Zeno's more celebrated arguments, those concerning spatial movement, are not preserved in his own words, but only as paraphrased by later philosophers, particularly Aristotle. The loss of the exact words is comparatively unimportant, however, because the logical shape of the argument is what counts, and this is discoverable from the paraphrase which Aristotle has given in the sixth book of his *Physica* (T 2).

FRAGMENTS

1.   If things are many they must be finite in number. For they must be as many as they are, neither more nor less; and if they are as many as they are, that means they are finite in number.

On the other hand, if things are many they must be infinite in number. For there are always other things between any that exist, and between these there are always yet others. Thus things are infinite in number.   (3)

2.   If a thing exists, then either it has magnitude or it does not.

A.   Say it has no magnitude. Then if added to another existing thing it would not make the latter any larger. That is to say, if something without magnitude is added to another thing, the other thing cannot thereby increase in magnitude. It follows that the thing added is nothing. For if something does not lessen the thing it is subtracted from, and does not increase the thing it is added to, then surely that something is nothing.

B.   [We conclude from the foregoing argument that] if anything lacks size [and bulk] it does not exist. If something

exists, then, its parts must have size and bulk, and moreover
they must be at a certain distance from each other. By the same
reasoning each part of a part must have size and bulk, and the
same is true of each lesser part, and so on. In short, the same
reasoning holds good without limit: no part, however small,
can be the ultimate part, nor will any part ever lack parts of
its own. Therefore, if things are many, they must be both small
and large—so small as to have no size, so large as to be infinite.
(2, 1)

3. *If anything is moving, it must be moving either in the*
place in which it is or in a place in which it is not. However,
it cannot move in the place in which it is [for the place in
which it is at any moment is of the same size as itself and hence
allows it no room to move in], and it cannot move in the place
in which it is not. Therefore movement is impossible.   (—)

4. *If place existed, it would have to be* in *something, i.e.,*
in a place.   (—)

TESTIMONIA

FROM PLATO:

T 1.   I see, Parmenides, said Socrates, that Zeno wishes to
associate himself with you not only in friendship but also in his
writings. What he has written represents virtually the same position as your own, but by altering the form of his arguments he
tries to delude us into thinking he says something new. For you
in your verses declare that the All is One, and you set forth
admirable proofs in support of your thesis; while he, on the

other hand, says that the All is not many, and he too adduces many weighty proofs in support. One of you affirms unity, the other denies plurality. Your expressions are so diverse that on the surface your arguments appear to have nothing in common, although you are really both saying almost the same thing. Such ingenuity of expression is quite beyond the power of most of us.

Yes Socrates, Zeno replied, but you have not quite grasped the true purport of my writings. In pursuing arguments you are like a Spartan hound tracking his quarry, but it escapes your notice that my treatise is not by any means so pretentious as to have been written with the aim you ascribe to it. I was not trying to dress it up to make it appear a great performance in men's eyes. The appearance that you speak of is mere accident. Actually the purpose of my writings has been to support the argument of Parmenides against those who try to make him look foolish by deriving absurd consequences from his doctrine that all is one. What my arguments are designed to do is turn the tables on those who believe in plurality; I try to show that on close examination their thesis involves more absurd consequences than the doctrine of the One. In just that argumentative spirit I wrote my book when I was a young man, but after it was written someone stole it, so that I did not have the option of deciding whether or not I wanted to make it public. (*Parmenides* 128A-E)

FROM ARISTOTLE:

T 2. Zeno argues fallaciously that since a body is [defined to be] at rest when it is in a place of the same size as itself, and since a [supposedly] moving body would be at any given instant in just such a place, it follows that the arrow in flight does not move at all. This is a false conclusion, however; for time is not made up of instantaneous moments. . . . Actually there are four logical conundrums which Zeno has formulated with regard to spatial movement, and there is need to find solutions to them.

The first of his arguments denies that movement exists on the ground that a moving body would have to go half the distance before it could go the entire distance.

The second is the so-called "Achilles" argument. It declares that even the swiftest runner will never overtake the slowest, because the pursuer must first reach the point from which the pursued has set out [at which moment the latter will have reached a new point, which the pursuer will then have to reach, and so on], so that the slower runner will always be some distance ahead. The argument is essentially the same as the one that depends on repeated bisection; the difference is that in this one we are not limited to dividing the distance into halves.

The third is the argument that an arrow in flight is really stationary. The proof rests upon the assumption that time is composed of instantaneous moments; if this is not granted there will be no syllogism.

The fourth argument deals with two equally spaced columns of men in the stadium marching in opposite directions, the one column starting from the outset of the race-course and the other from the turning-point. Marching at equal speeds they pass an equally placed column of stationary men. [On the ground that the two moving columns pass each other, man for man, in half the time that the men of each moving column take to pass those of the stationary column] the conclusion is drawn that the half is equal to the whole. The fallacy lies . . . in failing to distinguish between a comparison with something moving and a comparison with something at rest.   (*Physica* 239b 5 ff.)

T 3.   It is not hard to solve Zeno's difficulty that if place is something it must be *in* something; . . . for the vessel is not part of its contents.   (*Physica* 210b 20, 28)

FROM LATER GREEK SOURCES:

T 4.   Zeno was a citizen of Elea. Apollodorus in his *Chronology* speaks of him as the son of Teletagoras by birth but of Parmenides by adoption. At any rate he was a pupil of Parmenides and was his special friend. Aristotle attributes to Zeno the discovery of dialectic.

He was a man of excellent character both as philosopher and as citizen. His extant books bear the marks of a deep intellect. As a citizen he plotted the overthrow of Nearchus the tyrant but was arrested. On being questioned after his arrest as to who his accomplices were who smuggled arms into Lipara he gave the names of the tyrant's own friends, in order to deprive him of supporters.

Zeno was as indifferent to worldly reputation as Heraclitus had been. He spent his life in his native town of Elea, whose only outstanding virtue was the rearing of brave men, preferring it to the splendors of Athens which he visited very rarely. He flourished in the seventy-ninth Olympiad [464-460 B.C.].

Zeno was the first to propound the "Achilles" argument, although Favorinus ascribes its origin to Parmenides. Some of the beliefs that he held are as follows. [From the standpoint of appearance] there are many universes, but there is no empty space between them. The nature of things arose out of the pairs hot and cold, dry and moist, and these get transformed into one another. Man's coming-to-be is from the earth, and the soul is formed by a union of the qualities just mentioned, so blended that no single element predominates. (Diogenes Laertius IX. 25-29)

T 5.   Aristotle regarded Parmenides' pupil Zeno as the originator of dialectic. (Sextus Empiricus, *Against the Logicians* I. 7)

T 6.   A puzzle which Zeno the Eleatic propounded to Protagoras the Sophist. Tell me, Protagoras, he said, does one grain of millet make a noise when it falls? Or at any rate does one-tenth of a grain? On receiving a negative reply Zeno went on: Does a bushel measure of millet make a noise when it falls? Protagoras assented, and Zeno continued: But surely what is true of a quantity of millet must be true of its components—that is, of the single grain and even the ten-thousandth part of a grain. Must there not be some noise, then, in every case? For surely the noise must be proportionate to the conditions that produce the noise. It follows, then, that since a bushel measure of millet makes a noise, a single grain and a ten-thousandth part of a grain must also make a noise. (Simplicius *Commentaria*)

iii. Melissus

Melissus, the last of the eminent Eleatics, was a native of Samos. During his lifetime he won renown as a naval strategist and hero, when as admiral of the Samian fleet he was chiefly responsible for the decisive naval victory of 442 B.C. which enabled Samos to throw off the Athenian yoke.

As an author Melissus produced a book entitled *On Nature and Being,* in which he appears to have upheld the strict monism of Eleaticism but with a tone and with approaches that are his own. Experience, he argues, testifies to ongoing change, in which light gives way to dark, dark to light, moist to dry, dry to moist, and so on. But can such testimony be true? Look at what lies before you, he demands, and consider what it is that experience immediately presents to you. In terms of some given perceptual experience you discover, let us say, that being is moist. It *seems* moist, there is no doubt about that. But can it really *be* moist?

At this point the traditional Eleatic procedure would be to argue, by abstract dialectic, that if you mean "moist as distinguished from dry" then you are saying that something is not dry, and to say that anything "is not" is self-contradictory. Melissus proceeds differently. Think what you mean by the distinction between "is" and "seems," he demands. The seeming comes and goes; but if a thing really *is* moist and not merely *seems* so, then it is moist essentially. If moist is the very essence of the thing, then time cannot remove or alter that quality. What "is" moist, as distinguished from what "seems" moist, must therefore be moist always and unremittingly, for all eternity. Thus, even while retaining the basic Eleatic affirmations, Melissus comes closer than any of his predecessors to adopting an outlook and method of approach that we might nowadays describe as epistemological.

FRAGMENTS

1.   Anything that ever was must always have been and will always be. For if it had come into being, then before its coming-to-be it must have been nothing. But if ever there was nothing it would have been impossible out of nothing for anything to arise.   (1)

2.   Well then, since what is real could not have come into being, it not only now is but always was and always will be; and since it has neither beginning nor end it is [temporally] *unlimited.*

If it had come-to-be, then indeed it would have both a beginning and an end—a beginning, because its coming-to-be must have occurred at one moment of time rather than another; an end, because what has come-to-be will eventually terminate. Such is not the case, however. It never began and it never will terminate, but always was and always will be, without beginning or end; for it is impossible for anything really to be unless with utter completeness. (2)

3. *Not only must it always be* [*and hence be unlimited in time*], *it must likewise always be unlimited in magnitude.* (3)

4. *Nothing that has a beginning and end is either eternal or unlimited.* (4)

5. *If it were not one, it would be bounded by something else.* (5)

6. *If it is real it would have to be one; for if it were two, it would be bounded by something else.* (6)

7. *(A) Accordingly it is eternal and unlimited and everywhere alike. As it cannot perish, so it cannot become larger, nor undergo change, nor suffer pain or grief. For if it suffered any such modifications it would no longer be One. If it were altered in any respect, then necessarily it would not always be like itself; which would mean that something which once was had passed away and that something which once was not had come-to-be. If in ten thousand years it were to change by even so much as a hair's breadth, it would all perish for all time.*

(B) Even any reordering of it is not possible; for the order which it once had cannot perish, nor can any new order come-to-be. Since there cannot be any increase, nor any perishing, nor any alteration, how could there be any reordering of What Is? If anything at all were to be altered it would involve alteration of the entire cosmos.

(C) It does not suffer pain. For a thing in pain lacks full being, and does not have the same power as a healthy thing does of continuing to be. Moreover, if it were in pain it would

not always be alike, for to feel pain involves the addition or re-moval of something, and that would destroy its homogeneity. What is healthy cannot feel pain, for pain is a destroyer of health, and hence a destroyer of being and a producer of not-being. This same reasoning applies not only to pain but to grief as well.

(D) There cannot be any emptiness; for what is empty is nothing, and what is nothing cannot be. Accordingly What Is does not move; there is nowhere to which it can go, because everything is full. If there were some emptiness a thing could move into it, but since the empty does not exist there is nowhere for a thing to go. This means that neither can the dense and the rare exist; for to be rare is to be less full than to be dense, and is therefore to be comparatively empty. The difference be-tween what is full and what is not full is simply this. If a thing has room to receive anything else into itself, it is not full; but if it has no room to do so it is full. What Is must necessarily be full, since the empty does not exist; and since it is full every-where it cannot move.   (7)

8.   If there existed a many, the many existing things would have to be of the same kind as the One is. For suppose there existed, just as we see and hear them, such things as earth and water, air and fire, iron and gold, living and dead, black and white, and all the other different whatnesses which we speak of as existing: then each one of these perceived phenomena would be as it first appeared to us, perpetually just as it was at the first moment, without any alteration whatever.

Now in our everyday life we assume that we see and hear and understand more or less rightly; nevertheless we believe that what is warm becomes cool and what is cool becomes warm, that soft things become hard and hard things become soft, that what is living dies and that each new living thing is born out of non-living materials—in short, that all things are changed, and that there can be a vast difference between what they formerly were and what they are now. We suppose that even something as hard as iron gets worn away a little when rubbed, and we suppose the same of gold, stone, and other things that we regard as relatively durable. We suppose, too, that earth and stone come-to-be out of water. In such ways we show our ignorance of things as they are.

Our beliefs are not even consistent with one another. Having accepted many things as eternal and as possessing forms and durabilities of their own, we still imagine that all things undergo alteration, and that they become different from what we see on any given occasion. It follows, then, that we did not see correctly after all, and that we get no true apprehension of the things we believe to be many. For if [the appearances] were real, they would not change, but each of them would have to [continue to] be exactly such as it first appeared. For nothing is stronger than what is real.

In short, if there were any change, then what was has passed away and what was-not has come-to-be. Consequently even if many things existed they would have to be of the same nature as the One. (8)

9. *If anything is, it would have to be one. Thus if something really is, it cannot have body; for if it had body it would consist of parts and hence would no longer be one.* (9)

10. *If Being were divided it would be in motion, and if it were in motion it would not Be.* (10)

TESTIMONIA

FROM ARISTOTLE:

T 1.   Melissus says that Being is unlimited.   (*Physica* 185a 33)

T 2.   Melissus argues fallaciously, as can readily be seen. Starting from the premise, "Whatever comes-to-be has a first-principle," he draws the conclusion, "Whatever does not come-to-be lacks a first-principle."   (*ibid*. 186a 12)

T 3.   Those who believe in the existence of empty space argue that nothing could be in motion unless there were empty space for it to move into. The full cannot allow anything to move into it, because otherwise any number of bodies could coincide; for if two bodies could thus coincide, then so could three, and so on. Melissus, in support of his doctrine that there is no movement in the universe, uses this very argument in reverse: he accepts the premise that movement implies the existence of void, but he denies the possibility of any such existence, arguing that "void" implies non-existence. (*ibid*. 213b 3, 13)

T 4.   A plenum might undergo qualitative alteration without the aid of any vacuum—an obvious possibility which Melissus overlooks.   (*ibid*. 214a 2)

T 5.   Parmenides seems to have argued more validly than Melissus, for he conceives of the Whole as having boundaries and being equipoised at the center, whereas Melissus declares that the Whole is infinite. But the meaning of "infinite" is inconsistent with the meaning of "all" or "whole."   (*ibid*. 207a 15)

T 6.   It seems that whereas Parmenides conceived of the One by definition, Melissus conceived of it in terms of matter. (*Metaphysica* 986b 19)

T 7.   Melissus argues that the All is infinite, on the ground that the All does not come-to-be (since there cannot be any production from not-being), that it therefore lacks a starting-principle, and therefore is infinite. (*De Sophisticis Elenchis* 167b 13)

FROM LATER GREEK SOURCES:

T 8.   Melissus, son of Ithaegenes, was a native of Samos. He became a pupil of Parmenides. He was also a man active in political life, and became so highly valued by his fellow-soldiers that they chose him as admiral of the Samian fleet, in which capacity he won even more renown by reason of his valor.

He held the view that the universe is unlimited, unchangeable, immovable, an undifferentiated unity, and entirely full. He held that movement does not exist, but merely seems to. And he used to say that we ought to abstain from talking about the gods, because there is no knowledge to be had of them.

According to Apollodorus he flourished in the eighty-fourth Olympiad [444-440 B.C.].   (Diogenes Laertius IX. 24)

T 9.   Melissus' book was entitled either *On Nature* or *On Being*.   (Simplicius *Commentaria*)

T 10.   When Pericles had embarked for an attempted invasion of Samos, Melissus, son of Ithaegenes, a philosopher who was in charge of the Samian fleet, observing disdainfully the small number of Athenian ships and the weakness of their commanders, persuaded his free followers to make the initial onslaught. In the resulting battle the Samians were victors. They captured great numbers of the enemy and destroyed enough

Athenian ships to give them command of the sea and to enable them to prosecute the war with better equipment and supplies than previously. (Plutarch, *Life of Pericles*)

T 11. Melissus has been criticized for speaking of "starting-principle" (*archê*) not in a temporal sense as involving actual generation, but in a conceptual sense as having nothing to do with a changing world. He seems to have preceded Aristotle in grasping the point that all body, even when it is eternal, is limited and has limited capacities, and always in itself marks the end of a time-series as well as a beginning (*archê*), since there is an ever-moving beginning of what passes. Now whatever has a beginning and end in time, he reasons, must have a beginning and end in magnitude (and vice versa, too); for that which begins and ends in time is not everything simultaneously. Thus he bases his proof on the idea of beginning and end in time. (Simplicius *Commentaria*)

5

Qualitative Pluralism

THE STRENGTH OF PARMENIDES' influence upon Greek philosophical thought is shown not only in the writings of his followers but also by thinkers and schools of thought that either rejected or seriously qualified his monism. One principle in particular—the cosmological axiom *Ex nihilo nihil fit,* that nothing can be produced out of nothing, that Being cannot arise out of Not-Being —stands at the forefront of the Eleatic legacy. It may well be, as various interpreters have held, that the *ex nihilo* principle is to be found implicitly in the Milesian attempts to explain change; but there is no record of anyone before Parmenides having declared the principle, and surely if anyone had done so either Aristotle or the doxographers would have mentioned the fact. Heraclitus, in postulating that change is the fundamental reality rather than something derivative to be explained, was in effect denying the *ex nihilo* principle, and thereby he provided a challenge which the strongly logical mind of Parmenides seized upon and opposed. The result of this first great clash of opposing ideas in Greek thought was to set up a fundamental problem demanding solution. It was the problem of how to "save the appearances" of everyday experience without violating the principle of *ex nihilo*—the problem of reconciling the inescapable testimony of experience, that qualitative change does somehow occur, with the peremptory demand of logic (as conceived by Parmenides and his followers and subsequent opponents alike) that absolute coming-to-be must be rejected as an utter impossibility.

Despite their various disagreements the non-Eleatic philosophers after Parmenides agree upon a general principle of procedure. In one way or another their solution consists in postulating that reality, however they define it, does not change; and by contraposition that whatever does change is merely appearance. They must then, of course, devise a plausible explanation of the relation between the unchanging Real and the changing appearances. Of the various attempts, between Parmenides' time and the death of Aristotle in 322 B.C., five are most noteworthy: (1) the qualitative pluralism of Empedocles and Anaxagoras, (2) the atomism of Leucippus and Democritus, (3) the Pythagorean doctrine, in its later form, of certain pairs of opposites as ontologically intermediate between the One and the manifold world, (4) Plato's doctrine of unchanging Forms and changing appearances, and (5) Aristotle's analysis (in *Physica* I. 7) of change as triadic. The last two developments lie outside the scope of the present volume; the first three are to be examined in this and the next two chapters.

The first of the five solutions to be considered is that of qualitative pluralism. Despite the greater familiarity, to our own ways of thinking, of atomism on the one hand and Platonic idealism on the other, both of which deny that qualities are ontologically real, it should be realized that a qualitative explanation was the most typically Greek of any of the five types, and other things equal it would tend to have the greatest plausibility for the Greek mind. To think of blue and red, hot and cold, moist and dry as real states of existence, indeed more real than the abstract and quantitative concepts which are nowadays adduced to explain them, is natural for a child, for a primitive man, and probably for all of us when we are taken offguard in our everyday, non-theoretical moods. The Greeks, when not dissuaded by the logical asceticism of Eleatic and post-Eleatic abstractionists, took qualities at face value, despite their impermanence and frequent unreliability. Empedocles and Anaxagoras sought what was to their minds the most reasonable solution of the post-Eleatic problem when they undertook, each in his individual way, to provide an explanation in terms of qualities themselves. Three requirements were implicitly acknowledged by them both. (1) The ontologically real qualities must be plural; for the attempts by Thales and Anaximenes to explain in terms of a single quality had failed to provide any explanation of how the manifold variety of things could arise out of that one quality, and thus their theories were vulnerable to Parmenides' criticism. (2) Whatever qualities are postulated as ontologically real must be accepted as having permanent existence, neither coming-to-be nor perishing, and hence neither increasing nor diminishing in amount. (3) The fundamental qualities operate by intermixing and separating, and the changing world as we perceive and know it is the result of that mixture and separation.

i. Empedocles

Empedocles was a native of Akragas in Sicily, more often called by the Latin version of its name, Agrigentum. The traditional dates of his lifetime are 484 to 424 B.C. He practiced medicine, and in his native Sicily he founded a school of medicine which became known as the Sicilian school. He was the author of two books: the one, *On Nature,* scientific in purport (as science was then understood); the other, entitled *Purifications,* of a more rhapsodical and religious character, prophetic rather than investigative in tone.

Setting out from an acceptance of Parmenides' principle that What Is cannot be created or destroyed, but rejecting his denial of plurality, Empedocles postulates four basic physical realities—fire, air, water, and earth, the traditional "four elements" of popular cosmology. He describes them as "roots" of things; and the metaphor, considered in the light of his biological interests, suggests that he may have thought of the visible world as growing from the four roots somewhat on the analogy of a tree with luxuriant foliage and fruit in relation to the roots hidden underneath. If his metaphor of roots does indicate some such way of thinking, we must then recognize two elements in his theory—an essentially chemical concept of mixture and an essentially biological concept of growth. From the former standpoint the world of manifold particulars is produced by an intermingling of the elements in different proportions. Considered in that perspective alone the manifold objects of perception are mere appearances—except perhaps in those ideal instances when one of the four elements is encountered in its purity. When, on the other hand, the elements are considered as roots, out of which the manifold particulars of experience grow like the foliage of a tree, there is no longer any opposition between the real and the apparent. In the case of a tree the foliage is no less real than the roots, although it is less permanent. Much of the distinctive character of Empedocles' approach to natural problems seems to come from the tensive relation between these two modes of envisaging the relation between elements and phenomena.

Although the idea of potentiality was not developed as a precise abstract concept before Aristotle, the gist of the idea, clothed in one kind of concrete imagery or another, is probably as old as human thinking. After all, men are always interested in growth and development, in possibilities and the not-yetness of situations. No doubt Thales' maxim, "All things are full of gods," and Anaximander's "the Unlimited" represented the idea of potentiality expressed as two different concrete universals. Empedocles in speaking and thinking of the four basic elements as roots is expressing the idea of potentiality in yet another guise. Potentiality is a biologically centered concept, drawing much of its experiential meaning from the observation of growing organisms; and it is perhaps no accident that it was Aristotle, the greatest zoologist of ancient times, who gave to the idea of potentiality its first clear definition. Empedocles, as a physician and an observer of nature's curiosities, was sensitive to biological categories, even though he lacked both a suitable vocabulary and a methodological tradition; and the biologically oriented metaphor of "roots" was his way of expressing his sense of undetermined possibilities of change and growth in the natural world.

Viewed in this manner the idea of roots coheres with that other major tenet of Empedocles' philosophy, the opposition of Love and Strife. Aristotle, in his zest for schematizing the ideas of his philosophical predecessors, overstressed the difference between the four roots and the love-strife antithesis, characterizing the former as "material causes," the latter as a pair of "telic causes." That plain differentiation will serve the interpreter well enough up to a point, and there is nothing to contradict it in such Fragments as 15 and 16 or in such a Testimonium as T 29. Difficulties arise, however, when we reflect on his indication that the elements grow (Fr. 33), and on his personification of the elements (Fr. 12) in relation to Aëtius' testimony that "he calls the elements gods" (T 33) and in relation to the arresting statement (Fr. 50) that divine forces ("daemons") joined in sexual union and thus produced variety and novelty in the world. We seem to be close here to the strange doctrine which Simplicius attributes to Thales, that "all things are blended with gods."

Now the nature of divinity is such that it cannot remain unambiguously plural; it tends to evince some aspect of unity as well. The conception of God as the perfectly rounded Sphere (Frs. 23, 24), unencumbered by anthropomorphic traits (Fr. 26), expresses perhaps the ultimate conceptual reach of Empedocles' religious thought. But how is Divinity as the perfect sphere related to Divinity as the power of love and harmony symbolized by Aphrodite? As a guiding notion one might suggest that God the Sphere represents the harmony of divine perfection conceived in its essential nature, whereas God as the power of Love represents the harmony of divine perfection in the making. At all events Empedocles' conception of ultimate divine nature, while it implies perfection, does not imply omnipotence. The essential antagonist, "dreadful Strife," is no less real than Love is real. Their warfare is never ended; now the one prevails, now the other. The ancient notion of cosmic cycles becomes reenvisaged in those terms: long periods when the universe is tending toward adjustment, harmony, peaceful togetherness, and even (it would seem) a blending of diversities to such a degree that only the primordial diversity of the four elements remains; preceded and followed by long periods in which strife and the force of competing individuations give rise to the most manifold diversities, which endure and propagate until they have run their allotted course; and their alternation repeats itself through endless time.

Among Empedocles' ideas regarding specific operations of nature some readers will find a particular interest in his primitive pre-Darwinism expressed in Frs. 47, 48. Anaximander had already speculated on the significance of fish fossils embedded in inland quarries, and on that basis he had proposed the general hypothesis that the human race had somehow evolved from lower forms, particularly from marine animals. And now, half a century later, Empedocles speculates on the "how" of the process, and he seems to have attained, by a kind of inspired guess, to a rough version of the hypothesis of natural selection. Over two millennia before Darwin, and lacking anything like Darwin's wealth of systematized data, Empedocles conceived the possibility that many diverse species might have arisen by sheer chance, that many and perhaps most of them were ill-adapted for survival, and that only the well-adapted species survived in the long run, so that their characteristics were transmitted to later generations and eventuated in the characteristics with which we are now familiar. Of course his particular examples of maladaptation are fantastic—heads put on backwards, eyes in odd places, half-human half-bestial figures, and the like. Such fanciful details are not surprising when it is remembered that the only known paleontological data were a few fish fossils. But the vitality of scientific imagination (not the whole of science, yet an essential part of it) which from such sparse materials could leap to so comprehensive a hypothesis that would one day be justified, is enough to assure Empedocles of an honored place among the early contributors to the development of natural science in the western world.

FRAGMENTS

ON METHOD

1. Meagerly scattered among the body's members are the means of acquiring knowledge, and many are the evils that burst in and blunt the edge of attentive thought. The life of mortals is so mean a thing as to be virtually un-life; their doom is swift, they are blown away and vanish like smoke. Each one forms opinions according to what he has chanced to experience as he drifts about, yet each vainly boasts of knowing the general nature of things. Such universal matters, however, are beyond the reach of sight and hearing, and even beyond the mind's grasp. (2)

2. Avert from my tongue the madness of such men, O gods, and let pure streams of speech flow forth from my reverent lips. And you, O Muse, white-armed and virgin, whom many invoke, come forth from the house of Piety in your well equipped chariot, bringing me such words as are right and proper for ephemeral creatures to hear. You will not be urged, by some mortal ambitious to scale the heights of wisdom, to tell more than is fitting. (3)

3. Come now, with all your powers discern how each thing

manifests itself, trusting no more to sight than to hearing, and no more to the echoing ear than to the tongue's taste: rejecting none of the body's parts that might be a means to knowledge, but attending to each particular manifestation. (3, ctd.)

4. *Stepping from summit to summit, not plodding along a single track to the end.* (24)

5. *What is right may properly be uttered even twice.* (25)

BASIC PRINCIPLES

6. *They are fools, with no ability to reach out with their thoughts, who suppose that what formerly Was Not could come into being, or that What Is could perish and be utterly annihilated.* (11)

7. *From what utterly Is Not it is impossible for anything to come-to-be, and it is neither possible nor conceivable that What Is should utterly perish. For it will always be, no matter how it may be disposed of.* (12)

8. *And I shall tell you something more. There is no birth in mortal things, and no end in ruinous death. There is only mingling and interchange of parts, and it is this that we call "nature."* (8)

9. *When these elements are mingled into the shape of a man living under the bright sky, or into the shape of wild beasts or plants or birds, men call it birth; and when these things are separated into their parts men speak of hapless death. I follow the custom and speak as they do.* (9)

10. *In the All there is nothing empty and nothing over-stuffed.* (13)

11. *In the All there is nothing empty; whence, then, could there be any increase?* (14)

THE FOUR ELEMENTS

12.   Hear first the four roots of all things: shining Zeus, life-giving Hera, Aïdoneus, and Nestis who with her tears fills the springs from which mortals draw the water of life.   (6)

13.   Pay heed and I will tell you the first-principle of the sun; moreover I will explain the sources from which everything that we now .behold has sprung—earth, billowy sea, moist air, and giant sky that binds all things in its embrace.   (38)

14.   Earth, riding at anchor in the safe harbors of Aphrodite, comes together in right proportions with Hephaestos, with moisture, and with widely gleaming air, perhaps with a little more of one, a little less of another. Thus are created [such things as] blood and the manifold forms of flesh.   (98)

15.   But if you are deficient in belief with regard to these matters—how out of water, earth, air, and sun, mingled together, there arose the forms and colors of all mortal things by the unifying power of Aphrodite. . . .   (71)

GENESIS AND CHANGE

16.   Twofold is the process of which I shall tell. At one time there grew to be a single One out of many, while at another time it divided itself to make many out of One. Two-sided is the coming-to-be of perishable things, and two-sided is their passing away. The uniting of all things both creates and destroys; while the contrary phase involves both growth and scattering as things become divided [in the process of individuation]. And this thoroughgoing interchange never ceases: at times all things are united by the power of Love, while at other times they are repulsed and borne apart by the hostile force of Strife. Thus in so far as their nature consists in growing out of many into one and then being parted asunder again out of one into many, they are changeable and have no lasting life; but in so far as they never cease from continuously interchanging, in that respect they are unalterable as they continue on their course.

But come now, hearken to my words; learning will enlarge your mind. As I said before, while stating the boundaries of my discourse, I shall tell of a twofold process. For at one time there grew to be a single One out of many, while at another time there came to be many by division out of One—fire, water, earth, and the lofty height of air. Apart from these and in balanced relation to them is dreadful Strife; while Love resides in their midst, throughout their length and breadth. Envision her with your mind, instead of sitting with glazed eyes. Mortals can know and recognize her, for she is implanted within their bodies. It is thanks to her that mortals enjoy thoughts of amity and do works of peace. They call her by the names Joy and Aphrodite. She moves in and out among men in such a way that no one ever catches sight of her. Nevertheless my ordered discourse does not deceive. Pay heed to it.

All of these are equal and of the same age, but each has its own kind of activity and its own character, and each gains ascendancy when its time comes round. Nothing is added to them nor taken away from them. For if they were continually perishing, they would at last no longer exist. And since there is nothing else, how could anything be added that would cause them to increase? And how could anything perish, since there is nothing empty? No, these are the only things that are; and

*by interpenetrating they become one thing in one place and
another in another.* (17)

17. [*Such basic things as*] *sunbeams and earth, sky and
sea, are at one with the parts that compose them, even though
thrown in different guises to mortals' apprehension. Those things
in which such affinity is most active are better adapted for mixing, being united in love by Aphrodite. But such things as are
most different in origin, in form, and in type of mixing, are
hostile; being children of Strife they are indisposed to unite
and such unions as take place among them are baleful.* (22)

18. *Come now, look at the things that bear witness to what
I said formerly, in case there was anything defective in my earlier account. Behold the sun, sending warmth and brightness
everywhere, and the countless things perpetually bathed by his
radiance; there is also the rain-cloud, dark and cold on all sides;
and there is the earth, from which solid bodies, the foundations
of things, come forth. When Hostility is at work, all these things
are distinct in form and separated; but they come together in
Love, and are desired by one another. Thence have sprung all
the things that ever were, are, or shall be—trees and men and
women, beasts and birds and water-dwelling fishes, and even
such honored beings as the long-lived gods. In reality there are
only the basic elements, but interpenetrating one another they
mix to such a degree that they assume different characteristics.*
(21)

19. *When painters wise and skilled in their craft are preparing sumptuous votive altars in a temple, they use pigments of
many colors and blend them judiciously, now a little more of
this and now of that; thereby they produce likenesses of all
things—of trees, of men and women, of beasts and birds and*

*water-dwelling fishes, and even of such honored beings as the
long-lived gods. The way in which all the actual things of the
world have come into existence, although they are incalculably
more numerous, is essentially no different from this; let not your
mind fall into the error of supposing otherwise, since you have
heard the tale from a divine source.*   (23)

COSMIC HARMONY AND ITS ANTAGONIST

20.   *These two forces, Strife and Love, existed in the past
and will exist in the future; nor will boundless time, I believe,
ever be empty of the pair.*   (16)

21.   *Now one prevails, now the other, each in its appointed
turn, as change goes incessantly on its course. These alone truly
are, but interpenetrating one another they become men and
tribes of beasts. At one time they are brought together by Love
to form a single order, at another they are carried off in different
directions by the repellant force of Strife; then in course of time
their enmity is subdued and they all come into harmony once
more. Thus in the respect that by nature they grow out of many
into one, then divide from one into many, they are changing
things and their life is not lasting, but in respect of their perpetual cycle of change they are unalterable and eternal.*   (26)

22.   *As things came together in harmony, Strife withdrew to
the outermost region.*   (36)

23.   *In that condition neither can the sun's swift limbs be
distinguished, no, nor shaggy mighty earth, nor the sea; because
all things are brought so close together in the perfect circularity
of the Sphere.*   (27)

24. *Equal on all sides and utterly unlimited is the Sphere;
which rejoices in its circular solitude.* (28)

25. *There is no discord and no unseemly strife in his limbs.*
(27a)

26. *There is no pair of wings branching forth from his back,
he has no feet, no nimble knees, no genitals; he is spherical and
equal on all sides.* (29)

27. *When, in the fullness of time set by the primordial oath,
Strife had grown to greatness in the limbs [of the Sphere] and
was flaunting his demands for honors and privileges. . . .*
(30)

28. *Then all of God's limbs in turn began to quake.* (31)

COSMIC PROCESS

29. *But now I shall go back again over the pathway of my
verses already set forth, drawing a new word out of the old.
When Strife had fallen to the lowest depth of the vortex and
Love had reached its very center, then all things came together
so as to be one single whole. This unity was attained not all at
once, but according to the wishes of the things that were uniting, as they came some from one direction, some from another.
Yet along with the things that became mixed and unified there
were many things that remained unmixed—all, in fact, of which
Strife retained possession; for Strife had not yet retreated entirely from them to the outermost limit of the circle, but he had
departed from some things while in others he remained. But in
the same degree that Strife was flowing out a gentle immortal
stream of blameless Love was pouring in. Straightway what had*

previously been immortal became mortal, [i.e.,] what had been unmixed became mixed—an exchanging of paths. And as the mingling went on, innumerable kinds of mortal creatures in great diversity of forms were produced and scattered forth—a wonder to behold! (35)

30. *Bounteous Earth, in the melting-pot of her broad bosom, received two portions from bright Nestis [Moisture], four from Hephaestos [Fire], and with eight parts in all, which she fitted together with the divine cement of right proportion, she created white bones.* (96)

31. *At that time Kypris [Aphrodite], who was engaged in preparing forms, after she had moistened the earth with water, gave it to swift fire to harden it.* (73)

32. *Know that effluences flow from all things that have come-to-be.* (89)

33. *Fire expands by means of fire, earth increases her own bulk, and air increases air.* (37)

34. *Thus sweet caught hold of sweet, bitter rushed to bitter, sour went to sour, and warm mingled with warm.* (90)

PHENOMENA OF NATURE

35. *The sun flashes back from Mount Olympus with serene countenance.* (44)

36. *The sunlight is gathered together and circulates around the vast heaven.* (41)

37. *It is the earth that makes the night by getting in the way of the sun's beams.* (48)

38. *The sharp-darting sun and the gentle moon.* (40)

39. *There circles about the earth a borrowed light.* . . .
(45)

40. *. . . as the hub of a wheel circles about the extreme center.* (46)

41. *She cuts off his rays as he goes above her, and casts a shadow on the earth which corresponds to the breadth of the pale-faced moon.* (42)

42. *[Whereas fire tends naturally upwards,]* the air (aether) *plunged into the earth with its long roots.* (54)

43. *That the depths of the earth and the height of the vast sky are unlimited is a foolish notion that has been unthinkingly passed from tongue to tongue by the many.* (39)

44. *Many fires burn beneath the earth.* (52)

45. *Sea is the earth's sweat.* (55)

46. *Iris [the rainbow] brings from the sea a wind and a great storm.* (50)

EVOLUTION OF LIVING FORMS

47. *There sprang up on the earth many heads without necks, arms wandering unattached to shoulders, and eyes straying about in want of foreheads. Isolated limbs were wandering about.* (57, 58)

48. *Many creatures were born with faces and chests turned in different directions. There were offspring of oxen with faces of men, while on the other hand there were human offspring that had the faces of oxen. And there were creatures in which the masculine and feminine natures were combined, the result of which was sterility.* (61)

49. *There were shambling creatures with innumerable heads.* (60)

50. *As daemon copulated with daemon things came together by pure chance, with the result that many novelties sprang into being.* (59)

51. *Listen now to my account of how fire, by separating, caused the night-born offspring of men and of tearful women to arise; for mine is no trifling or foolish tale. First there sprang up out of the earth whole-natured forms having a due share of both water and fire. The fire, desiring to reach up to its like, produced growth in the creatures, even before they had developed shapely limbs, voices, and generative organs.* (62)

ORGANIC PHYSIOLOGY

52. *This [the universal contest between Strife and Love] is manifest in the human body. At one time, in blooming life's high season, all bodily members are brought together by Love; at another, severed by Strife's cruel power, they wander separate and alone on the margins of life. Thus it is with plants and with water-dwelling fishes, with animals whose lairs are on the hillsides, and with seabirds that sail on wings.* (20)

53. *All living beings breathe in and out in the following manner. There are bloodless tubes of flesh which extend along the surface of their bodies. At the mouths of these the outer skin is punctured with numerous pores, so small and closely packed as to keep the blood from flowing out but still such as to let the air pass through. When the fluid blood recedes from these pores the air rushes impetuously in, and when the blood pulsates back again the air is breathed out. It is like when a*

girl, playing with a clepsydra of gleaming brass, takes the mouth of the pipe in her fair hands and dips it into the liquid mass of shining water: the water does not flow into the vessel, because the mass of air within, pressing on the numerous perforations, holds it back until she uncovers the compressed stream; but when the air gives way, an equivalent amount of water enters. Likewise when water occupies the depth of the bronze vessel and the small opening with its narrow passage is blocked by the human hand, the outside air, striving to get in, presses on the surface and holds the water back behind the gates of the murmuring tube, until she releases her hand. As soon as she does so, an equivalent amount of water rushes off as the air enters—the opposite of what happened before. In the same way, when the fluid blood that surges through the limbs pulsates backwards into the body's interior, at once the stream of air surges swiftly in, and when the blood returns the air is breathed out again in equal amount. (100)

54. *All creatures share in breathing and smelling.* (102)

55. *It is in the warm parts of the womb that males are born; which is the reason why men tend to be dark, hairy, and more rugged.* (67)

PERCEPTION AND THOUGHT

56. *As when someone preparing to set forth on a journey through a stormy night procures a lantern and lights it at the brightly blazing hearth-fire, a lantern fitted with protection against the blowing winds, which its flashing beams scatter, being finer than they; so it is that the primal fire was originally entrapped within the membranes and delicate tissues of the round eyeball. These are pierced by ingenious passages in such*

*a way as to prevent the abundant surrounding water of the eye
from entering, while at the same time allowing the fire, by reason of its superior fineness, to pass through.*   (84)

57.   *Out of these* [*the four elements?*] *divine Aphrodite
fashioned the tireless eyes. She fitted them together with rivets
of love. Their beneficent flame is mixed with only a slight
amount of earth.*   (86, 87, 85)

58.   *One vision is produced by the two eyes.*   (88)

59.   *It is by earth that we see earth, by water water, by air
divine air, and by fire destroying fire; by love we perceive love,
and hate by dreadful hate.*   (109)

60.   *Out of these* [*the four elements?*] *all things are formed
and fitted together; it is by means of them that men think, suffer, and enjoy.*   (107)

61.   *The heart dwells in a sea of blood which flows back and
forth around it. That encircling blood is what men experience
as thought.*   (105)

62.   *It is by chance that men have come to have conscious
thought.*   (103)

63.   *According as men live differently the thoughts that
come to their minds are different.*   (108)

64.   *The notion that men exist, enjoy and suffer only during
their so-called lifetime, and that before they received human
shape and after their dissolution they are nothing at all, is a
notion that no wise man would entertain in his heart.*   (15)

SCATTERED OBSERVATIONS

65.   *Water fits readily into wine, but it will not mix with
oil.*   (91)

66.   *Wine is the water that has seeped through the bark and has been purified in the wood.*   (81)

67.   *It is moisture that makes evergreens flourish with abundance of fruit throughout the entire year.*   (77)

68.   *In heavy-backed sea-dwelling shellfish, in snails, and in strong-skinned turtles you can see instances of where the earthy part swells at the skin's uppermost surface.*   (76)

69.   *The black color at the bottom of rivers arises from the shadow; a similar phenomenon is found in hollow caves.*   (94)

70.   *One and the same thing are hair, leaves, thick feathers of birds, and the scales that grow on claws.*   (82)

71.   *The hair of hedgehogs takes the form of sharp-pointed bristles on their backs.*   (83)

72.   *Tracking out the traces of animals' limbs from the scent which their feet have left in the soft grass.*   (101)

ADMONITION AND PROMISE TO A DISCIPLE

73.   *It is too readily the way of petty minds to disbelieve their superiors. Hear and understand the truths of this book, and let my reasoned argument penetrate your innermost heart, as my trustworthy Muse bids you.*   (4)

74.   *If, supported by your steadfast mind, you will contemplate these matters with serious devotion and faultless care, then you shall have during your lifetime all those blessings [of which I have spoken] and many others too. For such blessings grow up by their own power in the heart, where each man's true nature resides. If, on the contrary, you strive after things of another kind, as men tend to do who let countless trivialities blunt the precision of their thoughts, then those blessings will desert*

you when the time comes round; for blessings, insofar as they partake of thought and wisdom, desire to return to their own kind. (110)

75. *And you shall learn the cures for all evils, and protection against old age; it is for you alone that I will bring this about. You shall be able to stop the force of the untiring winds that sweep over the earth and destroy crops; or, at your pleasure, you shall summon them back again. Out of dark storms you shall produce drought, and out of summer drought you shall bring pouring rains from the sky to nourish the trees. You shall be able to lead out of Hades the spirit of a man who is dead.* (111)

THE BOOK CALLED PURIFICATIONS

INVOCATION

76. *O Kalliopeia, immortal Muse, if when looking down on ephemeral things you have ever deigned to notice my endeavors, stand by me once again, I pray, while I utter a worthy discourse about the blessed gods.* (131)

77. *Friends, I know well that truth resides in what I shall utter; but it is hard for men to accept it, for they are hostile to beliefs that challenge their ways of thinking.* (114)

ON DIVINITY

78. *Blessed is the man who has gained the riches of divine wisdom; wretched is he whose heart holds dim opinions about the gods.* (132)

79. *It is not possible to reach out to God with our eyes, nor to take hold of him with our hands—the two most usual ways of persuasion that lead into men's minds.* (133)

80. *He has no human head fitted on to his body, nor does a pair of wings branch out from his back; he has no feet, nor hairy parts. He is purely mind, holy and ineffable, flashing through the whole world with swift thoughts.* (134)

THE ANCIENT AGE OF INNOCENCE

81. *[In those days] there was not any Arês, nor Kydoimos (Uproar), nor royal Zeus, nor Kronos, nor Poseidon. There was only Queen Kypris (Aphroditê). Men worshiped her with holy offerings, with painted figures, with perfumes having skillfully contrived fragrance, pure myrrh and sweet-smelling frankincense, and with libations of brown honey poured on the ground. The altars did not reek with bull's blood, and the practice of eating the raw limbs after ripping out the life was held in utter abomination.* (128)

82. *All creatures, beasts and birds alike, were tame and gentle to man, and friendly feelings were kindled everywhere.* (130)

THE PRESENT AGE OF STRIFE

83. *A land without joy, where bloodshed and wrath and agents of doom are active; where plagues and corruption and floods roam in the darkness over the barren fields of Atê.* (121)

84. *Ah, wretched unblessed race of mortals! Such were the strifes and groanings out of which you were born.* (124)

85.   *A father seizes a dear son, who has changed his outward shape, and slays him in ritual, so great is his folly. He is deaf to the beseeching cries of the victims as they are driven to the sacrifice; he slays them and prepares the evil feast. In like manner a son disposes of his father, a daughter of her mother; tearing out the life they devour the kindred flesh.*   (137)

86.   *Such a one will never be welcome in the vaulted palace of aegis-bearing Zeus, nor even in the house of Hades.*   (142)

87.   *Accordingly the weight of your wickedness makes you frantic, and you cannot ease your bitterly troubled souls.*   (145)

REINCARNATION

88.   *A daemon-goddess wraps them in a strange garment of flesh.*   (126)

89.   *[She] took them and changed them from living creatures into dead ones.*   (125)

90.   *From what high place of honor and bliss have I fallen, so that I now go about among mortals here on earth?*   (119)

91.   *In the past I have been a boy and a girl, a bush, a bird, and a dumb water-dwelling fish.*   (117)

92.   *I wept and mourned when I discovered myself in this unfamiliar land.*   (118)

93.   *We have come into this low-roofed cavern.*   (120)

94.   *There is an oracle of Necessity, an ancient decree of the gods, eternal and tightly sealed by broad oaths: that whenever anyone defiles the body sinfully with blood, or has fallen into the way of Strife, or has broken his oath, such a man, [when he becomes] a daemon endowed with a long stretch of life, must wander thrice ten thousand seasons shut off from the*

abode of the blessed, during which period he is reborn in all sorts of mortal shapes, exchanging one grievous kind of existence for another. The force of air swirls him into the sea, the sea spits him out on to dry earth, the earth tosses him into the beams of the fiery sun, and the sun flings him back again into the eddies of air. All seize him, and all reject him. Such a man am I, alas, a fugitive from the gods and a wanderer at the mercy of frenzied Strife. (115)

95.   *When reincarnated as animals they become lions, such as make their lairs on the hills, sleeping on the bare ground; or they become laurel trees with goodly foliage.* (127)

ETHICAL JUDGMENTS

96.   *What is lawful is not binding only on some and not binding on others. Lawfulness extends everywhere, through the wide-ruling air and the boundless light of the sky.* (135)

97.   *Fast from wickedness!* (144)

98.   *Will you not cease from the evil noise of bloodshed? Do you not see that you are devouring one another in heedlessness of mind?* (136)

99.   *Abstain entirely from laurel leaves.* (140)

100.   *Wretches, utter wretches, keep your hands away from beans.* (141)

101.   *Alas that some day of doom did not destroy me before my lips committed the sin of wrong devouring!* (139)

THE PROPHET ON EARTH

102.   *Hail, friends! You who inhabit the great city looking down on the yellow rocks of Akragas and extending up to the*

citadel; who exercise yourselves with good works, offering a harbor to worthy strangers and being ignorant of meanness: I greet you. I come among you no longer as a mortal but as an immortal god, rightly honored by all, and crowned with fillets and floral garlands. When I enter a flourishing town, with my attendant youths and maidens, I am received with reverence; great throngs of people press upon me, seeking benefits. Some desire a revelation; others, who have long been pierced by various kinds of painful illness, want me to tell them effective remedies. (112)

103. *But why do I stress such matters, as if there were anything surprising in the fact that I am superior to mortal perishable men?* (113)

104. *In the course of time there come to earth certain men who are prophets, bards, physicians, and princes; such men later rise up as gods, extolled in honor, sharing hearth and table with the other immortals, freed from human woes and human trials.* (146, 147)

105. *There was among them a man of rare knowledge, highly skilled in all kinds of wise words, possessing the utmost wealth of wisdom. Whenever he reached out with all his mind, he was easily aware of every particular thing that exists, spanning even ten or twenty generations of men.* (129)

TESTIMONIA

FROM PLATO:

T 1. *Socrates:* Evidently, then, you believe in Empedocles' theory of effluences?

Meno: Indeed I do.

Socrates: And of passages [in the sense-organs] to which the effluences come and through which they pass?

Meno: Yes.

Socrates: And that certain of the effluences fit into certain of the passages while others are either too large or too small?

Meno: Exactly.

Socrates: And is it agreed that there is such a thing as sight?

Meno: Yes.

Socrates: Well, so Empedocles in offering us these notions seems to be telling us, in Pindar's words, "Read my meaning." I take it to be something like this: "Color is an effluence from shapes commensurate with sight and perceptible by it."

Meno: That, Socrates, is admirably stated. (*Meno* 76c)

FROM ARISTOTLE:

T 2.   One may postulate a plurality, as when Empedocles says that matter (*hylê*) consists of four bodies (*sôma*). . . . The trouble with such a view is, we see things being generated from one another in such a way as to suggest that neither fire nor water goes on always retaining its own bodily identity. (*Metaphysica* 989a 21)

T 3.   Empedocles supposes four elements, adducing earth as a fourth to those already mentioned. These, he holds, always remain existent and never come-to-be; increase and diminution he explains as the compounding into and the separation out of one another. (*ibid.* 984a 8)

T 4.   Anaxagoras and Empedocles are opposed with respect to the elements. The latter declares that fire, earth, and the other things of the same rank are the elements of bodies and that everything is composed of them. (*De Caelo* 302a 28)

T 5.   Some, such as Empedocles, say at the outset that there are four [elements]. But in practice he reduces them to two, by making a contrast between fire and the other three.   (*De Generatione et Corruptione* 330b 19)

T 6.   He was the first to state that there are four material elements. In practice, however, he treats them not as four but as two—fire by itself, as contrasted with earth, air, and water taken together.   (*Metaphysica* 985a 33)

T 7.   As for the source of motion, Empedocles took issue with his predecessors in not regarding it as one but dividing it into two contrary forces.   (*ibid*. 985a 29)

T 8.   Empedocles says that things are sometimes in motion and sometimes at rest: when Love is producing the One out of many and Strife is producing many out of the One, things are in motion, but in the intervening periods they are at rest. (*Physica* 250b 27)

T 9.   If Strife had not been present in things, he says, then all would have been one; for it is when things come together in unity that Strife retreats into the background.   (*Metaphysica* 1000b 1)

T 10.   If one studies Empedocles critically in order to get at his real meaning and not be blocked by his obscure language, it will be found that Love is the cause of good things and Strife of evil things. Thus one might truly say that in a sense Empedocles was the first to speak of evil and good as first-principles. (*ibid*. 985a 5)

T 11.   Empedocles' argument breaks down when he makes Friendship (*philia*) the chief good. For he treats this as a first-principle in a double sense: as moving cause, in that it draws things together, and as matter, in that it is part of the mixture. (*ibid*. 1075b 2)

T 12.   Empedocles posits Strife as the kind of first-principle which causes destruction; nevertheless it would seem that Strife is the begetter of everything that exists except the One.   (*ibid.* 1000a 26)

T 13.   Empedocles is not entirely consistent with respect to the causes of things. At any rate [he admits that] Love often sets apart and Strife often combines. For when the All is differentiated into its elements by Strife, then fire and each of the other elements collects itself into oneness; on the other hand, when the elements are brought together into the One by Love, then each thing is drawn away from its own individuality. (*ibid.* 985a 21)

T 14.   Some say that there are alternating periods of coming-to-be and perishing, and that this alternation goes on unceasingly. Such is the view of Empedocles of Akragas and Heraclitus of Ephesus.   (*De Caelo* 279b 14)

T 15.   Empedocles begins [his description of the cosmic process] at a period after Love has been in the ascendancy. He could not think of a universe simply as constructed out of separate parts which were to be united by the power of Love, for the separateness of the constituent parts of the world as we know it presupposes a previous state of unity and togetherness. (*ibid.* 301a 16)

T 16.   Empedocles says that air is separated upwards not with uniform regularity but as it may chance; which is the point of the remark in his *Cosmogony:* "At one time it happened to run in that way, but frequently in other ways." He says also that the parts of animals developed very largely by chance. (*Physica* 196a 21)

T 17.   Others, such as Empedocles, take the view that like seeks like.   (*Ethica Nicomachea* 1155b 7)

T 18.   When he was asked why a certain dog always used

the same tiles for sleeping, Empedocles replied that there must be a likeness between the dog and the tiles, the likeness explaining why the dog was drawn to them. (*Magna Moralia* 1208b 11)

T 19. It would be absurd if someone such as Empedocles were to suppose he was offering a clear-cut statement in describing the sea as the sweat of the earth. Such a metaphorical way of speaking, while suitable for the purposes of poetry, contributes nothing whatever to our knowledge of nature. (*Meteorologica* 357a 24)

T 20. Empedocles says that the light from the sun has to pass through the intervening space before it reaches the earth and our organs of vision. (*De Sensu* 446a 26)

T 21. Some, such as Empedocles, say that the rotating movement of the heavens impedes the movement of the earth, like water in a rotating vessel. (*De Caelo* 295a 17)

T 22. Of those who deny the existence of a void there are some, such as Anaxagoras and Empedocles, who make no attempt to explain clearly the meaning of heavy and light. Those who do make such an attempt, if they still deny the existence of a void, are unable to explain what heavy and light are in themselves—in other words, why some things move downwards and others upwards. (*ibid*. 309a 19)

T 23. Empedocles was in error in going on to say that plants grow downwards with their roots because earth goes naturally down but that they themselves grow upwards because fire goes naturally up. (*De Anima* 415b 28)

T 24. Anaxagoras and Empedocles say that plants are moved by desire, even declaring that they have perception and can feel pleasure and pain. Empedocles and others said that plants have intelligence and knowledge. (*De Plantis* 815a 15, b 17)

T 25.   Some believe that each impression is taken in from the last outward agent through certain pores, and that this is how we see, hear, and exercise our other perceptions. They explain our ability to see through air, water, and other translucent substances on the ground that such substances contain numerous pores, too small to be seen and very close together; the more numerous the pores, they say, the greater the translucency. The theory has been held by Empedocles among others. (*De Generatione et Corruptione* 324b 26)

T 26.   Many difficulties are involved in saying, as Empedocles does, that each thing is known by the corporeal elements it contains, each being known by a like element [in the sense-organ].   (*De Anima* 410a 28)

FROM LATER GREEK SOURCES:

T 27.   Empedocles, a native of Akragas [Agrigentum] was, according to Hippobolus, the son of Meton and grandson of Empedocles. Timaeus, in the fifteenth book of his *Histories,* confirms this statement and adds that the elder Empedocles, the poet's grandfather, was a distinguished man. Likewise Heraclides, in his treatise *On Diseases,* declares that the family was an illustrious one and adds that the grandfather bred race horses. Eratosthenes, in his chronicle of Olympic Games, cites Aristotle as authority for the statement that the father of Meton was a victor in the seventy-first Olympiad. . . . The knowledge that he was a citizen of Akragas in Sicily is based upon his own testimony   [Fr. 102].

Timaeus further declares that Empedocles had been a pupil of Pythagoras but that he had been convicted of publishing some of the Pythagorean verses, for which reason he was disbarred from the discussions held by the school. Neanthes tells that down to the time of Philolaus and Empedocles all Pythagoreans were admitted to the school discussions. But after Empedocles had revealed some of the teachings to the public by speaking of them in his poem they passed an edict that he should not be allowed to hear any more of them.

Theophrastus says that Empedocles was an admirer of Parmenides and imitated him in his own verses after Parmenides had published his treatise *On Nature*. On the other hand Hermippus asserts that Empedocles was not so much an admirer of Parmenides as of Xenophanes, with whom he lived for a time and whose verses he imitated, before he became connected with the Pythagoreans. Alcidamas in his treatise *Natural Science* declares that Zeno and Empedocles were both pupils of Parmenides at about the same time and afterwards left him, Zeno to develop his own philosophy, Empedocles to become the pupil of Anaxagoras and Pythagoras, emulating the one in his investigations of nature, the other in the nobility of his life and bearing.

Aristotle in his *Sophist* calls Empedocles the founder of oratory, Zeno of dialectic. Satyrus in his *Lives* says that Empedocles ranked high both as physician and as orator, and that even Gorgias of Leontini, a man prominent in oratory and author of a treatise on that art, had once been his pupil.

The city of Akragas had at that time, according to Timaeus, a populaton of eight hundred thousand. Speaking of his fellow-citizens Empedocles remarked, "The citizens of Akragas eat as sparingly as if they were going to die tomorrow, but they build their houses as sturdily as if they were going to live forever." His poem *Purifications* was recited at Olympia by the rhapsode Cleomenes: so Favorinus tells in his *Memorabilia*.

Aristotle says that Empedocles was a champion of freedom to such a degree that he was an opponent of every kind of restrictive law; and Xanthus in writing about him tells that he refused the royal power when it was offered to him, evidently because he preferred the frugal life.   (Diogenes Laertius VIII. 51-77)

T 28.   Empedocles the natural philosopher, by blocking up a certain mountain gorge which had permitted the south wind to blow a fatal pestilence down upon the plains, was believed to have shut the plague out of the country.   (Plutarch *Moralia* 515c)

T 29.   Empedocles of Akragas considers the elements of things to be four: namely, fire, air, water, and earth. They produce change, he says, by combining and separating. What sets them in motion is Love and Strife, alternately the one bringing them into union and the other dissolving them.   (Theophrastus, quoted by Simplicius)

T 30.   Fire is of a disintegrating and separating nature, while water is adhesive and retentive, holding and glueing together by its moisture—a fact to which Empedocles alludes in calling fire "destructive strife" and water "tenacious love." (Plutarch *Moralia* 952b)

T 31.   According to Empedocles, things do not remain continually in fixed situations, nor do the elements have fixed boundaries, but all things partake of one another.   (Aëtius)

T 32.   By Zeus he means the heavenly fire and the aether, by life-giving Hera the moist air, by Aidonius the earth, and by Nestis who from her springs supplies mortals with the water of life he means something like water and the moisture of seeds. (*ibid.*)

T 33.   He calls the elements gods, and their intermixture the universe.   (*ibid.*)

T 34.   Empedocles says that the universe arises and perishes through the alternating forces of love and strife.   (*ibid.*)

T 35.   According to Empedocles the elements are composed of tiny particles, the tiniest possible, which are, one might say, elements of the elements. He says that these particles are of the same kind as the larger elements of which they are part.   (*ibid.*)

T 36.   Empedocles, comparing all the different senses, says that perception occurs by means of a fitting into the pores of each sense-organ. Thereby they do not perceive one another's objects, the pores of some sense-organs being too wide and of others too narrow for a given kind of sense-object to fit into them, so that some things go through without touching while others are unable to enter.

He explains vision as follows. Within the eye are fire and water; the surrounding membranes are composed of earth and air, through which the light, being finer, enters in much the same way it does in the case of lanterns. Pores of fire and water are placed alternately; the fire-pores receive bright objects and the water-pores dark objects, the colors adjusting themselves to the pores. It is by effluences that the colors reach and enter the organs of vision.

Hearing is the result of noise coming from outside. When [the outer ear] is set in motion by the sound, there is an echo inside; thus the process of hearing is like one bell echoing another.

Thinking and perceiving are the same. It is mainly by blood that we think, for in blood all the elements are mingled.

Those in whom a fair and equal proportion of parts have been mixed—neither too diverse [nor too similar], neither too small nor too large—such men have the best intelligence and the most accurate perceptions. Some men are good orators, others are good craftsmen, according as the well-proportioned mixture is in the hands or in the tongue; and similarly as regards other powers.   (Theophrastus *De Sensu* 7)

T 37.   He says that desire arises in animals [including human animals] from a lack of the things that would render them complete.   (Aëtius)

T 38.   He says that the embryo resides in the belly without breathing, and that the animal's first breath occurs at the moment of birth, when part of the moisture of the embryo is transformed into air, which is then supplemented by air coming into the lungs from outside. (*ibid.*)

T 39. Death, he says, consists in a separation of the fiery particles of matter from out of the mixture of which the soul is composed, so that death of the body and death of the soul occur simultaneously; and sleep he explains as a temporary separation of this kind. (*ibid.*)

T 40. Empedocles declares that what gave our souls their being and first-principle was not a mingling of blood and breath; but that the body, earth-born and mortal, was shaped by the soul, which came to it from elsewhere, for which reason he describes birth as a journey. (Plutarch *Moralia* 607D)

T 41. The soul he declares to be a mixture primarily of air and aether. (Aëtius)

T 42. He holds that pure men who partake of the elements in a pure way are divine. (*ibid.*)

T 43. Empedocles holds that there are two fates, or spirits, which take each of us into their care at birth and guide us. They may appear as Chthonia and far-seeing Heliope [Earth maiden and Sun maiden], or as bloody Deris and grave-eyed Harmonia [Discord and Attunement], or as Callistro and Aeschra [Beauty and Ugliness], or as Thoösa and Denaea [Quickness and Sluggishness], or as lovely Nemertes and dark-eyed Asapheia [Truth and Uncertainty]. Their seeds are mingled at our birth, and thus there grow up in us instinctive tendencies of great unevenness. (Plutarch *Moralia* 474B)

T 44. He holds that the first generation of animals and plants lacked perfection because they were concocted out of ill-fitting parts; that the second generations were formed of parts mutually suitable; that the third had parts grown into one whole; while the fourth consisted not of ingredients which kept their own natures such as earth and water, but of substances that had already become blended together. (Aëtius)

T 45.   Some say that the sea is, as it were, a sort of sweat from the earth; for when the earth is warmed by the sun it gives forth moisture; moreover it is salt, just as the earth is salt. (Theophrastus, quoted by Simplicius)

T 46.   The sky, he says, is formed by air being congealed by fire into crystalline form, and it embraces whatever is of the nature of fire or of air on either of the earth's hemispheres. (Aëtius)

T 47.   The sun's eclipse he explains as caused by the moon rising in front of it.   (*ibid.*)

T 48.   Empedocles regards the moon as a mass of air congealed in the same way as hail and contained within a sphere of fire.   (Plutarch *Moralia* 922c)

T 49.   Empedocles holds that the moon is framed by air rolled up into a cloud, whose form is baked into solidity by an admixture of fire; that it has the shape of a disc, and that it gets its light from the sun.   (Aëtius)

T 50.   According to Empedocles the cause of the lightning flash is the kindling and extinction of light as it suddenly has contact with the compressed air of a cloud; thunder is the crashing noise produced by the break-up of the cloud.   (*ibid.*)

FROM LATIN SOURCES:

T 51.   Empedocles, among his other mistakes, was especially wrong in his conception of the gods. He ascribes divinity to the four elements of which he says everything consists; but surely we can see that those elements are born and die, and moreover that they are devoid of sense.   (Cicero *De Natura Deorum* I. 29)

T 52. Then there are those who conceive of the first beginnings of things as pairs of substances, coupling together air and fire on the one hand, earth and water on the other. And finally there are those who conceive of the first beginnings as four—namely, fire, air, water, and earth. Foremost among this latter group is Empedocles of Agrigentum, born on that island of three-sided coastline [Sicily] sprinkled by the salt spray of the green Ionian Sea, which with its windings and currents separates the island from the mainland of Italy. (Lucretius *De Rerum Natura* I. 712)

ii. Anaxagoras

Anaxagoras, the second of the two known qualitative pluralists of the time, was born at Clazomenae in Asia Minor, not far from Heraclitus' native city of Ephesus. Most scholars, following the testimony of Apollodorus as reported by Diogenes Laertius (T 28), accept 500 B.C. as his probable birthdate, although others have adduced reasons for placing it as much as a generation earlier. Aristotle's only statement on the matter is that while Anaxagoras followed Empedocles in date of publication he preceeded him in date of birth (T 7).

At any rate Anaxagoras came to Athens as a young man, and was the first philosopher to become known as a teacher in that city, which was soon to become the most famous of all cities for its philosophical activities. During his long residence at Athens there were among his pupils both Pericles, afterward to become the outstanding Athenian statesman, and Euripides the dramatist. Eventually a popular outcry was raised against him, no doubt by political enemies of Pericles, for his alleged atheism and impiety, particularly as expressed in his declaration that the sun, instead of being a god, was an intensely hot mass of molten rock and was larger than the Peloponnesus. When he was brought to trial the prejudice had grown so strong that not even Pericles' influence was able to save him from a sentence of banishment. Accordingly the last years of his life were spent in exile at Lampsacus, a city on the Hellespont, the citizens of which showed their recognition of his worth by burying him with highest honors.

Anaxagoras' qualitative pluralism, like that of Empedocles, has to be understood in relation to the Eleatic principle that Being cannot arise from Not-Being. Consider for example a simple case of qualitative change, the striking of fire from flint. After sufficient friction there spurts up a flame which shows itself to vision as largely yellow and to the touch as painfully hot, where no flame had apparently been before. Reflecting on this phenomenon in relation to the Eleatic principle we can discover three logically possible explanations of it.

A. It is possible to accept the phenomenon at face value and thus to deny the Eleatic principle. That is to say, it is possible to admit that something now exists (i.e., this particular flame with its perceptible qualities) which did not exist previously. Such is the answer given by Heraclitus; it seems moreover to be implicit in everyday modes of thought, since the obvious thing to say and think is that while no flame existed before the friction took place a flame does exist now and as a result of it.

B. A second solution is reductionism, which consists in evading the problem by dismissing the qualities of flame as unreal. Thales, in declaring that water is the single true nature of all existent things, was the first clear proponent of reductionist thinking in Greece. Parmenides and eventually Plato handled the dismissal more universally by declaring all change, by its very nature, to be unreal. In the metascientific philosophizing that got under way in the seventeenth century and has continued to dominate theoretical physics from then to the present day, a distinction is maintained between the spatially definite characteristics that can be traced and measured by scientific techniques and such non-measurable characteristics as the visible yellow and felt warmth which are the flame's manifest qualities. These manifest qualities become regarded as mere epiphenomena, mere subjective results, of the vibratory activities which alone are supposed to be real. When the qualities are taken as appearances rather than realities, the Eleatic principle does not apply to them, any more than to the content of dreams. The atomism of Leucippus and Democritus, to be presented in the next chapter, is an outstanding type of such reductionism in ancient Greece.

C. But what if simultaneously the Eleatic principle is upheld and the perceptual qualities of the flame are accepted as real? How is it possible on that double basis to explain the sudden appearance of a hot yellow flame? Assuming that there has not been any appreciable alteration in our visual organs, there seems to be only one possible answer. If the qualities hot and yellow are real in their own right, and if they are now observed to exist although formerly they did not exist, and if our visual powers remain virtually unchanged, then the only possible explanation is that the qualities were formerly in hiding and that somehow the act of rubbing released them and brought them into the open. The fire must have been lurking invisibly in the flint, or in the air, or in both, until a suitable operation brought it forth. That, in essence, is the type of explanation espoused by Anaxagoras.

Thus Anaxagoras can be regarded as having carried to its logical conclusion the type of qualitative analysis which Empedocles had begun. For Empedocles too had started from the assumption that the terms of an explanation must be qualitatively akin to the phenomenon to be explained. Earth, water, air, and fire with their recognizable differences are qualitatively nearer to the world of perceptual experience than either atoms or vibrations conceived as abstractly apart from such perceptible qualities as yellow and warm. But in applying the Eleatic principle Empedocles stopped halfway. The post-Eleatic qualitative principle that "like causes like" is partly but not fully upheld in Empedocles' theory. A theory of four qualitative elements does not go far enough to represent the world's incalculable diversity. The various things with which we come into daily contact are not merely the four elements, and perhaps never any of those in their purity. When the leaves of a tree are formed it is no adequate explanation to say that they represent a certain proportion of earth and water; for the qualitative thinker is concerned with the leafiness of those leaves—their greenness, fuzziness, and such. How can leaves in this sense come-to-be out of earth—green leaves out of brown earth? That is the qualitative thinker's problem. If the Eleatic principle is accepted, we should then have to reply in one of two ways: either renouncing qualitative realism and dismissing the green leafiness as unreal and merely a subjective impression, or else supposing the quality of green leafiness to have lain concealed in the earth, in the trunk and bough of the tree, and perhaps in the sunbeams and the air until (for whatever reason) it was brought forth and made manifest to the sight. Anaxagoras in taking this latter line of explanation was carrying the Eleatic principle to its logical conclusion in the interpretation of the qualitative world. For "how could hair come from not-hair" (Fr. 4), or green from not-green, or leafiness from not-leafiness?

Consider in Anaxagorean perspective the problem of digestion. A man eats brown bread and green lettuce; these are digested and among their products are white bones and red blood. How to explain the transformation? By Anaxagoras' Eleatic principle bone cannot be a product of not-bone, nor blood of not-blood. Hence, he reasons, there must already have been tiny particles of bone and of blood lurking in the bread and lettuce. Such particles Anaxagoras describes as "parts," "elements," and "seeds"—the last term suggesting what Aristotle was later to mean by potentiality. For a seed is that which contains certain definite potentialities of future growth and development. Seeds of blood and bone, according to Anaxagoras' theory, have been latent in the foods but in such tiny and dispersed amounts that they could not be seen or tasted; in the process of digestion these tiny particles are drawn forth to some degree from the foods, are joined with their kind in the human body, and thereby their real nature as blood and as bone become manifest. Meanwhile what is happening to the bread and lettuce that are consumed? By the Eleatic principle they cannot have been destroyed; therefore we must conclude that particles of them remain in the blood and bone which they nourish, while other particles go into the waste matter which passes off.

Generalizing from this situation Anaxagoras concludes that "in everything there is a little bit of everything else" (Fr. 7). Existing things are always composite. What distinguishes one thing from another is the relative amounts of the various ingredients of it. In water the water particles predominate, in bread the bread particles, in bone the particles of bone, and so on. To speak of "pure" water or pure anything else is forever inaccurate; when we characterize this water as pure we can only mean, on Anaxagoras' theory, that the water particles are unusually predominant and that the particles of many other kinds which it contains are proportionately so few as to be undetectable.

The doctrine of universal mixture implies as a corollary, Anaxagoras perceived, the doctrine of unlimited divisibility. The connecting link between the two doctrines is the idea of inexhaustibility. Clearly, if it is true that everything must always contain some particles of everything else, then no matter how much of these ingredients may be drawn off there will always be a little of each of them left in the given substance. In order to account for such inexhaustibility within a thing of finite magnitude Anaxagoras is obliged to postulate infinite divisibility: "Of the small there is no least, but always a lesser" (Fr. 10). Anaxagoras is groping, in terms of his qualitative theory, towards a concept of the infinitessimal.

To a modern reader, following his accustomed way of making distinctions particularly between thing and quality, there may appear to be an odd inconsistency between Fr. 4 and T 8 on the one hand and Frs. 12 and 19 on the other. In the former pair we find bone, flesh, and hair mentioned as typical instances of seeds, while the examples mentioned in the latter are pairs of opposite qualities such as moist vs. dry and hot vs. cold. It should be realized, however, that an ancient Greek reader would not have found any inconsistency in the situation, but only a shift of emphasis. The distinction between noun and adjective, and correspondingly between thing and quality, was by no means exact or firm in Anaxagoras' time; subsequently it became somewhat clarified by Plato, sharpened by Aristotle especially in his *De Interpretatione,* and finally codified by the grammarians of Alexandria. But it was still possible for the Presocratic mind, even as late as Anaxagoras, to think of bone, flesh, hot, cold, bright, dark, etc. as vaguely related common ingredients in a composite. Although repeated attempts were made to regularize the connections of the qualitative pairs moist-dry and hot-cold with the four natural elements, no single way of conceiving their relationship ever won universal acceptance.

Anaxagoras' general metaphysical theory offers a basis for his cosmogony—his theory of how the world began. Originally, he holds, all things were so thoroughly mixed together that nothing could be distinguished from anything else. To all intents and purposes nothing existed, simply because everything existed without discrimination. A final postulate is now introduced, based on the human analogy. In a human situation, when things are in confusion, it is by an activity of mind that they are distinguished and set in order. Analogously Anaxagoras conceives the ordered world, the cosmos, as having been set in order by a mind which is somehow active in it. Unlike the archetypal creator-god of the Hebraeo-Christian tradition, who created the world by issuing commands, the creator-god in Anaxagoras' theory is pure mind, characterized primarily by a power to distinguish and separate one quality or characteristic or thing from another, and thereby to create through the production of order.

FRAGMENTS

GENERAL PRINCIPLES

*1.   Because of the weakness of our senses we are not able
to judge the truth.*   (21)

2.   Appearances are a glimpse of the unseen.   (21a)

*3.   The Greeks do not rightly understand what they call
coming-to-be and perishing. A real thing does not come-to-be
or perish; occurrences that are so called are simply the mixing
and separating of real entities.*   (17)

*4.   For how could hair come from what is not hair, or
flesh from what is not flesh?*   (10)

ORIGINAL MIXTURE
AND THE SEEDS OF THINGS

*5.   Such being the case, we must suppose that composite
things contain many ingredients of the very greatest variety—
the seeds of everything, having all kinds of characteristics, colors, and ways of affecting the sensitivities.*   (4)

*6.   The things of the universe are not sliced off from one
another with a hatchet, neither the hot from the cold nor the
cold from the hot.*   (8)

*7.   In everything there is a portion of everything else, ex-
cept of mind; and in some things there is mind also.*   (11)

*8.   Whatever there is most of in particular things deter-
mines the manifest nature that we ascribe to each.*   (12, end)

*9.   Since the great and the small share equally with respect
to the number of parts they possess, here is a further reason*

why everything must possess a portion of everything else. Thus nothing exists apart; everything has a share of everything else. For since there is no smallest amount, it is impossible for a complete isolation to be brought about, and it is equally impossible for anything to come-to-be out of not-being. Accordingly they must be now as they were in the beginning. In everything there is always a multiplicity of different ingredients; and there are as many ingredients separable from the lesser as there are ingredients separable from the greater. (6)

10. In the small there is no least, but always a lesser; for being cannot be defined by reference to not-being. Likewise there is always something bigger than what is big. The large and the small are thus equal in amount. And each thing taken from its own standpoint is large and small simultaneously. (3)

11. All things were together, unlimited both in number and in smallness; for smallness too was unlimited. And when all things were together none of them could be distinguished because of their smallness. Air and aether, both of them unlimited, covered and dominated all else; for of the ingredients in the mixture these were the greatest, with respect both to number and to size. (1)

12. When all things were together, before any separating had taken place, not even any color was discernible. This was because of the utter mixture of all things—of moist with dry, hot with cold, bright with dark. And there was a great quantity of earth in the mixture, as well as seeds which were unlimited in number and of the utmost variety. For none of the products is ever like any other. And that being so, we must believe that all this variety of things was present in the original whole. (4)

13.   Neither in speculation nor in actuality can we ever know the number of things that are separated out.   (7)

14.   We should realize that when separation has taken place each kind of entity is fixed in amount, and becomes neither more nor less. For the different kinds of entity, as they become distinguishable, cannot add up to more than the totality, and the totality is equal to itself at all times.   (5)

15.   While other things have a share in the being of everything else, Mind is unlimited, autonomous, and unmixed with anything, standing entirely by itself. For if it were not by itself but were mixed with anything else whatever, it would thereby participate in all that exists; because, as I have said before, in everything that exists there is a share of everything else. If Mind were to share in the universal mixture, the things with which it was mixed would prevent it from having command over everything in the way that it now does, whereas the truth is that Mind, because of its exceptional fineness and purity, has knowledge of all that is, and therein it has the greatest power. (12)

16.   Mind, which exists perpetually, is surely to be found in the surrounding mass, where other things exist, both in the things that have already been individuated and in those that are in process of becoming so.   (14)

17.   All mind, whether great or small, is alike; but of other things nothing is quite like anything else.   (12)

COSMOLOGY

18.   And Mind took charge of the cosmic situation, so that the universe proceeded to rotate from the very beginning. At first the rotation was small, but by now it extends over a larger space, and it will extend over a yet larger one. Both the things that are mingled and those that are separated and individuated are all known by Mind. (12)

19. *And Mind set in order all that was to be, all that ever was but no longer is, and all that is now or ever will be. This includes the revolving movements of the stars, of the sun and moon, and of the air and aether as they are being separated off. It was the rotary movement that caused the separation—a separation of the dense from the rare, the hot from the cold, the bright from the dark, and the dry from the moist.* (12)

20. *When Mind first set things in motion, there began a process of separation in the moving mass; and as things were thus moving and separating, the process of separation was greatly increased by the rotary movement.* (13)

21. *The rotation and separation are characterized by force and swiftness. The swiftness makes the force. Such swiftness is not like the swiftness of anything known to us, but is incalculably greater.* (9)

22. *Air and aether are separated off from the mass that encompasses them, which is unlimited in amount.* (2)

23. *The dense, the moist, the cold, and the dark came together here where the earth now is; while the rare, the warm, the dry, and the bright departed towards the farthest region of the aether.* (15)

24. *Out of these things that are separated off the earth is condensed; water being separated off from the mists, and earth from water. From earth the stones are condensed by the cold, and these move outward more than water does [i.e., are individuated more than water is].* (16)

25. *It is the sun that puts brightness into the moon.* (18)

26. *What we call Iris [the rainbow] is a glimmer of the sun reflected on the clouds. It is therefore the sign of a storm; for the water flowing about it in the cloud may produce wind and may pour forth as rain.* (19)

27. *We should recognize the possibility that men may have been formed [within the seeds], as well as other organisms that possess souls; and that such men may perhaps dwell in cities and cultivate their fields just as we do, and that they have their sun and moon and other heavenly bodies as we do, and that their earth yields them vegetable life of all kinds, the most useful of which they harvest and take home to supply their needs. In other words, it may be that the separating and individuating process goes on not only in our own world but elsewhere too.* (4, ctd.)

TESTIMONIA

FROM PLATO:

T 1. *Socrates:* So I am accused of saying that the sun is a stone and the moon is earth. Really, Meletus, aren't you confusing me with Anaxagoras? You must have a low opinion of the jurors if you think them so ignorant of literature as not to know that the books of Anaxagoras of Clazomenae are full of such doctrines. (*Apologia* 26D)

T 2. If such a view were true we would then have to agree with Anaxagoras' statement, "All things were together." (*Phaedo* 72C)

T 3. I heard a man reading from a book which he said was by a certain Anaxagoras, to the effect that Mind arranges everything that occurs and is the cause of everything. (*ibid.* 97c)

T 4. On reading Anaxagoras' book I perceive that he does not make any use of his concept of mind, nor does he appeal to it in explanation of how things are ordered, but he treats air, aether, and water as the causes. (*ibid.* 98B)

T 5. In declaring that the moon gets its light from the sun Anaxagoras was evidently drawing upon a more ancient doctrine. (*Cratylus* 409A)

T 6. Anaxagoras says that Mind has absolute power, being mingled with nothing as it dispenses to everything, running through all time. (*ibid.* 413c)

FROM ARISTOTLE:

T 7. Anaxagoras of Clazomenae preceded Empedocles in date of birth but followed him in the production of written works. (*Metaphysica* 984a 11)

T 8. Here Anaxagoras' view is opposed to that of Empedocles, for he takes the elements to be *homoeomerês*—that is, such particular sorts of thing as flesh and bone, and he says that air and fire contain mixtures of these and all the other seeds. He holds, in short, that whatever exists is composed of invisible *homoeomerês* packed together, and that out of them all else is born, such as fire, which he calls aether. (*De Caelo* 302a 31)

T 9. Anaxagoras and certain others say that the number of elements is unlimited. He posits as elements the *homoeomerês*, such as bone, flesh, and marrow—anything, in short, of which a part has the same nature as the whole. (*De Generatione et Corruptione* 314a 18)

T 10.   . . . those thinkers, such as Anaxagoras and Democritus, who regard the elements as unlimited, the former conceiving them as *homoeomerês*.   (*Physica* 203a 19)

T 11.   Anaxagoras of Clazomenae . . . says that the "first-principles" are unlimited in number, and that in the case of homogeneous things like fire and water they are *homoeomerês;* and that [things as we know them] come-to-be and perish through compounding and separating—the only kind of coming-to-be and perishing that is possible, since the *homoeomerês* themselves exist eternally.   (*Metaphysica* 984a 11)

T 12.   Having found such alleged causes as these inadequate to generate the nature of things, they [Anaxagoras and his followers] felt obliged in the search for truth to locate the first-principle in that which lay nearest [to what could be observed]. After all, perhaps neither fire nor earth nor any other such thing can be a proper cause, nor should be thought one, of why certain things exist and others come-to-be. Nor can either volition or chance serve to explain the matter plausibly.   (*ibid.* 984b 8)

T 13.   Anaxagoras, in speaking of the permanence of the Unlimited, expresses the matter oddly. He says that the Unlimited establishes—sustains—itself and is in itself; there is nothing outside of it, he says, so that wherever [in whatever conditions] a thing may exist it does so by virtue of the Unlimited.   (*Physica* 205b 1)

T 14.   There appears to be a strange contradiction in his saying that *all things were originally mixed together.* For the idea of their being mixed together implies that they must have had individual natures in order to be mixed, hence that the ingredients of the mixture must have been unmixed in the first place. Only thus could their emergence from the mixture have been other than a happening of pure chance. Nevertheless, if you follow his reasoning closely, you will see that he is making an original point. For in the so-called mixture before separation there clearly could not have been any white or black or gray or any other color, but everything must have been colorless. Likewise with taste and other qualities. It is impossible that any of the so-called forms should have existed [i.e., that there should have been any specific natures] when all things were mixed together, for otherwise there would already have been separation [of one type of thing from another]. (*Metaphysica* 989a 33)

T 15.   Others, such as Anaxagoras, say that the opposites, which exist in the One, are separated out of it. . . . And Anaxagoras evidently supposed these to be unlimited. For he holds to the doctrine commonly held by physical scientists, that nothing can arise out of not-being; for which reason he declares that all things were together, and that coming-to-be is but a change of form. . . .

Such thinkers, because they saw everywhere things arising out of other things, have declared that everything is mixed with everything. When different things come into being, they are called by different names, although each of them is an unlimited mixture, which is to say that an individual whole is never purely black or white or sweet [or sour], or flesh or bone, but its apparent quality is given by that of which it contains most. (*Physica* 187a 20, 36)

T 16.   He says that all things are mixed together except Mind, which alone is unmixed and free. (*Metaphysica* 989b 15)

T 17.   Anaxagoras says that when all things were together and had been at rest for an unlimited time, Mind produced motion and caused separation. (*Physica* 250b 24)

T 18.   In taking Mind as the first-principle of motion Anaxagoras rightly says that it is unaffected by anything else and that it is the first principle of motion. For only thus by being unmoved can it cause motion [in everything else] and by being unmixed it can rule. (*ibid*. 256b 24)

T 19.   Anaxagoras stands alone in declaring that Mind does not undergo change, having nothing in common with anything else. (*De Anima* 405b 19)

T 20.   In order that it may rule and may have specific knowledge of what it is ruling, it must have essential knowledge of all things, and for this reason it has to be unmixed. (*ibid*. 429a 18)

T 21.   While Anaxagoras, as already remarked, appears to distinguish between soul and mind, he treats them as of the same nature except that he regards mind especially as the first principle of all things; for it is mind alone, he says, that is simple, unmixed, and pure. In declaring that mind is the mover of everything he therein assigns both knowledge and motion, both mind and soul, to the same first-principle. (*ibid*. 405a 13)

T 22.   Anaxagoras does not always make his view quite clear; for while he generally speaks truly of Mind as the cause, at other times he speaks of this or that moving principle as present in all animals, both great and small, both noble and mean. But since it does not appear that what is properly called mind is present in all animals (indeed, not even in all men!) he seems here to regard the moving principle as equivalent to soul in general. (*ibid*. 404b 1)

T 23.   His argument that as mind exists in animals so it exists in nature as the cause of the universe and of order made him sound like a sober man in the midst of loose talkers. (*Metaphysica* 984b 15)

T 24.   Anaxagoras says that by virtue of possessing hands man is the most intelligent of animals. (*De Partibus Animalium* 687a 7)

T 25.   He says that plants are like animals in feeling pleasure and pain—an inference which he draws from the fact that they shed their leaves and let them grow again; and that in addition to having motion and sensation plants breathe. (*De Plantis* 815a 16)

T 26. There are those who, conceiving the void in an unusual way, make the same mistake as Anaxagoras did in attempting to prove that it does not exist. What they actually prove, by blowing up skins and stopping the holes of a clepsydra, is that air does exist and exercises force. (*Physica* 213a 22)

T 27. In remarking that he would not be surprised if a man's true condition would appear strange to the many [if they could know it] Anaxagoras seems to have meant that neither the rich nor the powerful man is thereby happy; for he knew that the many judge by external appearances and cannot see what is in front of them. (*Ethica Nichomachea* 1179a 13)

FROM LATER GREEK SOURCES:

T 28. Anaxagoras, son of either Hegesibolus or Eubulus, was a native of Clazomenae, and was at one time a student of Anaximenes. He was noted not only for his wealth and high birth but also for his magnanimity, particularly in giving away his patrimony to his relatives. When they chided him for being neglectful of his wealth he replied, "On the contrary, haven't I entrusted it to your care?" Eventually he abandoned public life and devoted himself to natural science. When someone asked him, "Don't you have any concern for your native land?" he replied with a gesture toward the sky, "Speak better and say that my native land is just what does concern me."

It is said that he was twenty years old at the time of Xerxes' invasion and that he lived to the age of seventy-two. Apollodorus in his *Chronology* says that he was born in the seventieth Olympiad [500-497 B.C.] and died in the first year of the eighty-eighth [428]. In his early twenties he began to study philosophy at Athens, and he remained at Athens for thirty years; he was the first writer to publish a book containing diagrams.

There are two different accounts concerning the trial of Anaxagoras. On the one hand Sotion in his *Succession of the Philosophers* says that the charge was impiety, brought against him by Cleon, for having declared the sun to be a mass of fiery metal, and that after being defended by Pericles, who had been his pupil, he received a sentence of banishment and a fine of five talents. On the other hand Satyrus in his *Lives* says that Themistocles, who opposed Pericles politically, conducted the prosecution, that the charge involved treasonable dealings with Persia as well as impiety, and that the philosopher was condemned to death. He adds that when Anaxagoras was told of his condemnation he remarked, "Long ago Nature condemned to death both myself and my judges."

It is reported that while he was confined in prison pending execution Pericles asked the populace whether they had any fault to find with his own conduct of public affairs. When they replied in the negative he declared, "Well, I am a pupil of Anaxagoras; don't listen to slander and put him to death, but listen to me and release him." Pericles is said to have brought him into court so weak and wasted by illness that his acquittal resulted more from the judges' sympathy than from the merits of the case. At any rate he was released, but was so affected by the indignities he had suffered that he took his own life. (Diogenes Laertius II. 6-15)

T 29.   When someone asked Anaxagoras whether the hills at Lampsacus would ever become sea, he replied, "Yes, if you allow them time."

To the question why he had been born he replied, "In order to study the sun, moon, and starry sky."

To one who asked, "Don't you miss the society of the Athenians?" he replied, "No, it is they who miss me."

When looking at the tomb of Mausolus he remarked, "A costly tomb is an image of the estate."

To one who was grieved at the prospect of dying in a foreign land he replied, "The descent to Hades will be much the same wherever you start from."   (*ibid.*)

T 30.   To someone who found him gazing fixedly at the night sky, on being asked why he stood there so uncomfortably, he replied: "In order to study the universe."   (Philo)

T 31.   Very similar to Anaximander's theory is that of Anaxagoras, who declares that in the separation from the Unlimited things that are alike are brought together with one another: for instance, whatever gold there is in the All comes forth as gold, earth comes forth as earth—not in the sense of sheer coming-to-be, but in the sense that they become what they inherently already are.   (Theophrastus, *Physical Opinions*)

T 32.   Anaxagoras of Clazomenae, son of Hegesioboulos, declared regarding the first-principle of the All that as doer it is Mind (*nous*) but that as occurrence it is matter (*hylê*). For when all things were together Mind came and set them in order. The material first-principles are infinite [in number], and also their comparative smallness is infinite. Motion occurs when Mind operates by grouping like things together.   (Hippolytus *Refutatio* I. 8)

T 33.   Anaxagoras of Clazomenae declared that *homoeomerês* are the first-principles of things. For it seemed to him unintelligible that anything should come-to-be out of not-being or pass away into not-being. We eat some simple food, such as the bread of Demeter, and we drink water; out of such nourishment there grow hair, veins, arteries, sinews, bones, and other parts of the body. The fact that these various things do arise compels us to acknowledge that they are all present [as seeds] in the nourishment of which we partake, and that from them all things grow.

The existence of such elements in the nourishment which pro-

duce blood, sinews, bones, etc. is a truth arrived at by contemplative thought rather than by sense-perception; for sense-perception
by itself will not discover everything, and a knowledge of how
bread and water are transformed into the body is something
that requires contemplative thought.

Because the elements that exist in the nourishment are *like* the
results that are produced in the body they are called *homoeomerês,* and he declared them to be the first-principles of whatever exists. He described the *homoeomerês* as "matter" but the
active cause governing their development he called "mind."
And he began thus: "All things were together and Mind arranged and disposed them." (Aëtius)

T 34.   The Stoics agree with Anaxagoras in holding that the
nature of cause is not evident to human reason, inasmuch as
some things occur by necessity, some by fate, some by purpose,
some by chance, and some of their own accord. (*ibid.*)

T 35.   All nature (*physis*), he says, involves both composition
and separation—that is, both coming-to-be and perishing. (*ibid.*)

T 36.   He said that the sun, moon, and stars are fiery stones
borne about by the revolving movement of the aether. That below
the stars there are the sun, the moon, and certain invisible bodies
that move with them. That the moon is below the sun and nearer
to the earth. That the moon is eclipsed when either the earth or
one of the invisible bodies passes in front of it, and that the sun is
eclipsed when the new moon passes in front of it. That the moon
is composed of earth and has hills and valleys on it. (Hippolytus *Refutatio* I. 8)

T 37.   He said that the sun is many times larger than the
Peloponnesus. (Aëtius)

T 38.   He said that the melting of snow in the mountains of
Ethiopia in summer and its freezing in winter are what cause
[the periodic inundation of] the Nile. (*ibid.*)

T 39.   Diogenes [of Apollonia] and Anaxagoras both say that after the universe came into being and animals were generated out of the earth, there occurred a tipping of the earth toward the south. It was self-moving and was designed to render some parts of the earth habitable and others uninhabitable as a result of the differences in temperature.   (*ibid.*)

T 40.   He held that sensations occur as a result of a commensurate relation between the sense-object and the pores of a particular sense-organ.   (*ibid.*)

T 41.   Anaxagoras postulates the existence of Mind as the cause of motion and becoming; he says that by causing separation it produced distinct worlds and distinct objects of all kinds. (Theophrastus, *Physical Opinions*)

T 42.   Anaxagoras held that sensation occurs by opposite affecting opposite; for like is not affected by like. Elaborating the principle in detail he said that the process of vision involves a reflection of the object on the eye, and that such a reflection is possible only in a medium that is different in quality from itself. He adds that the reason why most creatures see better in the daytime than at night is because the night is more nearly of the same color as [the pupils of] their eyes, but that certain species of animals, which are sharp-sighted at night, are different in this respect. In our ordinary daytime vision, where light is the outward cause of the reflected image, we perceive whatever color is most opposite [to the color prevailing in the eye].

Similarly, sensations of touch and taste arise by reason of opposites. What is equally warm or equally cool with the body does not produce warmth or cold in it. Nor do men perceive sweet and bitter by themselves alone. On the contrary, we perceive cold by the warmth in ourselves, pure water by our own saltiness, sweet by bitter, and so on, according as the opposite of any presented quality prevails in us. For all qualities reside in us to some degree.   (Theophrastus *De Sensu* I. 27)

FROM LATIN SOURCES:

T 43.   Anaxagoras, who was a pupil of Anaximenes, was the first to teach that the character of each thing, produced by separation, is determined and arranged by the rational power of unlimited Mind.

[*Cicero's criticism:*]   If such Mind, like mind as we know it, involves sensation, then Anaxagoras' theory involves a theory of unlimited sensation; which is untenable, because every sensation that can be felt and can produce natural effects is always limited. . . . If, on the other hand, unlimited Mind is not joined with anything by which it can feel—which is apparently what Anaxagoras means to say in describing it as open and simple—such a concept of mind goes quite beyond anything our intelligence can grasp.   (Cicero *De Natura Deorum* I. 26)

T 44.   Let us examine the *homoeomerês* of Anaxagoras—a Greek word which cannot be translated into our Latin tongue because of the poverty of our vocabulary. Still, it is easy to explain by other words what it means. When Anaxagoras speaks of *homoeomerês* in things, what he evidently means is that bones are made of very tiny particles of bone, flesh of very tiny particles of flesh, and that blood is formed from numerous drops of blood coming together in union. Likewise he explains gold as consisting of grains of gold, earth as formed out of small bits of earth, fire of fire, water of water, and so of the rest. He denies that void can exist anywhere in anything, and supposes no limit to the subdivision of bodies.   (Lucretius *De Rerum Natura* I. 830)

T 45.   Anaxagoras supposes that everything is secretly mingled with everything else, and that when something appears to be of this or that specific nature it is because particles of that nature predominate in the mixture and can thus place themselves more favorably.   (Lucretius I. 876)

6

Atomism

THE THEORY OF ATOMISM as it arose in ancient Greece presents itself to the contemporary mind in two contrary guises. It tends to have a quite different look, a different philosophical weight and import, according as we consider it from the standpoint of our own conceptual habits and presuppositions or in the context of early Greek intellectual history.

In an obvious respect the atomism of Leucippus and Democritus is closer than any of the rival Greek views to what we now identify as scientific thinking. Largely as a result of the intellectual demands implicit in technological developments it has been a major trend in post-Renaissance scientific thinking to take as an altogether basic concept the idea of quantifiable space. Of course space in some sense or other is inevitable; the awareness and assumption of spatial relations is so deeply a part of all human experience that an utterly non-spatial kind of awareness is virtually unthinkable. That, however, is not to the present point; spatial quality as such—for instance, the "flowing space" which an architect may try to achieve in the shaping of a colonnade, or the receding spaces of a Cezanne painting, or the sense of awesome depth in looking into the Grand Canyon—lacks the exactitude which techno-scientific procedures demand. Science, especially physics, as it is conceived today, requires maximum exactitude, and the scientific importance of spatial relations is that they allow of certain operations by which dif-

ferences (unlike differences of pure time or of pure quality) can
be envisaged as consisting of homogeneous units. For it is possible
to know homogeneous units only when there is an available technique for making exact comparisons between them. Such near-
perfect comparisons (i.e., with a minimal margin of error) are
possible and can be relied on when we apply a ruler to a surface,
or compare the clock hands with the notches on the dial, or take
pointer-readings from any kind of precision instrument; and every
such measurement involves some form of spatial comparison. Consequently, although Leucippus and Democritus did not specifically
endorse the quantitative comparison of atoms and atomic movements (lacking any means of undertaking it), still their postulation
of material entities with no distinguishing characteristics except
the potentially measurable ones of size, shape, position, and loco-
motion, constituted a first step toward the conceptual formation
of a measurable universe.

As seen in relation to their Greek predecessors, on the other
hand, the ancient atomists were but two among several post-
Eleatic philosophers attempting a metaphysical reconstruction. Aristotle, despite the considerable attention he gives to the theory of
atomism as an ingenious novelty, dismisses it as "implausible" because too remote from the actualities of the world as it is perceived; and Plato does not so much as mention it among all the
many theories which find a place in his Dialogues. From the ancient
standpoint the role of atomism is best understood as representing
one attempt among several to construct a metaphysics that would
be able, in the wake of Eleaticism, to cope with the twin problems of oneness vs. multiplicity and persistence vs. change. In
meeting these problems atomism offers a solution which, as compared with the solutions of Empedocles and Anaxagoras, shows both
a major similarity and a major difference. All three of the philosophies in question postulate, in their reconstructive undertaking, a
plurality of certain entities which persist unchanged in their intrinsic nature but which by their changing relations produce the

fluctuating manifold which is ever present to us in experience. The outstanding difference is that while the elements which Empedocles and Anaxagoras postulated were distinguished from one another qualitatively, the elements postulated by atomism were not. Democritus explicitly declares that all qualities and qualitative differences constitute "obscure knowledge," and that "real knowledge" knows only atoms and the void. Thus the pluralism which Leucippus and Democritus uphold is a pluralism of spatial differences only; it is a monism so far as quality is concerned.

i. Leucippus

Little is known about Leucippus, the acknowledged founder of atomism. According to reports he was born at either Miletus or Elea; in any event it was at Abdera that he founded, probably somewhere near 540 to 530 B.C., the school with which his pupil Democritus was afterwards identified. In his youth he had studied in the school at Elea, but whether before or after the death of Parmenides is not certain; doubtless his most direct influence came from Zeno, in view of that philosopher's strong interest in the problems and paradoxes of space. The Eleatic vocabulary left its mark on the atomists, at least in the respect that they equate the atoms with being and the void with not-being. Leucippus concurred with the Eleatic argument that true being does not admit of vacuum and that without vacuum there can be no movement; but starting out from the more realistic assumption that movement does in fact exist, he contraposed the argument—contending that since movement exists there must be vacuum, but that since vacuum cannot really *be* it must be identified with not-being. Unlike the Eleatics he was not unduly troubled by such conceptual intermingling of being and not-being. It remained for Plato to make the needed distinction between grades of being and types of negation.

FRAGMENT

*1. Nothing happens at random; whatever comes about is by
rational necessity.* (2)

TESTIMONIA

FROM ARISTOTLE:

T 1.   Leucippus believed he had a theory which would be
consistent with sense-perception, in that it did not abolish coming-
to-be and perishing, nor movement, nor the multiplicity of things.
To that extent he accepted the testimony of appearances. On the
other hand he conceded to the monists that there could not be
movement without a void, that a void is not-being, and that
What Is cannot ever be What Is Not. Accordingly he agrees
that What Is must be a complete *plenum,* absolutely and continuously full; with this qualification, however, that there is not
just one plenum, there are numerous plena, in fact they are unlimited in number. Because of their extremely small bulk they
are invisible. They move in the void—for there is a void—and
by their coming together they cause coming-to-be, while by
their getting loose from one another they cause perishing. They
act and are acted upon when they happen to come in contact;
for they make contact without becoming one, and it is through
contact and hooking on to one another that they produce phenomena.   (*De Generatione et Corruptione* 325a 23)
   T 2.   Leucippus and his colleague Democritus declared that
the elements are the full and the empty, which they call Being
and Not-Being respectively. Accordingly when they say that Being
is no more [real] than Not-Being, what they mean is that solid
body is no more [real] than vacuum—[i.e., that vacuum exists

quite as truly as body does]. This pair of opposites they treat, in effect, as the material basis of all that is. . . . They hold that the real differences among the elements, which cause all other differences, are three: shape, arrangement, and position. As they express it, real being is differentiated solely according to *surface-rhythm, inter-contact,* or *inclination.* By "surface-rhythm" they mean shape, by "inter-contact" they mean arrangement, and by "inclination" they mean the direction of turning. Thus A differs from N in shape, AN from NA in arrangement, and Z from N in direction of turning. (*Metaphysica* 985b 15)

T 3. Leucippus and Democritus say that all things are composed of indivisible bodies, and that these are infinite both in number and in their various shapes; and that compounds get their different characters from the shape and arrangement of the constituents. (*De Generatione et Corruptione* 314a 21)

T 4. They [Leucippus and Democritus] say that the primary magnitudes are infinite in number but not infinite in divisibility of magnitude; that the many does not come-to-be from the one or vice versa, but that all things are generated by the action of these primary magnitudes in catching on to each other and letting go. (*De Caelo* 303a 5)

FROM LATER GREEK SOURCES:

T 5. Leucippus was born at Elea, although there are some who say it was at Abdera, others who say it was at Miletus. He studied under Zeno. He held that the manyness of things is unlimited, and that they all become transformed into one another [by rearrangement of parts]. The All includes both the empty and the full. Worlds are formed when atoms fall into the void and become entangled with one another. He was the first who postulated atoms as first principles.

In the All, which is infinite, the full and the void are what he calls the elements. Out of them arise worlds infinite in number, and into them the worlds are dissolved. This is how the worlds are formed. In a particular area many atoms of the most diverse shapes are tossed out of the Unlimited into a vast empty space. They gather together and form a vortex, in which, as they whirl about in all sorts of ways and jostle one another, some get separated off, as the atoms which are like one another form particular unions. When the atoms are too numerous to revolve effectively, the lighter ones are thrown off into the outer void, as if they were being winnowed. The atoms that remain behind become more and more entangled, and their collectivity takes the form of a revolving sphere. The crust of the sphere encloses whirling atoms of all kinds, which, by the force of the vortex that whirls about the center, produce further combinations. Meanwhile the outer crust becomes thinner and expands, while other atoms from outside get drawn into its interior as they come in contact with the crust. By the interlocking of parts an aggregate is formed; it is damp and muddy at first, but after it dries and revolves with the universal vortex the sphere catches fire, and that is how the special character of the stars is formed. (Diogenes Laertius IX. 30-33)

T 6.   Leucippus of Elea or of Miletus (for it is told of him both ways) had been a student of philosophy with Parmenides; in his theory of Being, however, the road which he took was not that of Parmenides and Zeno, but appeared to be quite opposed to theirs. For as against their view that the All is one, motionless, unborn, and limited, and as against their agreement not to admit Not-Being as a possible object of investigation, he postulated that there are elements infinitely many and in perpetual motion, which are atoms [not further divisible]; and he maintained that the number of their shapes is infinite, too, on the ground that there is no more reason for an atom to have one shape than another. It was also a part of his theory that everything goes on coming-to-be and changing incessantly. Moreover he affirmed that Not-Being exists quite as much as Being does, and that both of them together are the cause of why things occur. The atoms, which he called "being," in their individual character are compact and full; they move about in empty space, which he called "not-being," and which "is," he says, no less than being.   (Simplicius *Commentaria*)

ii. Democritus

Democritus of Abdera has become far better known to subsequent history than Leucippus, the founder of the doctrine. It is hardly possible, on the basis of our limited evidence, to judge how much Democritus added to the teachings which he inherited; but at any rate it was he who succeeded in bringing the doctrine to public notice and making it a matter of philosophical controversy. The fact that Aristotle gives so much more detailed attention to Democritus than to Leucippus is doubtless explained partly by his closer temporal relation to the former and partly also by the greater degree to which Democritus had developed the implications of the doctrine.

While Democritus is chiefly distinguished and remembered by his theories of atomic behavior and human perception, represented by the first eight Fragments, he left in addition over two hundred brief general observations and ethical maxims, a selection from which is presented in the following pages. Most of the maxims are fairly trite ("Similar outlook encourages friendship," "Continual procrastination gets nothing done," etc.) and seem hardly worthy of a mind that could work out the conceptual implications of atomism. They serve as an indication, however, that

Democritus' philosophy did have, even if with scant imagination, its human side. The principles of atomism themselves, buttressed by the unqualified determinism which Leucippus expresses in his sole extant Fragment, appear not to allow any room for moral choice; for if everything, to the smallest iota, must be exactly as it is, there is futility in saying it ought to be otherwise. Nevertheless ethical choice is indispensable, and Democritus' philosophy shows its vigor and its pragmatic workability in holding fast to human values and human assumptions even at some little cost to logical consistency.

FRAGMENTS

ON KNOWLEDGE AND REALITY

1. The truth is that what we meet with perceptually is nothing reliable, for it shifts its character according to the body's dispositions, influences, and confrontations. (9)

2. By this criterion man must learn that he is divorced from reality. (6)

3. It has been demonstrated more than once that we do not discover by direct perception what the nature of each thing is or is not. (10)

4. My argument makes it evident that we know nothing authentically about anything, but each one's opinions are simply what flows into him. (7)

5. In reality we know nothing, for truth lies in the abyss. (117)

6. Of knowledge there are two types: the one genuine, the other obscure. Obscure knowledge includes everything that is given by sight, hearing, smell, taste, touch; whereas genuine knowledge is something quite distinct from this. Whenever [an investigation reaches the point where] obscure knowledge can no longer see the objects because of their smallness, and also cannot hear or smell or taste them nor perceive them by touch, [the investigator must then have recourse] to a finer means of knowing. (11)

7.   *By convention there is sweet, by convention there is bitter, by convention hot and cold, by convention color; but in reality there are only atoms and the void.* (9)

8.   *A dialogue between the intellect and the senses.*

INTELLECT: *It is by convention that color exists, by convention sweet, by convention bitter.*

SENSES: *Ah, wretched intellect, you get your evidence only as we give it to you, and yet you try to overthrow us. That overthrow will be your downfall.* (125)

9.   *If a cut were made through a cone parallel to its base, how should we conceive of the two opposing surfaces which the cut has produced—as equal or as unequal? If they are unequal, that would imply that a cone is composed of many breaks and protrusions like steps. On the other hand if they are equal, that would imply that two adjacent intersecting planes are equal, which would mean that the cone, being made up of equal rather than unequal circles, must have the same appearance as a cylinder; which is utterly absurd.* (155)

10.   *Do not try to understand everything, lest you thereby be ignorant of everything.* (169)

11.   *I would rather discover one cause than possess the kingdom of Persia.* (118)

GENERAL REFLECTIONS

12.   Man is a small "ordered world" [kosmos].   (34)

13.   Homer, gifted with a divine nature, built numerous verses into an ordered world.   (21)

14.   To give obedience to the law, to the ruler, and to him who is wiser than oneself, marks the well-ordered man.   (47)

15.   Animals live together with their kind—doves with doves, cranes with cranes, and so of the rest. It is the same with [some] inanimate things. It seems as if a tendency to unite may lie in the very similarity of things.   (164)

16.   In the most important concerns we are pupils of the animals. We learn spinning and mending from the spider, building from the swallow, and imitative singing from songbirds as well as from the swan and the nightingale.   (154)

17.   If the body were to bring suit against the soul for all the pains and ill-treatment it had received from her, and if I myself were the judge in the case, I would take pleasure in finding the soul guilty, on the ground that she had gravely injured the body by her heedlessness, had dissolved it with drunken revels, and corrupted and torn it apart by her lust for pleasure— in the same way that I would blame one who handled carelessly some valuable but fragile instrument.   (159)

18.   In the womb it is the navel that forms itself first, as an anchorage to prevent tossing and wandering.   (148)

19.   Coition is a slight attack of epilepsy, in which man gushes forth from man and breaks loose with the violence of a blow.   (32)

20.   *He who wishes to have children, it seems to me, would
do better to adopt them from families with which he is on
friendly terms. Thereby, being able to select, he can get the kind
of child he wants. And the child whom he chooses as most suitable should be one who best follows the true bent of his nature.
There is a great advantage to this procedure, whereby a man
selects out of many the child whom he prefers; for if he begets
a child of his own, the risks are many and he is bound to accept
whatever comes.*   (277)

21.   *It is well to realize that human life is fragile, short, and
mixed with many cares and difficulties; thereby one learns to
possess in moderation and to measure hardship by real need.*
(285)

22.   *It is needful either to be good or else to imitate the
good.*   (39)

23.   *Magnanimity consists in enduring tactlessness with com-
posure.*   (46)

24.   *The envious man torments himself like an enemy.*   (88)

25.   *The man who is enslaved by wealth can never be honest.*
(50)

26.   *Virtue consists not in avoiding wrong-doing, but in being without any wish for it.*   (62)

27.   *Good and true are the same for all, but pleasant differs
from one man to the next.*   (69)

28.   *Immoderate desire marks the child, not the man.*   (70)

29.   *Untimely pleasures result in displeasure.*   (71)

30.   *Old age is scattered mutilation: it still has all its parts,
but each of them is somehow lacking.*   (296)

31.   *Some men, with no understanding of how our mortal*

nature dissolves [at death] but keenly aware of the ills of this life, afflict life still more with anxieties and fears by making up false tales about the time that comes after the end. (297)

32. There is no lightning-flash hurled by Zeus that does not contain pure light from the aether. (152)

33. I came to Athens and no one knew me. (116)

34. I am the most widely traveled man of all my contemporaries, and have pursued inquiries in the most distant places; I have visited more countries and climes than anyone else, and have listened to the teachings of more learned men. No one has surpassed me in the drawing of lines accompanied by demonstrations, not even the rope-knotters of Egypt, with whom I passed five [?] years on foreign soil. (299)

TESTIMONIA

FROM ARISTOTLE:

T 1. Democritus says that one thing cannot come-to-be out of two, nor two out of one; for he identifies substances with indivisible magnitudes. (*Metaphysica* 1039a 9)

T 2. [Identical with Leucippus, T 2].

T 3. [Leucippus, T 3].

T 4. [Leucippus, T 4].

T 5. Democritus apparently thinks that there are three kinds of real difference. His view is that while the underlying nature of material body is the same in all instances, bodies differ from one another in *surface rhythm* (shape), *inclination* (direction of turning), and *intercontact* (arrangement). (*Metaphysica* 1042b 12)

T 6.   Democritus declares that one type of primary nature does not come-to-be out of another type; accordingly, that universal body is the first principle of all [atoms], which differ according to size and shape.   (*Physica* 203a 33)

T 7.   According to the theory of Democritus it is the nature of the eternal objects to be tiny substances infinite in number. Accordingly he postulates also a place for them that is infinite in magnitude, which he designates by these names—*the void, the nothing,* and *the infinite;* whereas he speaks of each individual atom as *the yes-thing, the dense,* and *being.* He conceives them as so small as to elude our senses, but as having all sorts of forms, shapes, and different sizes. Treating these as elements he conceives of them as combining to produce visible and otherwise perceptible objects.

As they move about in the void the particles are at variance with one another because of their dissimilarity and the other mentioned differences; hence in their motion, as they bump or even as they brush against one another, they tend to get ensnarled and interlocked. The process of interlocking never makes them into a single nature however, for it would be absurd to think that two or more things could ever become one. When these substances remain joined for some time, it is explained by the fact that they fit snugly and so catch firm hold of one another; for some bodies are scalene while others are sharply hooked, some are concave, others convex, and there are numerous other differences. His [Democritus'] theory is that they cling together and remain in certain combinations until they are shaken apart and separated by outside forces.   [From Aristotle's lost work *On Democritus*]

T 8.   Both Anaxagoras and Democritus say that unlimited Being involves an infinitude of contacts—contacts among qualitative similars according to the one, contacts among the spermatically universal shapes according to the other.   (*Physica* 203a 20)

T 9.   Those who regard the ultimate parts of things as solids have a better basis [than those who regard them as planes]
for declaring that the larger body is the heavier. Since, however, in composite bodies the weight does not correspond in
this way to the size—a body of lesser size being often the heavier,
as bronze is heavier than wool—there are some of them who
explain the cause of the discrepancy as follows. When emptiness
gets imprisoned in bodies, they explain, it makes them light,
and may make a larger body lighter than a smaller. The reason
is that there is more emptiness within. (*De Caelo* 309a 1)

T 10.   All the thinkers under discussion assume certain pairs
of contradictories. . . . Thus Democritus speaks of the full and
the void [solidity and vacancy], the one as being, the other as
not-being. Furthermore, in speaking of position, shape, and arrangement he implies that they subsume certain pairs of contraries: position involves above and below, ahead and behind;
shape involves angular, straight, and curved. (*Physica* 188a
18)

T 11.   Democritus points out the impossibility of all things
having come-to-be, inasmuch as time could not have come-to-be.
(*ibid.* 251b 15)

T 12.   For this reason [the unreliability and inconsistency of
sense-impressions] Democritus declares that either there is no
truth or at any rate to us it is not evident. Such thinkers as he
suppose that knowledge is sensation and that sensation is physical alteration; thus they conclude that whatever appears to the
senses must be true. (*Metaphysica* 1009b 11)

T 13.   Democritus declares that the soul is a sort of fire or
heat. For the atomic shapes are unlimited, and those which are
spherical he says make up fire and soul. They are like the so-
called motes in the air which show themselves as sunbeams
entering our windows. Such seeds taken all together, he says, are

the constituent elements of the whole of nature. So far he agrees with Leucippus. He adds that those of them which are spherical compose the soul, because such shapes can penetrate all things, and because being in motion they set things in motion.

The atomists suppose it is the soul that imparts motion to animals, for which reason they regard life as depending on respiration. When the surrounding air presses upon animal bodies and tends to squeeze out those atomic shapes which, being never at rest themselves, impart motion to the animal, they are reinforced by other atoms from outside to produce the respiratory process. The respiration prevents the escape of atoms that are already in the animals; and, they explain, just so long as it has the strength to do so life continues. (*De Anima* 404a 1)

T 14. In animals that breathe, according to Democritus, their respiration has the result of preventing the soul from being squeezed out from the body. He does not say, however, that nature contrived the arrangement to this end; he totally fails to reach any such explanation. What he says is, that the soul and the hot are identical, in that they are the primary forms among spherical particles. When these are crushed together by their surroundings and are about to get forced out, it is respiration, according to his theory, that comes to their aid. For in the air there are many such [spherical and extremely tiny] particles which he identifies with mind and soul. When we breathe and air enters, these enter along with it, and by withstanding the pressure they prevent the soul in the animal from being forced out.

Democritus thus explains why life and death are bound up with respiration. Death occurs when the surrounding air [in the lungs] presses upon the soul to such a degree that the animal can no longer respire, which is to say, that the air from outside the body can no longer enter and counteract the compression. Death is the departure of [mental] forms because of pressures from the air that surrounds them. It occurs not at haphazard, but by reason either of old age, which is natural, or of violence, which is unnatural. But Democritus does not offer any clear explanation of why this process goes on and why all must die. (*De Respiratione* 471b 30)

T 15.   Democritus completely identified soul and mind, holding that whatever appears to us in sense-perception is truth. (*De Anima* 404a 28)

T 16.   Some have identified soul with fire on the ground that fire is the element which is made up of the finest particles, being most nearly incorporeal, and also that it is preeminently the element which is in motion and sets things in motion. Democritus has expressed plausibly the reason for these characteristics. He regards soul and mind as the same thing, and this he holds to consist of those primary indivisible bodies which because of their fineness and smooth shape are the cause of motion. Since the shape which is most susceptible of motion is the spherical, it is of this shape that the atoms of mind and of fire consist.   (*ibid*. 405a 5)

T 17.   Some say that the soul moves the body in which it resides, by imparting its own motion to it. Democritus, for example, takes this view, and in such a way that he appears somewhat like Philippus the comic poet who tells of how Daedalus endowed a wooden statue of Aphrodite with motion simply by pouring quicksilver into it. Democritus' account shows a certain similarity to this. For by his theory the spherical atoms, which by their very nature never remain still, tend by their intrinsic movement to set in motion the entire body.

We might raise the critical question as to whether these atoms [which constitute the mind] can produce rest as well as motion. It is difficult or even impossible to see how this can be so. In general it is not in any such [mechanical] way that the soul appears to set an animal in motion, but with reference to some kind of purpose.   (*ibid*. 406b 15)

T 18. Democritus is mistaken in saying that if the intervening space were entirely empty and if there were an ant in the
remote sky we would be able to see it. (*ibid.* 419a 15)

T 19. Democritus is right in his theory that the eye is composed of water [rather than fire], but wrong when he proceeds
to explain the action of sight as simple mirroring. (*De Sensu*
438a 5)

T 20. Democritus, like most other natural philosophers who
deal with sense-perception, makes the mistake of regarding all
sense-objects as something touchable. (*ibid.* 442a 30)

T 21. They reduce things as directly perceived to the "common sensibles," as Democritus does in the case of black and
white, for instance: black, he says, is the rough, and white is
the smooth. Smells he identifies with atomic configuration.
(*ibid.* 442b 10)

T 22. Democritus of Abdera says that it is determined in
the womb whether the offspring is to be male or female. He
denies, however, the theory [of Empedocles] that heat and
cold are what make the difference; it depends, he thinks, upon
which of the two parents' generative fluid prevails—i.e., that
part of the fluid which has come from the distinctively male or
female parts [rather than the part which has come from the
body as a whole]. Of the two theories that of Democritus is
the better; for he is trying to discover and specify the exact way
in which the sexes become differentiated; but whether he is
right or not is another matter. (*De Generatione Animalium*
764a 6)

T 23. A writer such as Democritus is mistaken in maintaining that the external parts of an animal become distinct first
and the internal ones afterwards. Such a theory might better
apply to animals carved out of wood or stone; for in them

there is no first principle whatever; but in all living animals there is a first principle and it is inside them. (*ibid*. 740a 13)

T 24. The reason that an animal embryo stays so long in the maternal uterus is because it is rooted there by the blood-vessels, through which it gets its nourishment; not, as Democritus alleged, in order that its parts may become formed like the parts of the mother. (*ibid*. 740a 36)

T 25. The reason for the sterility of mules, according to Democritus, is that the parents have been of different species, and this condition destroys the genital passages in the offspring. However, there are cases of other species of animals which are born by the same kind of intermating and are still able to generate; whereas if Democritus' theory were true we should expect to find those other species sterile also. (*ibid*. 747a 30)

T 26. Monstrosities are produced, according to Democritus, when there is a double action upon the womb, an earlier and a later, and the second of them enters the uterus in such a way that new parts are superadded and the natural course of the embryo is changed. (*ibid*. 769b 31)

T 27. Democritus' theory of why the baby animal sheds its first teeth is that these teeth are developed prematurely in the infant by the action of sucking, but that later on, as the animal matures, it develops teeth according to nature. (*ibid*. 788b 12)

FROM LATER GREEK SOURCES:

T 28. Democritus was a native of Abdera, or, according to some accounts, of Miletus. As a boy he was taught theology and astronomy by deputies of King Xerxes [of Persia], who had been entertained by Democritus' father. Later he met Leucippus and also, it is said, Anaxagoras who was forty years his senior. He is reported, in Favorinus' *Miscellaneous History*, to have

said of Anaxagoras that his theories about the sun and moon
were not original but of great antiquity, and that he had simply lifted them. Democritus likewise disparaged Anaxagoras'
theories of the cosmos and of the mind. There was a lack of
sympathy between them amounting to hostility; so how could
there have been truth in the tale that he was Anaxagoras' pupil?

It is stated in two books—in Demetrius' *Men of the Same
Name* and in Antisthenes' *Succession of Philosophers*—that Democritus journeyed to Egypt in order to learn geometry from
the priests, and that he visited the Chaldaeans in Persia and
made a trip to the Red Sea. It is even said that he associated
with the gymnosophists in India and traveled to Ethiopia. Being
a third son and thus entitled to only a small share of the family
inheritance, he chose to take it in money [instead of property]
in order to pay his travel expenses. It is said that his elder brothers were crafty enough to foresee his choice and profit by it;
at any rate according to Demetrius' reckoning Democritus' share
was over one hundred talents, which he spent in its entirety.
He despised fame, and when he visited Athens he did not make
himself known to Socrates, although knowing well enough who
he was. [Here follows Fr. 33.]

Thrasylus declares: "He appears to have been an active admirer of the Pythagoreans, and in a book which he named after
them he gives high praise to Pythagoras himself. In fact he
draws so many ideas from Pythagoras that he might even have
appeared to be his pupil, except that it is chronologically impossible." Glaucus of Gherium, who was his contemporary, says
definitely that he was a pupil of one of the Pythagoreans, and
Apollodorus of Cyzicen says that he was on intimate terms with
Philolaus.

Antisthenes tells how he would undertake various expedients
to make trial of his sense-impressions, such as occasionally iso-
lating himself in tombs. The same author states that after spend-
ing all his money on travel Democritus was so poor that for a

while he had to accept support from his brother Damascus. However, he then developed a reputation by correctly predicting certain future events, with the result that the populace came to regard him as worthy of divine honors.

There was a law [in Abdera], according to Antisthenes, to the effect that no one who had squandered all his patrimony was to be buried within the city precincts. Knowing of the law, and fearing to be at the mercy of envious and unscrupulous executors, Democritus gave a public reading of *The Great Universe,* the best of all his books. As a result they raised a stipend of five hundred talents for him, and they gave him some valuable bronzes in addition. Furthermore when he died, at the age of over a hundred, he was given a funeral at public expense.

Aristoxenus, in his *Historical Notes,* tells that Plato wanted to burn all the writings of Democritus that he could collect; but that Amyclas and Clinias the Pythagoreans dissuaded him, pointing out that the books were already in such wide circulation that his attempt could not succeed.

According to Apollodorus in his *Chronology* Democritus was born in the eightieth Olympiad [460-457 B.C.], but according to Thrasylus in his short pamphlet entitled *Preliminary Exposition of the Works of Democritus* it was the third year of the seventy-seventh Olympiad [470 B.C.]—by which reckoning he would have been born a year earlier than Socrates. He mentions the monistic doctrine of Parmenides and Zeno in such a manner as to suggest that they were lively topics of current discussion while he was writing, and he alludes similarly to Protagoras, whose teachings are known to have been contemporaneous with those of Socrates.

Athenodorus, in the eighth book of his *Promenades,* describes a visit which Democritus paid to Hippocrates. On asking his host for some milk, which was promptly brought to him, he examined it and pronounced that it had come from the udder of a black goat which had lately given birth for the first time.

Hippocrates is said to have acknowledged, with wondering surprise, that the facts were correct. And there was a young maidservant of Hippocrates, whom Democritus on first arrival greeted with "Good morning, Maiden!" but on the next day with "Good morning, Madame!" As a matter of fact it turned out that the girl had been seduced during the night.

How Democritus conducted himself at the approach of death is described by Hermippus. He was extremely old, and just as the festival of Thesmophoria was about to begin his death appeared to be imminent. His sister was vexed, because it looked as if his dying would prevent her from attending the festival and devoting herself to the worship of the goddess. On learning of her concern he told her not to fret but to give orders that he be supplied with hot appliances every day. By holding these to his nostrils he contrived to outlive the three-day period. When it was over he stopped his treatment and allowed his life to flow out of him painlessly. Hipparchus asserts that he had lived to be a hundred and nine years old. (Diogenes Laertius IX. 34-43)

T 29.   [Partial catalogue of Democritus' writings, as quoted from Thrasylus by Diogenes Laertius:]

i.   Ethical treatises: *Pythagoras; Disposition of the Wise Man; Souls in Hades; Tritogenia*—so named because it deals with the three things on which reflective human life chiefly depends; *On Manly Excellence; The Horn of Plenty; On Tranquillity; Ethical Reflections*. And there is said to have been a work entitled *Well-Being*, of which no trace is to be found.

ii.   Physical works: *The Great Cosmos* (attributed by the school of Theophrastus to Leucippus); *The Lesser [Treatise on the] Cosmos; Descriptive Cosmology; On the Planets; On Nature*, Book I, followed by Book II entitled *On the Nature of Man, or, On Flesh; On Reason* and *On the Senses*, combined in later editions into a single treatise entitled *On the Soul; On*

Flavors; On Colors; On Differences of Rhythmic Surface; On Changes of Rhythmic Surface; summaries of the foregoing works; *On Images, or Prognostications; On the Criteria of Logic,* Books I, II, III; *Unsolved Problems.* (*ibid.,* 46-49)

T 30.   Democritus holds the following opinions. The first principles of the Whole are atoms and the void; anything else is merely mental supposition. The worlds are infinite in number; they come-to-be and perish. Nothing can come-to-be from not-being nor pass away into not-being. The atoms are infinite in number and in differences of size. As they are borne along in the universe they form vortices, and thereby they generate all composite things, which include fire, water, air, and earth; for these are conglomerations of certain atoms. Because of their absolute solidity the atoms are impassive and unchangeable. The sun and moon are composed of especially smooth and spherical atoms, and this is true also of the soul and, what he takes to be identical with it, the mind. Sight is produced by the impact of images upon the eyes. Everything happens by necessity; and this necessity, particularly the causes of why things come-to-be, he ascribes to vortex [i.e., to vortices of whirling atoms].

The end of human action he declares to be tranquillity; which is not merely pleasure, as some have wrongly taken it to mean, but consists in an enduring calm and strength of the soul, free from fear, superstition, or other emotion. He also calls it well-being, and uses certain other names as well. Qualities exist only by convention, he maintains; in nature [i.e., in reality] there are only atoms and the void. (*ibid.* IX. 44-45)

T 31.   Plato and Democritus both maintain that only intelligibles are true—Democritus on the ground that nothing sense-perceptible has any natural existence, inasmuch as the atoms of which everything is composed have a nature which is completely devoid of any sense-perceptible quality. (Sextus Empiricus *Against the Logicians* II. 6)

T 32.   There are two characteristics [of atoms], according to Democritus, namely size and shape. These primary bodies, which are absolutely solid, have no weight, but they move about in infinite space according as they collide with one another. (Aëtius)

T 33.   The only kind of motion, according to Democritus, consists in vibration.   (*ibid.*)

T 34.   Differences of heaviness and lightness are explained by Democritus as ultimately differences of size. For if we could get down to atomic units, we would see that [since every atom is absolutely solid] the only standard of an atom's weight must be its size. In the case of compounds, on the contrary, two bodies of the same size might be of different weights; for the body containing more emptiness would be lighter, while that containing less would be heavier.

He speaks in similar terms of hard and soft. According to his theory a thing is hard when its parts are compact, soft when they are loose, and differences of degree are explained proportionately. The reason why differences of hard and soft are not always commensurate with differences of heavy and light is that they are not produced by the same positions and groupings of empty spaces. Thus although iron is harder than lead, lead is heavier than iron. That is because the iron is of uneven composition, and its empty spaces are more numerous and bigger although the particles are more condensed in some places than in others. But its average of empty spaces exceeds that of lead.

As for other sensory qualities he argues that none has objective reality, but that all of them are effects of our sensuous faculty as it undergoes alteration; it is bodily alteration that produces images. Nor does he regard hot and cold as having an objective nature; they are merely a matter of configuration [of the groupings of atoms]. What we experience as qualitative change within ourselves is the effect of incoming atomic configurations being massed together so as to produce intensity of effect. What is massed together [on entering our sense organs] prevails [as a conscious experience], while what is widely diffused is imperceptible.

His proof of the unreality of sensory qualities is based on the fact that they do not appear the same to all: what is sweet to some is bitter to others, while to yet others it is sour or pungent or astringent; and sense-qualities of other types may be characterized similarly.

Anything sour, he holds, is composed of atoms that are angular, tiny, thin, and twisted. By its sharpness it slips in and penetrates everywhere, by its angular roughness it draws the parts [of the tongue] together and binds them. As a result of the same properties it heats the body by producing emptiness within; for whatever has most empty spaces amongst its atoms is most heated. But sweet consists of atomic figures that are rounded and not too hard; it softens the body by its gentle action. (Theophrastus *De Sensu* I. 61)

T 36.   Vision is explained by Democritus in terms of optical reflection, of which he gives an unusual account. As a result of the effluences which, of one sort or another, arise from everything, the air is compressed between the object and the eye, and thus receives an imprint. This imprinted air, because it is now more solid and is of a color-hue which contrasts with that of the eye, is reflected in the moisture that exists within both eyes. . . .

Democritus, describing how the visual impression is received, says that it is as if one were to imprint a shape upon wax. (*ibid*. I. 50)

FROM LATIN SOURCES:

T 37.   Perhaps you cannot accept that view which is set down as the opinion of the revered Democritus—that the first-beginnings of body and those of mind are placed beside each other alternately, thereby holding the living organism together. (Lucretius III. 370)

T 38.   Then Cotta took up the argument, . . . "For my own part I believe that even that very eminent man Democritus, the fountain-head from which Epicurus derived the streams that watered his little garden, has no fixed opinion about the nature of the gods. At one moment he holds the view that the universe includes images endowed with divinity; at another he says that there exist in this same universe the elements from which the mind is compounded, and that these are gods; at another, that they are animate images, which were wont to exercise a beneficent or harmful influence over us; and again that they are certain vast images of such a size as to envelop and enfold the entire world."   (Cicero *De Natura Deorum* I. 43)

7

Pythagoreanism

WHILE THE PYTHAGOREAN SCHOOL OF PHILOSOPHY had a long and permeating but varied influence in the ancient world, its founder himself, from whom its name was taken, is a virtually legendary figure. A few facts about him can be accepted as historically probable, however. He was born on the island of Samos about 580 B.C. Like many another ancient philosopher he journeyed in his youth to Egypt, where for an indefinite number of years he pursued studies in astronomy, geometry, and theology under the tutelage of Egyptian priests. After further extensive travels, which some ancient commentators say took him as far east as India (a claim which lacks adequate support, however) he returned to his native insular province only to find it in the grip of a dictatorship. So now, as a man of mature years, he migrated to Crotona in southern Italy, probably accompanied by younger men who had become his disciples.

The city of Crotona, which had been founded as early as the eighth century B.C. by Greek colonists, possessed a good natural harbor, which made it a center of sea trade and thereby economically prosperous. Moreover it was said to possess the best school of medicine in any of the Greek colonies of the west. In this attractive location Pythagoras established a school of his own, distinguished by its pursuit of higher studies in mathematics, astronomy, music, metaphysics, and polydaemonistic theology; by a disciplined community life, which included both a daily regimen of activities and studies and the practice of non-possession by sharing unreservedly all the necessities of living; and by carefully guarded conditions of membership which nevertheless allowed (for the first time in history, so far as is known) the admission of women as members. Unfortunately the inhabitants of Crotona regarded the school as an intruder and its head as a dangerous wizard who was rumored to have a golden thigh and to possess various queer magical powers. Hostilities mounted, and at length when Pythagoras had become a very old man there was a mob uprising, which made a vicious attack upon the school, burned the buildings, and murdered or exiled the members.

The nature of daily living in the school, both its moral and its intellectual disciplines, can perhaps best be understood as an intellectualized development from earlier mystery cults such as the Eleusinian. The main Eleusinian practices involved two steps—purification and revelation, the ritualistic sea-bathing by boys undergoing initiation and the dramatic exhibition in a dark room of the sacred grain stalk in a flash of light. Granted that the ritual and the mystery had a symbolic character for the ancient Eleusinian worshipers, Pythagoras in taking over the basic pattern minimized the ritual and stressed the symbolic character of the religious formulations. Ritual gave way to purposively guided action. The practice of silence each morning, between rising from bed and the ascetically sparse community breakfast, was a means on the one hand of reawakening one's inner affinity with the divine, and on the other hand of exercising and strengthening one's power of memory by daily practice in recalling the ordered events of the preceding day, then of the day before that, and so on. Community meals, readings aloud, and the practice of sharing were at once a zestful part of daily living and a symbolic reaffirmation of the participative nature of life—the human soul's participation in the divine reality that envelops us and thereby in the aims and needs of fellow members of the Pythagorean brotherhood. Within this harmonious social framework the higher studies—philosophical, mathematical, musical—were pursued, with the hope (and perhaps the occasional realization) of the ultimate Pythagorean aim —to hear in its full glory, and with an intuitive grasp of its hidden meaning, the Music of the Spheres.

MUSIC AND MATHEMATICS

The legend is that once while passing a blacksmith's shop Pythagoras was struck by the diversity of tones coming from within as the hammers hit the anvils. Investigating he discovered that a heavier hammer produced a lower pitch while a lighter hammer produced a higher. Since weight, as he already knew, could be measured on a balance, where smaller weights could be taken as units by which to measure a larger weight, he thus found in the smithy clear evidence of a working identity between musical intervals as heard and numerical relations as identified visually.

Furthermore it had been discovered empirically, by practicing musicians, that changes in pitch could be produced by pressing down a vibrating string or by blowing through different lengths of otherwise identical pipe. It remained for Pythagoras to discover that if one string is twice the length of a second of the same character, the result in acoustical terms is that unique harmony of sounds, the octave. Again, if the first string is made one and a half times as long as the second (that is, when the ratio of lengths is 3:2) the result is another harmonious interval, the fifth, or the *do-sol* relation. And a ratio of 4:3 in the lengths produces the *do-fa,* or the *sol-do* relation. Allowing for some looseness of early syntax we can understand the triumphant generalization at which Pythagoras arrived when he proclaimed the identity of music with number.

But Pythagoras did not stop there. To extend one's generalizations is tempting, and the musical generalization became broadened into a metaphysical one, which virtually came to serve as the badge of the school: that *All is number*. Research into the nature of number and its associated ideas was made the central theoretical discipline, with the result that the word *mathêmatika* (a neuter plural connected with *mathêma,* "learning," and so originally signifying "things taught and learnt") gradually became attached to the more restricted meaning which the word "mathematics" has carried subsequently.

As conceived and practiced in the Pythagorean school mathematics had a more qualitative character than has been involved in conceptions of that science since the seventeenth century. In the first place it was predominantly geometrical. A square number meant the area of a square erected on a given line, and a cube number meant the volume of a cube erected on a square; the notion of a fourth and of higher powers was therefore not entertained. Pythagoras discovered the determination of increasing dimensionality by an increasing number of points—that two points determine a straight line, that three points not on the same line determine a plane surface, and that four points not on the same surface determine a three-dimensional figure. Even when lines, areas, and columns were not in question, numbers were still conceived spatially by means of dots; which gave rise to the peculiar Pythagorean conception of masculine numbers, feminine numbers, and triangular numbers. The first two can be understood by imagining dots arranged in perpendicular rows and columns, regularly spaced, starting at a lower left corner and extending indefinitely upward and to the right. An important instrument called the *gnomon,* an L-shaped ruler, would be placed so as to cut off one dot at the extreme lower left. Let the gnomon then be moved step by step so as to cut off one more row and one more column at each step. On the first move 3 dots will be added to the original one, then 5 more, then 7, 9, 11, and so on. In the process the gnomon will move in a straight diagonal line, as it cuts off successively larger squares. The uniformity of direction and the square perfection of the successive results were regarded as masculine characteristics; accordingly the odd numbers, since they operate in the process of geometrical creation and growth of regular squares, are called "masculine numbers." If now we start with two dots instead of one, and move the gnomon as before, there will be added successively 4 dots, then 6 more, than 8, 10, 12, etc. The resultant figures are oblong (imperfect approximations to the square), and the gnomon as it moves must change its direction, in an ever diminishing curve. Even numbers, therefore, since they produce this imperfect and varying result, are called "feminine numbers."

Masculine progression   *Feminine progression*

There are also "triangular numbers" to be considered, the nature of which becomes evident from imagining the growing triangular shape that results when, starting with a single dot, two dots are placed under it, then three dots under that, then four, and so on.

The Tetractys

The triangle with a four-unit base was called the Tetractys, and was held in high reverence; as shown by the fact that Pythagorean initiates were required to swear their allegiance, including their promise not to reveal the secret mysteries of the Order, by the Oath of the Tetractys, which ran: "I swear by Him who reveals Himself to our minds in the Tetractys, which contains the source and roots of everlasting nature." Among the reasons for so high

a regard were these: that the number 4 represents justice, which
is the most fundamental of human virtues and, some would add,
is essential to the governance of the universe; that the numbers
which the Tetractys contains determine respectively the point, the
line, the plane, and the tetrahedron; that each pair of adjacent
lines exhibits the ratio of one of the three main musical harmonies
(1:2, 2:3, 3:4); that the units of the Tetractys add up to ten,
the Decad, itself a sacred number on independent grounds; and
that the Tetractys creates both masculine and feminine numbers—
masculine when two adjacent lines are added together, feminine
when one line is skipped in making a sum. Fanciful ingenuities of
this kind made up a large part of Pythagorean number theory.
Their interest for us lies largely in the evidence they give as to
the central importance of the concept of number for the Pythagoreans; which helps to explain the intellectual bewilderment into
which they were thrown by the discovery of incommensurables.

THE MYSTERY OF INCOMMENSURABLES

When the Pythagoreans spoke of number they were thinking of
whole numbers and the ratios between them; fractions were conceived, properly enough, as ratios between whole numbers. A special ratio of whole numbers which Pythagoras had learned during
his youthful pilgrimage to Egypt, was the 3:4:5 ratio as exempli-
fied by the two sides and hypoteneuse of a right-angled triangle.
Later, as ancient tradition affirms, Pythagoras discovered how to
demonstrate the general theorem (subsequently known as the Pythagorean Theorem) that in *any* right-angled triangle the squares
erected on the two sides will have a combined area equal to that
of the square erected on the hypoteneuse; or (what is exactly the
same theorem) that the square erected on the diagonal of a square
has twice the area of that original square. Obviously the Egyptian
3:4:5 triangle offers a particular case of the general relational
law. But another special case mainly drew the attention of the

Pythagorean number analysts, who like all Greeks found high virtue in symmetry—the case of the isosceles right-angled triangle, in which the two sides are of equal length. Here by the general theorem it is readily seen that the ratio of the larger square on the hypoteneuse to the smaller square on either of the sides must be 2:1. But immediately the question arose for them: What is the ratio between the *length* of the hypoteneuse and the length of a side? The fact that nowadays we can reply glibly by means of the symbol $\sqrt{2}$ fails to meet their problem; for the meaning of that symbol has been worked out subsequently during centuries of mathematical study, and it was the early Pythagoreans who inaugurated that study by posing the problem. Their question was whether any two whole numbers could be found that would give the exact ratio between the length of the hypoteneuse (h) and the length of a side (s). If one approaches the matter empirically, without preconception, it might appear at first sight that h is about one and a half times s, but measurement will prove the estimate to be too high. The ratio 4:3 might next be tried, but here the estimate proves to be too low. As higher numbers and more refined ratios are tried, an experimenter eventually passes beyond the possibilities of verification by measurement; and for the early Greek experimenter, with his crude types of measuring instrument, that point must have been reached quite soon. Probably, then, in the early years following the discovery of the Pythagorean Theorem there was genuine questioning as to whether any numerical ratio between h and s could be found.

Then someone, whether Pythagoras or a disciple, discovered the deductive proof, later formulated by Euclid, that no such numerical ratio is possible. The result was consternation. It had been a basic tenet of the school that All is Number, and here for the first time was a demonstration that certain ratios between lines were incommensurate—could not be measured by reference to a common numerical unit. What was to be done? The Pythagoreans in their bewilderment decided to treat the information as a top secret, to be revealed only to trusted members of the school who had taken the vow of silence; and when one of them, Hippasus, exposed the secret to outsiders, he was solemnly excommunicated from the Pythagorean fellowship, and a legend says that the gods then took a hand by causing him to perish at sea in a shipwreck.

COSMOLOGY AND ASTRONOMY

Pythagorean musical and mathematical conceptions found their highest expression in the cosmological doctrine of the Music of the Spheres. When Pythagoras declared that there is a universal harmony, a grand musical pattern, in the movements of the universe, he was expressing, in his own style of concrete imagining, a conviction that rational law governs the universe. For to the Pythagorean mind, it must be remembered, music was identical with number, and number in turn was conceived geometrically. Consequently what the Music of the Spheres primarily affirmed was the presence of a geometrical order among the motions of sun, moon, planets, and fixed stars. Since the circle, in its perfection and simplicity, made the strongest appeal to the unsophisticated mathematical sensibilities of the Greeks, the meaning of astronomical law became naturally affixed to it. There was no serious trouble in conceiving the observed movements of sun, moon, and fixed stars as basically circular, although the deviations between summer and winter required some explanation; but the apparent irregularities of the five known planets (Mercury, Venus, Mars, Jupiter, and Saturn) created a serious difficulty. At any rate, that some kind of geometric pattern must exhibit itself in all those movements was an article of faith for the Pythagoreans, maintained with religious conviction—partly suggested by experience, from observing the half-circle movements of sun, moon, and constellations, but in any case demanded as a guiding concept for the rational interpretation of whatever astronomical phenomena might be observed. To Pythagoras it appears that such astronomical order was conceived both geometrically and musically— that is, by means of visual and auditory imagination combined— for it is recorded of him that on a few memorable occasions in his life he entered into the transcendent experience of actually "hearing" that celestial music.

The general number theory gave rise also to a more particular astronomical result. Adding the orbits of the five known planets to those of the sun and moon and that of the fixed stars gave a total of eight orbits, each of which must be conceived of as basically circular or as somehow explanable in terms of a combination of circles. Eight, however, was not a good Pythagorean number; the next good number above it was ten, the Decad. Two more revolving bodies had therefore to be found or postulated; the need was met by conceiving of the earth itself as a planet, revolving about the same center as that about which the sun and other planets revolved, and by postulating that behind the earth (on the side opposite to that on which the Greeks and all known peoples resided) there was a tenth revolving body which they called the counter-earth. A cosmic center had to be assumed which all ten orbits encircled, and this ultimate center was conceived as the Central Fire. Of course inhabitants of the known earth (i.e., Europe, near-Asia, and north Africa) were unable to see either the counter-earth or the central fire; and this inability was explained by supposing that the earth, while revolving around the central fire, kept its inhabited face turned away from the fire and the counter-earth, with the result that they were perpetually invisible to earth people. If the hypothesis seems a curious one to contemporary habits of thought, let it be considered that the Greeks, lacking telescopes, possessed no example of a body rotating on its own axis, whereas experience did show them one example of a revolving body keeping one face toward, and hence one face away from, the center of its orbit—namely the moon.

THE SOUL AND ITS DESTINY

To a degree and in a manner which it is difficult for a modern thinker to realize, trained as he is in the ways of specialism, the Pythagoreans regarded mathematical and astronomical studies as inseparable from moral and religious disciplines and from personal self-examination. Behind the practices of self-discipline and self-examination which were part of the daily life there lay a profound set of convictions about the nature and destiny of the soul.

First, the soul is immortal: it existed before what we call birth and will go on existing after what we call death. The present life is a sojourn, a temporary stage in a long pilgrimage; and the body (*sôma*) was likened to a tomb (*sêma*) in which they held that the soul has to live out a sort of shadow-life, a half-life, which is more nearly death than it is life. Starting from these premises a man's primary purpose will be, not a pursuit of the so-called goods which the present life offers, but a preparation, through self-discipline and self-harmonization, for the larger life into which he may be destined to enter hereafter.

However, the larger and hoped for life is not attained immediately and automatically after our departure from this life. Each soul is weighted down to a greater or lesser degree by its impurities and disharmonies, so that consequently it must (according to the ancient Orphic doctrine which Pythagoreanism took over) first go through an ordeal of purification and then be reborn into some other human or animal shape, in which it is given a new opportunity to meet the challenges of bodily circumstance and through them to purify itself for its ultimate destiny. This is the doctrine known as metempsychosis, transmigration, or reincarnation.

From the belief that we have lived before, and in better circumstances than now, an educational corollary follows. Learning in the present life is really recollection. The fundamental truths are already known to us, in the depths of our unconscious selves, and the purpose of education should therefore be to stir these hidden parts of us into activity, rather than to impose truths upon them from outside sources. As the mind becomes meditative and withstands the corruptive influences of its everyday environment it becomes better able to behold and recognize the truths which, although they appear to be given by experience, are really already within each individual, awaiting the right stimulus and challenge to dislodge them.

Finally, it appears that the soul, both in the present life and hereafter, was regarded not so much substantively as functionally —not as a thing of gaseous materiality residing in the head or the heart, but as a harmony. The degree to which the harmonious music of the soul is realized determines the direction of its destiny and what other bodily sojourns it must undergo before it has purified itself of all unharmonious elements in order that it may become one with the great cosmic harmony which is the ultimate destiny of all existence.

The present chapter, unlike its predecessors, begins not with fragmentary quotations of the philosophers in question, but with a set of testimonia; for there are no extant fragments of Pythagorean philosophy earlier than those attributed to Philolaus (Sec. iv), who was roughly contemporary with Socrates. The *Symbola* (Sec. ii) and the *Golden Verses* (Sec. iii) represent important elements of Pythagorean moral and religious teaching; but coverage of the metaphysical doctrine is furnished only by the Testimonia (Sec. i). Probably the ratio of what can be known in relation to the whole body of teaching is smaller in the case of Pythagoreanism than in any of the doctrines that precede.

i. Aspects of the Doctrine

TESTIMONIA

FROM PLATO:

T 1. *Socrates:* As I conceive the matter, our eyes are designed to look up at the stars, while our ears are designed to hear the harmony of their movements; and these are kindred modes of investigation, according to the Pythagorean teachings. (*Republic* 530D)

T 2. *Simmias:* As you probably already know, Socrates, most of us [Pythagoreans] believe somewhat as follows about the soul. We say that the body is held together by the tensive relation that exists between the hot and the cold, the dry and the moist, and other such [pairs of opposites]; while the soul is a blending and attunement of those same elements when they are mixed in right proportion. Well now, if it is true that the soul is a harmony, then when the body gets unduly relaxed or tightened by illness or some other cause, it follows from our assumption that the soul, even if we grant it to be divine, must then necessarily perish, as happens in other cases of attunement, whether musical or involving some other activity of craftsmanship. The body, however, will continue to exist for quite a long while, until it either rots or is cremated. What reply, then, can you make to this argument that the soul, if it is a blending of bodily elements, will be the first thing to perish when what we call death occurs? (*Phaedo* 86B)

T 3. *Socrates:* Perhaps Euripides was right when he remarked, "Who knows if life be death and death be life?" I have heard a [Pythagorean] philosopher say that in our present state we are really dead, that our body (*sôma*) is our tomb (*sêma*), and that the part of the soul in which the desires have their abode is of such a nature as to be blown to and fro—metaphorically in this life but actually after death. Some clever fellow, probably from either Sicily or Italy, making a play with words, called the soul a jar, because it can easily be jarred by persuasive words into believing this or that. The people who let themselves be persuaded without thinking are called "the uninitiated," and he of whom I speak described the uncontrolled and unretentive part of their souls by comparing them to a jar full of holes, on the ground that they can never be filled and satisfied. Moreover in Hades, he said referring to the unseen after-world, the uninitiated will be dreadfully unhappy, for they will be constantly occupied pouring water from a leaky pitcher into a leaky sieve. He compared the souls of such persons to a sieve because of its leaky nature, whereby it is unable to retain anything because of its lack of purpose and its forgetfulness. (*Gorgias* 492e)

T 4.   *Cebes:* But tell me, Socrates, why is suicide held to be unlawful? Philolaus, about whom you were just asking, has affirmed this doctrine in my hearing, and so have other [Pythagoreans]; but I have not quite understood the reason for it.

Socrates: You are troubled, I suppose, by the paradox that although a [good] man is better off after dying, he is not permitted to seize that benefit by an act of his own, but must await the hand of another? . . . Let me tell you of a doctrine which [the Pythagoreans] teach in religious secrecy, to the effect that man has been stationed here in a kind of prison, from which he has no right to release himself and run away. There is something profound in the doctrine which goes beyond my understanding; but at any rate I believe with them that the gods are our guardians, and that we mortals are justly in their possession. (*Phaedo* 61e)

FROM ARISTOTLE:

T 5.   At the same time as the philosophers of whom I have been speaking [the qualitative pluralists and the atomists] or even earlier, the so-called Pythagoreans, who were earnest students of mathematics, were first developing it as a science; and by reason of this special interest they came to think of its first-principles as the first-principles of everything whatever. Accordingly, since by the very nature of mathematics it is numbers that stand first among the basic principles, it seemed to the Pythagoreans that they could discover in numbers, more truly than in fire or earth or water, many analogues by which to explain both existences and occurrences. For instance, they explained justice as a certain property of number [four, the square], soul and mind as another such [one, unity, the point], the "decisive moment" (*kairos*) as another [seven]; and they gave the same kind of interpretation to virtually everything else as well. Furthermore they observed empirically that the properties and ratios of harmonious musical tones depend upon numbers. Since they found, in short, that everything else, too, in its intrinsic nature, seemed to be essentially numerical, and thus that numbers appeared to be the ultimate meaning of everything that exists, they concluded that the elements of numbers must be the elements of everything, and that the visible heavens in their entirety consist of harmony and number.

Accordingly they collected and employed all the analogies they could find which would represent the relation of numbers and harmonies to the properties or parts of the visible heavens and even to the entire universe; and if they came up against any gaps in such analogies they would snatch at whatever additional notion they could find to bring an orderly connection into their total explanation. For example, since the decad [the number ten, considered archetypally] is believed to be perfect, and to embrace the essential nature of the whole system of numbers, they conclude that the number of things existing in the sky must therefore be ten; but since in actuality there are only nine that are visible, they postulate the existence of a counter-earth as the tenth. The matter is one which we have dealt with in greater detail elsewhere. (*Metaphysica* 985b 22)

T 6. The elements of number, according to their theory, are the even and the odd, the former being unlimited, the latter limited. Unity consists of both, partaking of the nature of both even and odd. Number derives from unity; and numbers, as we have said, constitute for them the entire visible universe.

Other members of the Pythagorean school regard the first-principles as consisting of ten pairs of opposites, which they set forth in contrasting columns: limit vs. the unlimited, odd vs. even, unity vs. plurality, right vs. left, male vs. female, rest vs. motion, straight vs. curved, light vs. dark, good vs. evil, square vs. oblong.

Alcmaeon of Crotona seems to have developed his theory along the same lines: either he took the theory from them or they from him, for his expressions are quite similar to theirs. Like them he says that most things in human experience are found in contrasting pairs; unlike them, however, he does not give a definite list of such pairs, but contents himself with mentioning any examples that happen to occur to him, such as white vs. black, sweet vs. bitter, good vs. evil, and large vs. small. Concerning other significant contrasts he offers only indefinite suggestions, whereas the Pythagoreans specify both how many and of what nature they are. From both sources, then, we receive the teaching that pairs of opposites are the first-principles of things, but it is only from the Pythagoreans that the number and nature of them are specified. (*ibid.* 986a 18)

T 7.   The Pythagoreans, having observed that the things presented to us in sense-perception have many attributes of number, leapt to the theory that existing things are numbers— not just in the sense that they entail numbers as something distinguishable from themselves, but in that they actually consist of numbers. And why so? On the ground that the properties of number are inherent in musical harmony, in the movements of the visible heavens, and in many other things besides.   (*ibid*. 1090a 20)

T 8.   The Pythagoreans, while maintaining the doctrine of duality [manifested in the table of opposites] as a basic principle, added this further notion, which is peculiar to themselves, that the limited and the unlimited are not entities of a different order, but that the unlimited and unity-as-such are the subject (*ousia*) of whatever is predicated. Which is why they consider number to be the substance (*ousia*) of all things.   (*ibid*. 987a 13)

T 9.   The Pythagoreans believe in a single kind of number, the "mathematical"—conceiving such numbers not as something abstracted [from the world of sense-experience] but as actual constituents of perceptible things. They even construct the entire visible universe out of numbers—not numbers in the abstract, but spatially extended units of magnitude.   (*ibid*. 1080b 16)

T 10.   The Pythagoreans held that being and unity are nothing else than the very nature (*physis*) of the thing itself—as though the "specific character" (*ousia*) of anything could be the same thing as unity and existence!   (*ibid*. 1001a 9)

T 11.   All reputable philosophers who have dealt with this type of physical question have discussed the problem of the Unlimited, which in one way or another they treat as a first-principle. The Pythagoreans, followed by Plato and certain others, do so in the sense that they conceive the Unlimited as a self-subsistent entity (*ousia*), rather than as a derivative attribute. The Pythagoreans are peculiar in regarding the Unlimited as existing in perceptible things; and they add that what lies beyond the "heavenly vault" (*ouranos*) is the Unlimited.

Moreover, the Pythagoreans identify the Unlimited [in the sense of the indeterminate] with the Even. For the even series, when it is cut off [by successive positions of the *gnomon*], produces something unlimited. When we begin with the One and make successive additions of odd numbers [by moving the *gnomon*], the resultant series of shapes preserves a single form; but when we begin with an even number and make such successive additions of even numbers around it, the resultant shapes do not preserve any form (*eidos*)—which is to say, they are [indeterminate, or] unlimited. (*Physica* 203a 2)

T 12.   The Pythagoreans affirm the existence of a void, explaining that it comes into the "visible universe" (*ouranos*) out of limitless breath. It is the void that distinguishes natural objects from one another, by making a separation and division among things that are neighbors. This is true especially with regard to numbers, for it is the void that gives numbers their specific nature. (*ibid.* 213b 24)

T 13.   A magnitude that is divisible in one dimension only is a line, divisible in two dimensions a plane, in three a body. There are no further possibilities, for three dimensions are all that exist, and to divide in three dimensions is all that can be done. For as the Pythagoreans say, the All and everything in it are determined by the number three, since beginning, middle, and end constitute the basic triad that is the number of the All. (*De Caelo* 268a 9)

T 14.   In Plato's theory of participation the only original contribution is the change of name; for where the Pythagoreans say that things exist by imitation (*mimêsis*) of numbers, Plato prefers to say they exist by participation (*methexis*) in them. (*Metaphysica* 987b 10)

T 15.   Those in Italy who are called Pythagoreans say that at the center there is fire, the earth being in effect one of the planets, which moves in a circle about the center and thus produces night and day. They hold the theory that there is another earth, behind and facing this one, which they call the counter-earth.

Moreover the Pythagoreans think it altogether fitting that the most lordly position in the universe, its center, should be well guarded. Hence they call the fire at the center the "watch-tower of Zeus"; by which name they mean to indicate that it is not only the center of space but also the center of matter and of life.   (*De Caelo* 293a 7, b 2)

T 16.   Moving in orbit about the center there is first the counter-earth, then the earth, and after the earth the moon. (From his lost work *On the Pythagoreans*)

T 17.   They say that the soul is a sort of attunement (*harmonia*); for attunement is a synthesis and blending of opposites, and the body is composed of opposites.   (*De Anima* 407b 28)

T 18.   Pythagoras paired the virtues with numbers, but he did not clarify what he meant by that.   (*Magna Moralia* 1182a 11)

T 19.   To some, like the Pythagoreans, reciprocity is taken as equivalent to absolute justice; for they define the just as what is mutually reciprocal.   (*Ethica Nicomachea* 1132b 21)

T 20.   Evil belongs to the unlimited, the Pythagoreans think, and good to the limited.   (*ibid*. 1106b 29)

T 21.   The Pythagoreans put the One in the column of goods. (*ibid*. 1096b 5)

FROM LATER GREEK SOURCES:

T 22.   Italian philosophy was begun by Pythagoras, a native of Samos, and son of Mnesarchus an engraver of gems. From

Samos he journeyed to the island of Lesbos, to become a student of Pherecydes, after whose death he returned to Samos. In his youthful eagerness for knowledge, however, he left his native land, and participated in both Greek and foreign mystery cults, undergoing all the steps of initiation. He went to Egypt, taking with him three silver bowls as gifts for the priests, and there he learned the Egyptian language—so Antiphon tells in his book *On Men of Outstanding Merit*. He gained admittance to the Egyptian sanctuaries, where he was taught the secret doctrines of the gods. He traveled also to the Chaldaeans and the Magi, and while in Crete he made the descent into the Cave of Ida in the company of Epimenides.

On returning to Samos he found that the government had been usurped by Polycrates. Consequently he embarked for Crotona in Italy, where he established a community and constitutional government for the exiled Greeks, who held him in high regard. They were about three hundred in number, and they conducted their government so well that it was in truth an aristocracy in the best sense. (Diogenes Laertius VIII. 1-3)

T 23. [At Crotona], as his reputation grew, he won many followers—both men and women from the city itself as well as many foreign princes and chieftains from the surrounding countryside. One of the local women was Theano, who afterwards became celebrated. No one knows what Pythagoras said to his followers, for silence with them was no casual matter. (Porphyry, *Life of Pythagoras*)

T 24. Those who committed themselves to the guidance of his doctrines acted as follows. They performed their morning walks alone and in places where there was appropriate solitude and quiet; for they considered it contrary to wisdom to enter into conversation with another person until they had rendered their own souls calm and their minds harmonious. It is turbulent behavior, they believed, to mingle with a crowd immediately on arising from sleep. But after their solitary morning walk they would associate with one another to discuss the teachings and to exchange suggestions for improving the style of behavior. Then they would walk together, visiting temples and other worthy places.

Their next step was to care for the health of the body: some would anoint themselves for the race course, others would compete at wrestling in the gardens and groves or at high-jump with leaden weights in their hands, while others would practice the art of pantomime. Contrasting types of exercise were sought with a view to improving the strength and health of the body.

Luncheon was extremely simple, consisting of bread and honey; they did not drink wine during the daytime. In the afternoon there were further studies. As evening came on they again took walks—no longer singly as in the morning, but in groups of two or three; they would practice walking in graceful rhythm together, while they discussed the studies that had occupied them during the day.

After walking they bathed, and then assembled in a place where they ate supper in small groups, no group being of more than ten. Supper was regularly preceded by appropriate libations and sacrifices, and was brought to a close just before sunset. They drank wine, ate maize, bread and the various kinds of food that are eaten with bread, as well as herbs both raw and boiled. They ate the meat of such animals as were considered lawful.

After supper there were further libations, and then readings followed, the youngest reading what the eldest selected. When they were ready to disperse, a cupbearer poured out another libation for them, and the eldest would then discourse, on such questions as our duties to the divine and to the lower orders— to the daemons, to the heroes, and to parents and benefactors. They wore pure white night-garments and slept in pure white beds under light coverlets, avoiding those made of wool. By attending to the state of their bodies they remained always in the same condition, not at one time lean and at another overburdened with flesh.

By such disciplines the Pythagoreans sought to arrange their lives entirely for the purpose of following God. They held that all things are possible with the gods, and that one ought to seek benefits only from the divine Lord of all. But since it is not easy for man to know what are the things in which God takes joy, they studied the art of divination, which is the art of interpreting the benevolence of God as manifested in the world.

Music, medicine, and divination were the sciences most highly esteemed by the Pythagoreans. They practiced the habit of silence, and were alert to listen. In medicine they studied the values of symmetry, of labor, food, and repose. On right preparation of food and the proper manner of eating it they placed much importance. They avoided incisions and burnings when they could. Some illnesses they cured by incantations; they considered health to be greatly benefitted by music when rightly employed.

To strengthen their memory the students began each day, on first waking up, by recollecting in order the actions and events of the day before; after that they tried to do the same for the preceding day, and so on backwards as far as they could go, taking care to make the order of recollection correspond with the order in which the events had actually occurred. For they believed that there is nothing more important for science, and for experience and wisdom, than 'the ability to remember. (Iamblichus, *Life of Pythagoras*)

T 25.   The Pythagoreans used to marvel when they met with a city-bred man who had never seen a divine being. (Apuleius)

T 26.   Aristotle says that the people of Crotona used to speak of Pythagoras as the Hyperborean Apollo. He adds that on a certain occasion Pythagoras was seen by many people at both Metapontum and Crotona on the same day and at the same hour. And that during the games at Olympia he arose in the stadium and displayed one of his thighs, which was golden. (Aëlian)

T 27.   Pythagoras wrote nothing, as was also the case with Socrates. (Plutarch, *Lives*).   None of the Pythagoreans have noted down anything in all the generations up to the time of Philolaus; he was the first, and he published those three well-known books which Dion of Syracuse is said to have bought at Plato's request for a hundred minae.   (Iamblichus, *op. cit.* 199)

T 28.   Although certain persons have spread the silly rumor that Pythagoras left absolutely no writings, that view is opposed by Heraclitus the physical philosopher, who declares emphatically: "Pythagoras, son of Mnesarchus, pursued his researches farther than anyone else. In his compilation of writings he concocted a queer wisdom of his own, which showed much learning but poor constructive ability." The remark is elicited by what Pythagoras had reputedly written at the outset of his supposed treatise *On Nature,* namely: "Now by the air I breathe and by the water I drink, may I never suffer blame for this work!" The fact is, however, that while the book in question commonly passes for the work of Pythagoras, it was really written by a Pythagorean named Lysis of Tarentum, who left the group and went to Thebes. Pythagoras himself had written three books—*On Education, On Statecraft,* and also one entitled *On Nature*.   (Diogenes Laertius VIII. 6)

T 29.   In accordance with Pythagoras' maxims, "Friends share all things in common" and "Friendship is equality," his disciples gave all their possessions into one common fund. During the first five years of discipleship they were under obligation to keep silent, listening to Pythagoras' discourses without seeing him; but at the expiration of that time, on passing an examination, they were admitted to his house and to the sight of him. About six hundred auditors used to attend his lectures at night; and those who were privileged to see him would write to their friends congratulating themselves on their great good fortune.

The prohibition against killing animals and more especially against eating their flesh was based not only on the ground that animals share with men the privilege of having a soul. Such was the announced reason, but mainly why Pythagoras prohibited a meat diet was in order to strengthen his followers' power of will and accustom them to simplicity of life. Furthermore he wished them to restrict their diet to what was easily procurable, eating uncooked foods and drinking nothing but pure water; such, he believed, was the way to a healthy body and a keen mind. The only altar at which he worshipped was that of Apollo the Life-Giver, behind the Altar of Horns at Delos. What he placed on the altar as offerings, according to Aristotle in his *Constitution of Delos,* was uncooked cakes made of grain; he did not sacrifice animal victims.

Pythagoras had a wife named Theano, a daughter Damo, and a son Telauges who succeeded his father [as head of the school] and who, according to some accounts, became the teacher of Empedocles. Pythagoras died at the age of either eighty or ninety. The story of his dying at eighty fits in with his theory [of man's life as falling into four twenty-year periods]; but other accounts say that he lived to be ninety. It is told that he met his death in the following manner. While he was sitting with friends in his house at Milo a fire broke out. The blaze may have been started by resentful applicants who had been denied admission to the brotherhood, or maybe, as other reports have it, by citizens of Crotona seeking to preserve their government from Pythagorean domination. Pythagoras in escaping from the fire was pursued by assailants. On finding himself in front of a field of beans he stopped, declaring that he would let himself be captured rather than walk across it, and that he would let himself be killed rather than reveal the secret doctrines. Whereupon his pursuers caught and slew him, and in the same uprising they murdered about forty of his disciples, which represented more than half of the inner membership. (Diogenes Laertius, VIII, *passim*)

T 30.   The philosophy of which I shall now speak was first upheld by Pythagoras, sometimes called the Samian. His teachings are known as the Italian philosophy, because of the fact that in fleeing from the usurping government of Polycrates in Samos he settled in a city in Italy, where he spent the rest of his life. Astronomy, geometry, and music were combined in his scientific studies. After a careful study of the nature of number he declared that the universe produces musical sound and is put together by attunement; he was the first to show that the movement of the seven planets [including sun and moon] is characterized by melody and attunement.

He divided his disciples into two groups, which he distinguished as esoteric and exoteric. To those of the former group he entrusted the study of the more developed forms of science, to the latter the more moderate. He experimented with what is called magic, and it was he who first established the science of physiology.

What he principally taught about number was this. Number is the first-principle: it is unlimited and indefinable, and it contains within itself the infinite series of numbers. The decad, the perfect form of the sacred number ten, is present in the essence of each of the first four numbers, since they [when added] become ten. He declared that this sacred tetractys is the fountain which has its source in ever-flowing nature. In the tetractys all the numbers have their first-principle.   (Hippolytus *Refutatio*)

T 31.   In the first book of his work on the Pythagoreans Aristotle tells of their doctrine that while the universe is essentially one, it is permanently differentiated by time, breath, and the void, which are drawn from the Unlimited, and which distinguish the places where things are.   (Stobaeus)

T 32.   The Pythagoreans interpreted all antitheses in terms of their double column of opposites, the pairs of which stood for comparative goods contrasted with comparative evils. They confined the number of basic alternatives to ten, because the decad meant for them the whole essence of number. They regarded each of the ten contrasted pairs as revealing the shared nature of all of them.   (Simplicius *Commentaria*)

T 33.   In Alexander's *Successions of Philosophers* he has set down the following as Pythagorean beliefs which he found stated in some Pythagorean memoirs. The first-principle of all things is the Monad [unity]. From the monad there arises the indeterminate dyad [twoness in the abstract], which then serves as passive material to the monad, while the monad serves as active cause. From the monad and the indeterminate dyad there arise numbers; from numbers, points; from points, lines; from lines, plane figures; from plane figures, solid figures; from solid figures, perceivable bodies compounded of the four elements, fire, water, earth, air. These elements undergo full transformations into one another; they combine to produce a universe that is animate, intelligent, and spherical.   (Diogenes Laertius, *loc. cit.*)

T 34.   Aristotle in his work on the Pythagoreans says that for them the One partakes of the nature of both the odd and the even: for if you add it to an even number it produces an odd, and if you add it to an odd number it produces an even; which it would not be able to do unless it shared in both natures. For this reason they called it "the even-odd."   (Theo of Smyrna)

T 35. One is the point, two is the line, three is the triangle, four is the pyramid. All are primary and are first-principles of whatever particular things are of their kind. (Speusippus)

T 36. It is said that when Pythagoras visited Zaratas of Chaldaea he set forth his views as follows: that from the beginning there have been two causes of things, father and mother; that the father is composed of light, the mother of darkness; that light contains as its elements the warm, the dry, the buoyant, and the swift, while the elements of darkness are the cold, the moist, the heavy, and the slow; that these two groups represent male and female respectively, and that of them the universe is composed. (Hippolytus, *loc. cit.*)

T 37. Some of the Pythagoreans, as Aristotle writes in his book about them, explain the eclipses of the moon by the interposition of either the earth or the counter-earth. (Stobaeus)

T 38. He [Pythagoras] conceives the soul as comprising three parts—reason, intelligence, and passion. The two latter are possessed by other animals as well, but reason is in man alone. The bodily seat of the soul extends from the heart to the brain: the portion that is in the heart is passion, while the portions located in the brain are reason and intelligence. Sense-perceptions are drops distilled from these. Reason is immortal, all else is mortal. The soul draws nourishment from the blood. The rational powers of the soul are of the nature of breath; they and the soul itself are invisible, in the same way that the air is invisible. [In one's early life] the veins, arteries, and sinews are the determinants of the soul. But when the soul settles down into itself and becomes strong, then rational thoughts and the exercise of deliberate choice become its determinants.

When cast out upon the earth [after death] the soul wanders in the air, like a body. Hermes is the steward of souls; he is called the Escort, Keeper of the Gates, and the Hermes of the Underworld, because it is he who guides the souls by land and by sea to the uppermost region, whereas the impure are not allowed to come near to the pure nor even near to one another, but are bound by the Furies in unbreakable chains. The entire air is filled with [unembodied] souls which are called daemons and heroes. It is they who send dreams to mortals and portents of coming ills and blessings.

The most momentous thing in human life is the art of winning the soul to good or to evil. Salt should always be placed on the table and served with a meal, as a symbol and reminder of what is right; for salt preserves whatever it finds, and it arises from the purest sources, the sun and the sea.

We should be equally attentive in our worship of gods and of heroes. Worship of the gods should be performed in pure white robes, in reverent silence, and after purification. Heroes should be worshipped only after midday. Purification consists not only in ritual cleansing and baptism, but also in avoiding pollution by abstaining from animal flesh, beans, and other forbidden foods, and observing all the other religiously and ritualistically required abstinences.

These are among the things which Alexander reports having found in a scroll of Pythagorean memoirs. (Diogenes Laertius, *loc. cit.*)

FROM LATIN SOURCES:

T 39.   I am not disposed to approve of the practice which tradition ascribes to the Pythagoreans, who, when questioned as to the grounds for some assertion which they were putting forward in a discussion, are reported to have replied: "Himself has said so" (*Ipse dixit*), "himself" being Pythagoras. Thereby they sought to give weight to an opinion already decided, by making authority prevail unsupported by reason. (Cicero *De Natura Deorum* I. 10)

T 40.   There is a story that Pythagoras sacrificed an ox on having made a new discovery in geometry; I don't believe it, however, inasmuch as he refused even to sacrifice a victim to Apollo at Delos, being loath to sprinkle the altar with blood. (*ibid*. III. 88)

T 41.   Pythagoras, who believed that soul is diffused throughout the substance of the entire universe and that our individual souls are fragments of it, fails to reflect that such dismemberment of the world-soul among individuals would be a tearing of God to pieces; moreover that when our individual souls are unhappy, as happens to most of us, then the condition of God would be unhappy too.   (*ibid*. I. 11)

ii. The Pythagorean Symbola

The symbolic maxims which follow are chosen from the much larger number to be found in Pythagorean literature. Each of them carries an ethical and occasionally a metaphysical meaning, which in some cases a reader can discern for himself, in others perhaps not. Traditional and probable interpretations of the more obscure symbola are offered in the Notes.

S 1.   Step not beyond the center of the balance.

S 2.   Go not by the public road.

S 3.   Assist a man in lifting a burden, not in laying it down.

S 4.   Do not sit on a bushel measure.

S 5.   Do not tear away the crown.

S 6.   Do not poke the fire with a sword.

S 7.   Abstain from beans.

S 8.   Always serve salt with a meal.

S 9.   Do not throw stones into fountains.

S 10.   *Do not urinate in the direction of the sun.*

S 11.   *Do not stick iron into anyone's footprints.*

S 12.   *Let no swallows nest on your roof.*

S 13.   *Do not step over a calf's tether.*

S 14.   *Do not turn back in the middle of a journey.*

S 15.   *On rising from bed obliterate the print of your body.*

S 16.   *Leave no mark of the pot on the ashes.*

S 17.   *Keep away from the cypress chest.*

S 18.   *Do not wear a narrow ring.*

S 19.   *Do not sing without harp accompaniment.*

S 20.   *Wear no rings containing images of the gods.*

S 21.   *Pour your libations to the gods at the handle of the cup.*

S 22.   *Offer the gods no wine from an unpruned grapevine.*

S 23.   *Feed the cock and protect him, for he is sacred to the sun and moon.*

S 24.   *Do not obliterate the place of the torch.*

S 25.   *The wind is blowing; adore the wind.*

iii. From the Golden Verses

1.   *First honor the immortal gods, as they are established and ordained by the Law.*

2.   *Honor the Oath, with all religious devotion.*

3.   *Next honor the heroes, full of goodness and light.*

4.   *Honor likewise the terrestrial daemons, rendering to them the worship that is lawfully due them.*

5.   *Honor also your father and mother, and near relatives.*

6. *As for the rest of mankind, make those your friends who distinguish themselves in virtue.*

7, 8. *Give ear to a [Pythagorean] comrade's lightest word; avoid being irked by his incidental faults.*

12. *Above all, have respect for yourself.*

14. *Accustom yourself not to perform actions except as governed by reason.*

15. *Reflect always that it is ordained by destiny that all men must die.*

16. *Reflect that the goods of fortune are uncertain, and that as they are acquired so they may likewise be lost.*

31, 32. *Do not neglect the health of your body: give it drink and meat in due measure, and give it such exercise as it needs.*

35. *Accustom yourself to a way of living that is neat and tasteful but without luxury.*

36. *Avoid all that will stir envy.*

40-44. *After going to bed do not allow sleep to close your eyelids until you have first examined all your actions of the day, asking yourself: Wherein have I done amiss? What have I omitted that ought to have been done? If you find on reflection that you have done anything amiss, be severe with yourself; if you have done anything good, rejoice.*

48. *Never put your hand to any undertaking until you have first prayed to the gods that you may accomplish what you are about to attempt.*

49-50. *When you have made this habit [of prayer to the gods] familiar to yourself, then you will know the constitution of the immortal gods and of men.*

61, 62.   O Zeus, father of men, if you would deliver men from the evils that beset them, show them what daemon is to be invoked.

66.   By healing your soul you will thereby deliver it from all evils, from all afflictions.

71, 72.   When after divesting yourself of your mortal body you arrive in the pure upper aether, you will be a god, an immortal, incorruptible; and death shall have no dominion over you.

iv. Philolaus

Philolaus is not actually a Presocratic, since he was virtually contemporary with Socrates, whom he must have outlived by at least eleven years if it is true, as Diogenes asserts, that Plato while on a journey to Italy in about 388 B.C. had a conversation with him. Nevertheless he must be included here as representing the last known stage of the development of Pythagorean thought up to the time of Plato. Moreover he was reputed to be the first Pythagorean to put the essentials of the doctrine into systematized writing.

Since he was born in southern Italy, Philolaus may have been the son of one of those Pythagoreans who escaped the massacre at Crotona. In any case he is known to have studied under Lysis, who himself had escaped; and he passed the teaching on to Simmias and Cebes, the two young men who figure so prominently in Plato's *Phaedo*. In view of the close-knit continuity of Pythagorean thought it is not possible to be sure how much Philolaus added to its teachings; but the balance of evidence indicates that he either invented or gave a fresh emphasis and interpretation to two main doctrines: (1) that the soul is an immortal *harmonia,* and (2) that the earth is a planet revolving (like the sun and the other planets) around a central fire. He appears also to have made a number of important contributions to the development of mathematics, such as the method of constructing the five regular solids.

The Fragments that follow have traditionally been attributed to Philolaus, although in recent times a number of scholars have cast doubts on their authorship. A résumé of the main controversy may be found in Kirk and Raven, pp. 308-313. But while the authorship and exact date of the Fragments may lie open to question, their Pythagorean character is unmistakable, and for that reason they invite study in the present connection.

FRAGMENTS

1. In the universe everything is fitted together and harmonized out of the unlimited and the limiting—both the universe as a whole and all the things that it contains. (1)

2. It is necessary that all things must be either limiting, or unlimited, or both limiting and unlimited. Since things cannot consist either of the limiting alone or of the unlimited alone —so, at least, it plainly appears—we must obviously conclude that the universe and its contents are fitted together and harmonized by a combination of the limiting and the unlimited. (2)

3. For if everything that is were unlimited, there would not be anything of such a character that it could be recognized. (3)

4. Whatever can be grasped by the mind must be characterized by number; for it is impossible to grasp anything by the mind or to recognize it without number. (4)

5. *Number comprises two distinct forms, the odd and the even; there is also a third, compounded of both, the even-odd. Each of these forms takes many guises, as is shown by each different object.*   (5)

6. *As for nature and harmony, the situation is as follows. The real essence of actual things is eternal, and thus nature must partake of divine rather than of merely human intelligence. For it would be impossible for us to recognize any existing thing, unless each of the things of which the universe is composed had a real essence; this holds both for what is limiting and for what is unlimited. Since these two first-principles are basically unlike, it would obviously be impossible for the universe to have been put in order unless a harmony were supplied; it is thanks to this addition that the orderly universe came-to-be.*   (6, to line 6)

7. *The One is the first-principle of everything.*   (8)

8. *The first element of harmony, the One, is at the center of the Sphere, and is called the hearth.*   (7)

9. *Harmony involves a unity of mixed elements that are various, and an agreement of elements that disagree.*   (10)

10. *In studying the operations and the essence we must take account of the power and role of the Decad: it is great, completely self-realizing, and all-accomplishing; it is the first-principle of human life, in which it participates, and of which it is the leader. Its power is such that without it all things are unlimited, obscure, and indiscernible.*

For it is in the nature of number that the possibility of recognition resides; it gives direction and teaching to every man with respect to what is unknown and baffling. Nothing about existing things—neither they themselves nor their relations to one another—would be clear without number and the essence of number. It is Number which takes the things that we apprehend by sense-perception and fits them harmoniously into the soul, thereby making them recognizable and capable of being compared with one another, as the power of the gnomon makes possible. Thereby it gives body to things and distinguishes the different relations between things, whether unlimited or limiting. You can see the nature and power of number illustrated not only in spiritual (daemonikos) *and divine matters but also* [implicitly] *in human affairs and in language quite generally, including productive activities in all the crafts as well as in music.* (11)

11. *Falsehood does not inhere in the nature of number and harmony; for there is no kinship between it and them. Falsehood and envy partake of the nature of the unlimited, the unreasonable, and the irrational. Falsehood cannot be breathed into number, being hostile and inimical to its very nature; whereas truth is congenial to number and shares close family ties with it.* (11, ctd.)

12. *The elements of the Sphere are five: the fire in the Sphere, the water, the earth, the air, and the ship's hull in which it rests.* (12)

13. *It is an ancient teaching by theologians and inspired prophets that the soul, in being yoked to the body and buried in it as in a tomb, is suffering punishments for certain past misdeeds.* (14)

*14. The soul is established in the body through number;
which is to say, through immortal and incorporeal harmony.*
(22)

*15. The body is loved by the soul, because without the body
the soul cannot get sense-impressions. After the soul has been
separated from the body in death, its existence in the world is
incorporeal. (ibid.)*

*16. Number is the ruling and self-creating bond which
maintains the everlasting stability of the things that compose
the universe. (23)*

8

The Sophists

THE ADVENT OF THE SOPHISTS marks a new turning in ancient
Greek philosophy. Metaphysical thought in its development from
Thales to Anaxagoras on the one hand and to the Atomists on
the other shows a fairly logical, almost a dramatic pattern. First
there are the naive attempts to find the ultimate explanation of
things in a single, perceptually recognizable kind of substance;
out of them a growing interest in the "how"—in the finding of a
principle by which to explain change; then the bold declaration of
Heraclitus that change itself is the ultimate reality and the ultimate basis for all explanation; the equally bold counter-declaration
by Parmenides that change, being intellectually unacceptable,
simply "is not"; and finally the three main and diverse attempts
to reconcile the manifest fact of change with the Eleatic principle
that what is ultimate is necessarily changeless. Greek philosophy
was soon to proceed, spurred and directed by the philosophical
genius of Plato, far beyond this compact group of inquiries and
solutions; but Plato's achievements of penetration and subtlety
were made possible by his having brought man and the problems
of human essentiality into the very heart of the metaphysical problem. Plato might be called, in a sense, a metaphysical anthropolo-
gist. What Plato might still have accomplished without the
example and goad of Socrates we do not know, nor what Socrates

might have been and done without the challenge and contrariety of the Sophists. At all events, taking the known facts as they are, we cannot ignore the fresh humanistic interest which the Sophists, by their radical emphasis upon the problems of man and his activities, obliquely contributed to the subsequent development of Greek philosophy.

That is not to say that the problems of man had been altogether ignored in earlier philosophies. But the pithy remarks about man and his destiny by such writers as Heraclitus and Empedocles are secondary to and generally derivative from their metaphysical systems. In both the Pythagorean and the Hippocratic philosophies there is a more pronounced humanistic concern, but in the one it is limited to the confines of a school-community and cult, in the other it is particularized by the exacting demands of medical practice. Both of these movements effected a partial modification of the older aristocratic faith that a man's essential *aretê* must have been transmitted by patrilinear inheritance and had originally been instilled by a divine progenitor—a view which has left its traces in the myth of Asclepius as the archetypic ancestor of all physicians and in the brotherhood clause in the so-called Hippocratic Oath. In any case it was left to the Sophists to go the whole way in secularizing and democritizing the ideal of *aretê*.

Protagoras of Abdera (ca. 480-411 B.C.) was the acknowledged initiator of the Sophistic movement. The word *sophistês* is composed by adding to the word for wisdom a suffix connoting a man who practices a profession, and who is thus in some way an expert; a sophist therefore means something like a "wisdom expert." There is a paradoxical shock in both the Greek and the English versions of the idea; for while there can perhaps be experts in any finite field of activity or inquiry, which is to say persons with the know-how to achieve specific results, it is as meaningless to speak of an expert in wisdom as to speak of an expert in goodness. Nevertheless Protagoras and his followers did in fact make the claim.

It is instructive to observe what happened to the idea of wisdom at the hands of the Sophists, as a result of their doctrine, and their energetic practice of it, that "wisdom can be taught." In traditional Greek thought wisdom was taken as one of the four cardinal human virtues, the others being temperance, courage, and justice. The general idea of *aretê* (inadequately rendered "virtue" or "specific excellence," or in a human context as "human excellence") was an idea, indeed an ideal, of supreme appeal and attractiveness to the Greek mind. Outside the area of human affairs it might refer to the distinguishing excellence of any species, natural or otherwise—the strength of a lion, the fleetness of a rabbit, the sharp cutting edge of a pruning hook enabling it to clip branches effectively. Within the human context it was almost synonymous with that other high-ranking Greek word *kalokagathia*—built from the words *kalos* (beautiful, admirable), *kai* (and), *agathos* (good). These two main value-words, *aretê* and *kalokagathia,* were applied to man in his wholeness, composed of body, psyche, and mind—to a victor at the Olympic games, provided he were both an athlete and something more, to a Parmenides and a Socrates, who were both thinkers and outstandingly more.

Involved in the meaning of *aretê* there was always an element or at least an overtone of political reference. A Greek of the fifth century B.C. lived in a *polis*—a civilized community the size of a small city but with the political autonomy (in most cases at most times) of a state. In such a situation a youth would grow to manhood feeling his constant interrelatedness with the life and aims of his *polis* and knowing that the principal road to success was likely to lie in a political (not, as in most cases today, a commercial) direction. The virtue, the *aretê,* the human excellence that the youth would wish to develop for himself would be personal and political at once. Naturally enough it was apt to include the glamor of outward displays with their tangible benefits, such as the winning of debates before the Assembly, no less than, perhaps somewhat more than, a pure development of the inward virtues. It was a rarer voice that issued from time to time a reminder that the most genuine riches are to be found within rather than outside: Heraclitus (Fr. 8); the Delphic maxim, "Know thyself"; Socrates' "The unexamined life is not worth living."

When Pericles assumed power in Greece in the middle of the fifth century the political aspect of the ethical problem took on a new relevance and a new tone. Under his leadership Athens entered into the larger political life of Greece, changing from the older self-sufficient city-state to a more dynamic imperial state. As Werner Jaeger remarks, a rationalization of Athenian life thereby began to take place, and the rationalization of political education at the hands of the Sophists was only a part of it.

The principal skill which the Sophists taught, and of which an ambitious Greek youth would be eager to acquire mastery, was the ability to win debates and to influence public opinion through the art of persuasive speech. At least the two leading Sophists, Protagoras and Gorgias, evidently performed such teaching with marked success: for both of them lived to be very old and in their long careers they amassed considerable wealth; moreover both of them produced successful orators, statesmen, and other men of eminence from among their pupils. The visible and tangible evidences of their success could not be denied.

The temptation was, as sometimes happens with successful men, to push their claims of success too far, failing to distinguish between the specific skills which they were demonstrably able to teach and that general human excellence which, while it may make use of, can never be reduced to a matter of know-how. Protagoras claimed for the sophist the ability to teach *aretê* by essentially the same method as he might teach the rules of grammar and the art of oratory. Ethics was thus, for him, but one field of investigation among others. Gorgias added to this a doctrine of ethical pluralism—that there are different virtues, not one human virtue in general, and that the different virtues are of varying importance according to one's station in life: a soldier needs courage, a lawgiver needs practical wisdom and justice, a philosopher needs contemplative wisdom. It was mainly Socrates who critically attacked Protagoras' claim, by his double insistence that virtue is essentially one, finding its unity in wisdom, and that virtue in the full human sense cannot be taught but can only be encouraged and challenged to grow. Subsequently Plato, in the third and fourth books of *The Republic,* undertook to meet Gorgias' ethical pluralism, by defining the sense in which the virtues pertain to different political classes and the sense in which a healthy republic requires human virtue in all its citizens, whatever their special aptitudes and special duties.

i. Protagoras

FRAGMENTS

1.   Man is the measure of all things: of things that are, that they are; of things that are not, that they are not.   (1)

2.   All matter is in a state of flux. A fluctuating thing may retain its shape, however, because the changes may be such that the additions compensate for the losses. It is our sense-impressions of the thing that get modified, because affected by age and other bodily conditions.   (Quoted by Sextus Empiricus).

3.   There are intelligible principles inherent in the matter of every phenomenon; because matter is essentially the sum of all the seemings that it has for any and all persons.   (ibid.)

4.   Learning requires both natural endowment and self-

discipline. It has to begin when one is young. It does not take root in the soul unless it goes deep. (3, 11)

5. *Skill without concern, and concern without skill, are equally worthless.* (10)

6. *As for the gods, I have no way of knowing either that they exist or that they do not exist; nor, if they exist, of what form they are. For the obstacles to that sort of knowledge are many, including the obscurity of the matter and the brevity of human life.* (4)

TESTIMONIA

FROM PLATO:

T 1. [*Protagoras is imagined to be speaking.*] Consider, Socrates, why it is that men inflict punishment on a wrongdoer, and you will see that in doing so they implicitly agree that human excellence (*aretê*) can be acquired. A sensible man in inflicting punishment does not do so in order to avenge a past wrong that is beyond recall, but looks rather toward the future, in that he wishes to deter both the culprit and those who witness his punishment from doing any further wrong in the future. Those who administer punishment, then, do so for the sake of prevention, which is tantamount to admitting that virtue (*aretê*) is capable of being taught.

But where are the teachers, you ask? In a sense it is like asking who teaches children to speak their own language, for in that too there are no specific teachers to be found. Consider, too, how the sons of artisans learn the craft of their fathers. Up to a point they learn it from the father as well as from the father's friends and fellow-craftsmen. But as they become ready for more advanced instruction it will probably be harder for

them to find suitable teachers than it was when they were nov-
ices. The same is true in the teaching of virtue or of anything
else. What we do [when we want advanced instruction] is to
look for a teacher who excels us even moderately in the kind
of excellence we want, and we are glad when we can find such
a one.

Well, that is the way in which I regard my own teaching—
as the activity of a man who is somewhat more competent than
the rest in helping his fellow-men attain to what is good and
admirable. I give my pupils full value for their money, as they
themselves agree. To make sure of doing so I have adopted the
following condition of payment. After receiving instruction from
me a pupil may, if he chooses, pay the fee that I have set;
but if he thinks it too high, he has only to go to the temple
and declare under oath how high a value he sets on what he
has learned, and he may then pay accordingly. (*Protagoras*
324A, 327E)

T 2. *Socrates:* Protagoras has said, as you will doubtless
recall, that man is the measure of all things—of things that
are, that they are; of things that are not, that they are not.
Presumably you have read the statement?

Theaetetus: Oh yes, often.

Socrates: Well, he means something like this, doesn't he?—
that particular things are for me just what they appear to me
to be, and are for you just what they appear to you to be. For
you and I are men.

Theaetetus: Yes, that is surely what he means.

Socrates: Then, since so wise a man is not likely to be talking nonsense, let us pursue his meaning. It is sometimes the
case, isn't it, that one of us feels cold while the other, although
blown by the same wind, does not? Or that one of us feels
mildly chilly while the other feels very cold?

Theaetetus: That is true.

Socrates: And when such a situation occurs are we to describe the wind itself as cold or not cold? Or shall we accept Protagoras' solution, that it is cold for him who feels it cold and is not cold for him who does not feel it so?

Theaetetus: The latter, I should think.

Socrates: And it does in fact sometimes appear cold to one observer and not cold to another simultaneously?

Theaetetus: Yes.

Socrates: In the case of qualities like warm and cold, do "it appears" and "it is perceived" have the same meaning?

Theaetetus: Evidently so.

Socrates: Protagoras means, then, that perception is always of something existent, and that the knowledge which it imparts is infallible?

Theaetetus: That seems clear.

(*Theaetetus* 152A)

T 3. [*Protagoras is represented as speaking.*] Of course I don't deny that there is such a thing as wisdom and that wise men exist. But what I mean by a wise man is one who can alter people's ways of judging so that what appears and is to them bad now will appear and will be to them good. It is like the case of some food which appears and is bitter to a sick man but appears and is quite the opposite to a man in health. It should not be said that either of the two men is more knowing or more ignorant than the other; they are simply different. Still, we agree that the one state is preferable to the other, and so we think that the sick man had better be changed into a healthy state. That's how it is with education (*paedeia*): its aim is to change men from a worse to a better condition. But whereas the physician brings about the change by means of drugs, the sophist does so by means of words.

The point is not that a man who thinks what is false is taught to think what is true. It is not possible to think what is false; because one can only think what he experiences, and what he experiences is true. Consider, however, the case of a man who has got into a bad [i.e., unhealthy] condition of soul and whose thoughts reflect that condition: if he can be brought to a good [i.e., healthy] condition of soul, his thoughts will be correspondingly better. The resulting appearances are sometimes ignorantly spoken of as "true"; I, however, do not call them truer than the earlier ones but simply better. Consequently, my dear Socrates, instead of comparing us sophists to jumping frogs as you did, you might better have recognized us to be a kind of physician.

Farmers in curing sickly plants simply try to replace unhealthy modes of assimilation by healthy modes. [No question of truth or falsity in such cases.] In like manner responsible rhetors seek to improve their city-state (*polis*) by instilling [in its citizens] workable notions of what is right in place of unhealthy ones.

My position, then, is that whatever seems right and admirable to a particular city-state is truly right and admirable—during the period of time in which that opinion continues to be held; and that it is the wise man's task, when the people are afflicted with unsound beliefs, to substitute others so that they seem true and therefore *are* true. Thus the sophist, who trains his pupils on the same principle, thereby shows his wisdom and justifies his claim to a large fee when the course of training is over. It is in this sense, and in this sense only, that some men are wiser than others; which does not affect the truth of the proposition that there is no such thing as thinking falsely. (*Theaetetus* 166D)

FROM ARISTOTLE:

T 4.   There is a doctrine of Protagoras in which he said that man is the measure of all things. He was saying, in other words, that each individual's private impression is absolutely true. But if that position is adopted, then it follows that the same thing is and is not, that it is both good and bad, and similarly for other contradictions; because, after all, a given thing will seem beautiful to one group of people and ugly to another, and by the theory in question each of the conflicting appearances will be "the measure." (*Metaphysica* 1062b 13)

T 5.   When Protagoras says that man is the measure of all things he presumably means the man who has both rational understanding of the matter and perceptual acquaintance with it. On this interpretation, since we do in fact accept thought and perception as the two "measures" of whatever we are dealing with, Protagoras in making so provocative a statement is really not saying anything at all. (*ibid*. 1053b 20)

T 6.   If it is equally possible to affirm and to deny anything whatever on any subject, then a given thing will be at once a ship, a wall, and a man: which is the necessary conclusion for those who hold the theory of Protagoras. (*ibid*. 1007b 20)

T 7.   In actual fact the circle touches the ruler not at a point [but along a tiny length], as Protagoras used to declare in arguing against the geometers. (*ibid*. 998a 3)

T 8.   They were right who rejected the kind of training that Protagoras offered; for this art was a deceptive one, in that it could not establish real probabilities but merely specious plausibilities. (*Rhêtorikê* 1402a 25)

T 9.   Protagoras classifies nouns as masculine, feminine, and nondescript. (*ibid*. 1407b 7)

FROM LATER GREEK SOURCES:

T 10.   Protagoras was born at Abdera, as Heraclides of Pontus states in his treatise *On Laws,* when remarking that Protagoras had made laws for the city of Thurii. He and Prodicus of Ceos gave public readings, charging fees for admission. He had once studied under Democritus.

Protagoras was the first to declare that there are two opposing sides to every question, and he was the first to build arguments on that basis. He began one of his writings with the words: [Fr. 1]. He used to maintain that soul is nothing apart from sense-experiences, and that everything is true. He began another of his writings thus: [Fr. 6]. Because he had begun his book in this way the Athenians banished him from their city; moreover they burnt his writings in the marketplace, after sending a herald to collect all copies of them that were in anyone's possession.

He was the first to demand a fee of a hundred minae; he was also the first to distinguish the tenses of verbs, to stress the importance of seizing the "opportune moment" (*kairos*), to set up contests in debating, and to teach tricks of argument to pleaders on both sides of a question. He was the first to introduce the Socratic type of argument; in practicing it, however, he tended to neglect the rational meaning in favor of verbal quibble, and thereby he gave birth to the tribe of eristics [controversialists, verbal quibblers] who are now to be met with everywhere.

We learn from Plato's *Euthydemus* that the so-called argument of Antisthenes, ostensibly demonstrating that contradiction is impossible, was first employed by Protagoras; and we learn from Artemidorus in his reply to Chrysippus that Protagoras was the first to teach the art of refuting whatever proposition might be offered. It was he who first classified the types of sentence into four: as expressing wish, question, answer, or command.

We are told by Aristotle in his treatise *On Education* that Protagoras invented the shoulder-strap on which porters can set their burdens. As a matter of fact he himself had once been a porter, as Epicurus mentions somewhere; and it was while working at this occupation that he attracted the attention of Democritus, who noticed how skillfully he tied up his bundles of wood.

The works of his which now survive are these: *The Art of Eristic; On Wrestling; On Mathematics; On the Commonwealth; On Ambition; On Virtues; On the Ancient Arrangement; On Those in Hades; On the Misdeeds of Men; Maxims;* and *A Book for Legal Advocates, with Opposing Sets of Arguments.*

There is a story that once when he sought to collect his fee from Euathlus, who had studied with him [and had agreed to pay if and only if he won his first case at law], Euathlus protested: "But I haven't yet pleaded a case." "Very well, then," Protagoras replied, "I will sue you. And if I win you will have to pay me by the judgment of the court, whereas if *you* win you will have to pay me by the terms of our agreement."

Some say that Protagoras lived to be ninety. Apollonius, however, says he died at seventy after a forty-year career as a sophist, and assigns his *floruit* to the 84th Olympiad [444-441 B.C.]. (Diogenes Laertius IX. 50-56)

T 11.   Protagoras of Abdera, the sophist, had studied under Democritus in their native city. Then, during Xerxes' invasion of Greece, he associated with magi from Persia. The Persian magi do not extend their teachings to non-Persians except by the command of their king. But Protagoras' father, whose name was Maeander, was one of the wealthiest men in Thrace; he entertained Xerxes in his home and presented him with gifts. As a result he obtained Xerxes' royal permission for his son to study under the magi.

When Protagoras declares his ignorance of whether or not the gods exist, I suspect he derived that heresy under the influence of Persian education. For while the magi invoke gods in their secret ceremonies, they avoid any public profession of belief in divine beings, not wishing it to be supposed that their own powers are dependent on an outside source.

Because of his remark about the gods Protagoras was cast out by the Athenians. Some say that he was brought to trial and was solemnly outlawed "from the entire earth"; others say he was banished without the formality of a trial. At any rate he wandered about among islands and mainlands, until at length, while sailing in a small boat and trying to evade the Athenian triremes which were deployed over all the seas, he was drowned.

Protagoras first introduced the custom of charging a fee for lectures. Thereby he bequeathed to the Greeks a practice which is by no means a bad one, since we set greater store on what costs money than on what comes free.

Plato recognized that while Protagoras spoke with impressive eloquence the underlying thought was far from impressive, and even the expression was sometimes unduly long-winded. In the course of a long myth Plato gives a caricature of Protagoras' style. (Philostratus, *Lives of the Sophists* 494-495)

T 12.   In a certain letter Epicurus tells of how Protagoras the sophist, from being a porter and hewer of wood, became the private secretary of Democritus. The latter had been struck by the distinctive movements of Protagoras as he piled wood, and so adopted him into his household, giving him his first start in life. Subsequently Protagoras taught reading and writing in a provincial village, and thereupon he began to develop his skill as a sophist. (Athenaeus, *The Deipnosophists* VIII. 354)

T 13.   It is told of Protagoras that he once made a whimsical agreement with his pupil Euathlus. He stipulated an inordinately high fee for the course of lessons, but with the proviso that Euathlus was to pay it only if he should be successful in the first case he pleaded in court, and not otherwise. Euathlus, who was of a shrewd and cunning mind, having easily mastered all the rhetorical tricks by which to soften judges and confound adversaries, and having by now learnt all he wanted to from Protagoras, became reluctant to put the matter of payment to the test, and put his teacher off with specious excuses, for a long while neither paying nor openly refusing to do so. At length Protagoras had the young man haled into court, and after explaining to the judges what the conditions of the agreement were, he propounded to Euathlus the following dilemma:

"If I win the case you will have to pay me by the decision of the judges, and if *you* win you will still have to pay me because of the terms of our agreement; thus win or lose you are equally condemned. So what are you expecting to gain?"

But Euathlus, as an accomplished disciple of so subtle a teacher, turned Protagoras' own argument against him. "Whatever the outcome of the suit," he said, "I am freed of having to pay what you demand. For either I win the case and thus am cleared by the court's decree, or I am beaten and thus am cleared by the terms of our original bargain."   (Apuleius *Florida* 18)

ii. Gorgias

FRAGMENTS

1.   Our struggle in life requires two virtues, bravery and wisdom—readiness to endure a danger and skillful knowledge of how to manage it. (8)

2.   In contending against adversaries, destroy their seriousness with laughter and their laughter with seriousness. (12)

3.   While a friend may often choose to serve his friend by unjust actions, he will never expect unjust actions from his friend in return. (21)

4.   Tragedy produces a deception in which the deceiver is more honest than the non-deceiver and the deceived is wiser than the undeceived. (23)

5. *Being is unrecognizable unless it manages to seem, and seeming is feeble unless it manages to be.* (26)

6. *The bright jewel of a city is courage; of a human body it is beauty; of the soul, wisdom; of human action, virtue; of speech, truth. To lack the quality in each case is to lack the specific excellence.* (11)

7. *She [known as Helen of Troy] acted as she did either (i) by a combination of chance, necessity, and the will of the gods, or (ii) because she was abducted by force, or (iii) because she was seduced by persuasion.*

If the first is the true explanation, then not Helen but her accuser is deserving of censure. For no human purpose can thwart the purpose of a god: the stronger cannot be thwarted by the weaker, and a god is superior to a man in power, in wisdom, and in everything else. Therefore if Helen's action is to be attributed to a god and thus to chance, she is not to blame.

If again, she was carried off by force and was lawlessly and unrighteously outraged, it is clear that not she but her assailant was in the wrong. The barbarian who barbarously abducted her should indeed be condemned, punished, and disgraced; but she, bereft of her country and her friends, is deserving rather of pity than of blame.

Finally, if it was speech that persuaded her by seducing her soul, her defence is no less easy. Speech is a powerful force which can achieve the most divine results with a very minimum of bodily effort: it is able to dispel fear, allay grief, arouse joy, and stimulate pity. Persuasion by speech is on a par with abduction by force: Helen in being persuaded was compelled, and hence it was not she but her seducer who was to blame. (11, ctd.)

8. *If all men had full memory of the past, awareness of the present, and foresight into the future, speech would not be as effective as it is. But since in fact men have little ability to remember the past, observe the present, or foretell the future, speech works easily; with the result that most speakers on most subjects offer only opinion as counsellor to the soul. But opinion is delusive and inconstant, and those who rely on it run grave risks. (ibid.)*

9. *When persuasion joins with speech it can affect the soul in any way it wishes. Consider first how astronomers, using "speech and argument"* (logos), *manage to dispel men's former opinions [about things of the sky and upper air] and to implant other opinions which had formerly seemed incredible and inconsistent with plain facts. Consider next how at a court trial an advocate's plea can succeed in swaying the listeners, not because of the truth of what he says but by the sheer power of speech and its skillful composition. And thirdly consider those contests between philosophical disputants, in which mental agility is what determines the acceptance of opinions. (ibid.)*

10. *The power of speech over the disposition of the soul is comparable with the effect of drugs on the disposition of the body. As drugs can expel certain humors from the body and thereby make an end either of sickness or of life, so likewise various words can produce grief, pleasure, or fear, which act like drugs when they give rise to bad persuasions in the soul. (ibid.)*

11. *Men who neglect philosophy while busying themselves with ordinary affairs are like the Suitors [in the* Odyssey] *who desired Penelope but went to bed with her maids.* (29)

TESTIMONIA

FROM PLATO:

T 1.   *Gorgias:* Whenever there is a political election it is
the orators who are successful in giving advice and getting
their opinions acted upon.

Socrates: That is what baffles me, Gorgias; in fact it is precisely why I have been asking you again and again to explain
to me what the power of rhetoric is. For when we reflect on its
power to influence men's opinions it seems to be something almost supernatural.

Gorgias: Oh Socrates, if only you knew the full extent of
its power—how it comprises in itself virtually all the other arts!
Let me give you a telling example. On many occasions I have
accompanied my brother or some other physician on visits to
their patients. Sometimes a patient would be reluctant to take the
medicine or to submit to cautery; and when the doctor was unable to persuade him it was I who succeeded—by no other means
than the art of rhetoric. I'll go further and declare that if both
a rhetor and a medical doctor were to visit some city, any city
at all, and were to take part in a debate before the assembly
as to which of them ought to be appointed the city's medical
director, the doctor would get nowhere in the debate whereas
the speech expert would be elected if he wished to be. It would
be the same if he were contending with a practitioner in any
other field whatever: the rhetor could always get himself elected
against any rival candidate, for there is no subject on which he
could not speak more persuasively than other men in the
populace, whatever their craft or profession. That shows you
what the power of rhetoric can perform.

Of course, Socrates, there is also the further question of how the art of rhetoric is to be employed, just as there is in the case of any other trained skill. Such special abilities to perform ought not to be used promiscuously. Suppose that a man has developed a skill in boxing or wrestling or armored combat to such an extent that he surpasses everyone, friend and foe alike: of course that does not give him the right to go about beating up his friends or knifing them. And if a man who had undergone training in a school of athletics, where he developed a strong physique and learned the art of boxing, were then to go home and strike his father and mother, or his other relatives and his friends, surely it would not be reasonable to get angry at his trainers and teachers and seek to have them exiled because of what he did. For when they taught him skill in boxing it was with a view to its rightful use against enemies and thugs; the pupil and not the teacher was the one who perverted that skill to wrong ends. Accordingly it is not the teachers who are wicked, nor is the art itself to be condemned and declared wicked, but only those who misuse it, I should think.

The same argument applies equally to rhetoric. It is true that a rhetor is able to refute everyone else and on any subject, in such a way that he can win the support of the crowd and so accomplish virtually any result he may wish. But that does not entitle him to destroy the standing of physicians or of other able men, just because he could do so if he chose. He should use his rhetorical skill fairly, as in the case of the trained athlete. (*Gorgias* 456A)

T 2. *Protarchus:* When I was attending Gorgias' lectures I heard him repeatedly declare that the art of persuasion was superior to all other arts because it gained power over its objects not by force but by their willing submission. (*Philebus* 58A-B)

FROM ARISTOTLE:

T 3.   The paid teachers of eristical [contentious] argumentation adopted a method of teaching like that of Gorgias. They would assign their pupils speeches to be learnt by heart, some of which were rhetorical, some eristical. In the latter the arguments of the competing sides would be included in what was to be memorized.   (*De Sophisticis Elenchis* 183b 37)

T 4.   In ceremonial oratory a speaker can decorate his speech from time to time with stray bits of eulogy. Which was doubtless what Gorgias had in mind when he remarked that [in making a speech] he was never at a loss for something to say.   (*Rhêtorikê* 1418a 33)

T 5.   Some metaphors have a too labored theatricality, as when Gorgias speaks of "events that are green and full of sap" or of "a foul deed sowed and an evil harvest reaped." On the other hand his rebuke to the swallow who let drop on him as she flew overhead was effectively theatrical in the best sense: "Shame on you, Philomela!" he said.   (*ibid*. 1406b 8, 15)

T 6.   In his treatise *On the Olympic Games* he says, "Men of Greece, you deserve to be admired." His praise was addressed to those who had instituted the solemn Olympic festivals.   (*ibid*. 1414b 31)

FROM LATER GREEK SOURCES:

T 7.   Sicily gave birth to Gorgias in the city of Leontini, and we may trace the art of the sophists back to him, who may be called its father. In much the same way that Aeschylus can be regarded as the father of tragedy because he introduced such innovations as appropriate costumes, padded buskins to increase height, messengers who report events occurring offstage, etc., so Gorgias may be seen as related to his predecessors in his own craft. For in his energy, his use of paradox, his inspired manner of speaking, and his adoption of an exalted style for great themes, he set an example for later sophists to follow. He distinguished himself also by his device of breaking off a sentence and making an abrupt transition, producing an effect that gave pleasure by its very insolence; by adorning his style with poetic language that was not only ornamental but also deeply impressive; and by his ability to improvise with the greatest facility. When in later years he gave discourses at Athens he won, as was to be expected, hearty applause from the crowd. Not only crowds, however, but also illustrious men yielded to his influence—among them Critias and Alcibiades in their youth, and Thucydides even as a mature man.

At the religious festivals of Greece, moreover, Gorgias played a distinguished part. He declaimed his *Pythian Oration* from the altar; as a result of which a gold statue of him was set up and dedicated in the temple of the Pythian god. His *Olympic Oration* was of fundamental importance for the state. In it, perceiving that Greece was divided against itself, he wrote with a view to reconciling the factions: he sought to turn their united energies against the barbarians, urging them to regard not one another's cities, but the barbarians' territories, as the booty to be won in war. His *Funeral Oration* was delivered at Athens in honor of those who had fallen in the war and whom the Athenians wished to honor with public funerals and panegyrics; it was most ingeniously constructed.

It is said that although Gorgias lived to be 108 years old, his body was not debilitated by age, but that to the very end of his life he remained in health, his senses as keen as a young man's. (Philostratus, *Lives of the Sophists* 492-494)

T 8. At that time the Sicilian city of Leontini, whose citizens had some kinship with the Athenians although politically it was a colony of Chalcis, found itself under attack by the Syracusans. Gravely encumbered and distressed by the war, and fearing to be overwhelmed by the superior forces of the enemy, the Leontinians sent an embassy to Athens, asking for prompt aid in order to rescue their city from danger.

At the head of the embassy they had appointed Gorgias the rhetor, because of his preeminent skill in speech. He was the first to have established rhetoric as an art, and he had developed so high a reputation as a teacher of it, which is to say as a sophist, that he commanded a fee of one hundred minae per pupil.

On arrival at Athens Gorgias was conducted to the Assembly, where he made a speech urging an alliance. The Athenians, who were clever by nature and had a taste for eloquence, were astonished at the novelty of his diction. It was the first time they had heard a speaker employ rhetorical tropes artistically combined with antitheses, balanced periods, controlled rhythms, parallel endings, and the like. The effect was so novel that it was received with enthusiasm, although nowadays it would seem mannered, repetitious, and ridiculously extravagant. At any rate, he thereby succeeded in persuading the Athenians to enter into an alliance with the Leontinians; and amidst wide acclaim for his rhetorical skill he took ship for Leontini. (Diodorus Siculus XII. 53)

T 9. It was Gorgias who founded the art of impromptu oratory. He would make a public appearance in the theater at Athens and say boldly to anyone, "Propose me a theme." He was the first to issue such a challenge, by which he virtually boasted that he had all knowledge at his fingertips and could speak on any subject that might be proposed, trusting simply to the "inspiration of the moment" (*kairos*). (Philostratus, *op. cit.* 482)

T 10. It is reported that Gorgias, after reading the dialogue

of Plato that bears his name, remarked to friends, "How beau-
tifully Plato knows how to satirize!" It is also reported that
after reading from Plato's dialogue aloud as part of a public
lecture Gorgias remarked that neither had he ever spoken the
words attributed to him nor had he heard Plato mention them
before. (Athenaeus, *The Deipnosophists* XI. 505)

T 11.   Although Gorgias of Leontini belonged to the same
philosophical circle as those who had abolished the criterion, he
did not employ the same mode of attack as Protagoras. In his
book *Concerning Not-Being,* whose subtitle is *Concerning Nature,*
he undertakes to set up three propositions in succession: first that
nothing exists, secondly that even if anything existed it could not
be known by men, and thirdly that even if anything could be
known by anyone it could not be communicated to anyone else.
(Sextus Empiricus, *Against the Logicians* I. 65)

The argument supporting the first argument, as presented by
Sextus Empiricus in what looks like direct quotation, is unduly
long, involved, and conceptually fussy, containing repetitions and
quibbles which serve no valid purpose. Consequently the remain-
der of T 11 is not a full translation but a somewhat abbreviated
paraphrase of Sextus.

Gorgias opens the argument with a trilemma: "If anything is,
then either Not-being is, or Being is, or a mixture of the two is."
[Or, translated differently:] "If anything exists, then either the
non-existent exists, or the existent exists, or a mixture of the two
exists." Gorgias has no difficulty in refuting the first as inconsistent. He then refutes the third on the ground that there can
be no mixture of the two because not-being has just been proved
not to be—or, the non-existent has just been proved not to exist!
These maneuvers leave only the second of the three alternatives
to be considered.

So Gorgias now proceeds to argue as follows. If Being is (exists), then two questions arise: it is either infinite (eternal) or

finite (having had a beginning in time) or a mixture of the two; and again, it is either one or many. The development of the first of these two "problems" turns upon a confusion between eternity and the spatially unlimited, and a corresponding confusion between original coming-to-be and spatial finitude. The second of the "problems" is handled by distinguishing four ways of being "one"—as a unit, as a continuum, as a magnitude, and as a physical body. He devises a seeming objection to each of the four alternatives: for instance, that a physical body cannot be "one," inasmuch as it has three dimensions!

There follows, as given by Sextus, Gorgias' defence of his second and third propositions. Here it makes for a little more clarity in English translation to employ the terminology of existence rather than that of being, even though the Greek is still *to on*. For it is confusing to contrast "what is thought" with "what is," but somewhat more intelligible to contrast it with "what exists."

It is now to be demonstrated that even if anything exists ("is") it is unknowable and even unthinkable by man. Gorgias argues: Since the objects of thought are not themselves the existents about which we are inquiring, it follows that those existents are something other than thought. Clearly there is a distinction between our thoughts themselves and the supposed existents to which they refer; for if someone thinks of a man flying or a chariot traveling over the sea, it does not follow that the man is really flying or that the chariot is traveling over the sea.

Moreover, if "to be thought" were itself a property of the existent, then "not to be thought" would be a property of the non-existent; for existent and non-existent are opposites, and it is the nature of opposites to have opposite properties. But it is not true that "not to be thought" is a property of the non-existent; for Scylla and Chimaera and many other non-existents are thought. It follows, then, that even if something is existent, it does not thereby have the property of being thought.

Finally, if something is grasped by thought as existing, its existence cannot be communicated to another person. For suppose it to be true that there are externally existent objects which we apprehend by sight, by hearing, and by sense-perception generally —visual objects by sight and audible objects by hearing, never the other way round—how can the character of these objects of perceptual experience be indicated to another person? For the means by which we indicate is speech (*logos*), and speech is not identical with the things that are spoken about. Therefore what we indicate to the person whom we address is not existing things but merely speech, which is something different from them. Just as a visible object will not become audible nor an audible object visible, so likewise an externally existent object will not become of the nature of speech; hence, not being speech, its nature cannot be communicated to another person.

After his lengthy statement of the foregoing arguments Sextus then comments: "If we accept Gorgias' arguments the criterion of truth is swept away, for there cannot be a criterion of what neither exists nor can be known nor can be communicated." (Sextus Empiricus, *Against the Logicians* I. 65-85)

iii. Fragments from Other Sophists

PRODICUS OF CEOS

1. *Sophists reside in the borderland between philosophy and statesmanship.* (6)

2. *Desire doubled is love; love doubled is madness.* (7)

THRASYMACHUS OF CHALCEDON

1. Justice is simply the advantage of the stronger. (Plato, *Republic* 338)

2. The gods evidently do not see human affairs: if they did they would not neglect to bestow justice on mankind, for it is the greatest of blessings and yet men make little use of it. (8)

ANTIPHON (PROBABLY OF ATHENS)

1. Justice consists in not transgressing the laws of the city in which one dwells. The best way of combining one's own interests and the demands of justice is to act according to justice when there are witnesses but according to nature when one is alone and unobserved. For the authority of the laws is imposed artificially, but the authority of nature is intrinsically binding. The former is established by general consent, not by natural growth, whereas action according to nature has nothing to do with general consent. Hence if a man transgresses the laws he can escape penalty and disgrace by avoiding detection. If, on the other hand, he defies possibility by transgressing the laws inherent in nature, the injury that results to him will not be lessened by going undetected nor increased by being generally known; for such injury is due not to opinion but to truth. (44)

2. In all men the mind has leadership over the body—with respect to health, to sickness, and to everything else. (2)

3. It [truth] is infinite in the sense that it needs nothing and receives no addition from anywhere. (10)

4. Time is both a conception (noêma) *and a measure* (metron), *not a substance* (hypostasis).   (9)

5. If one were to bury a bed and the rotting wood were to sprout, the thing that sprouted would be wood but not a bed.   (Aristotle *Physica* 193a 12)

CRITIAS OF ATHENS

1. He was no simpleton who remarked that chance favors the man of wise prudence.   (21)

2. If you will discipline yourself to make your mind self-sufficient you will thereby be least vulnerable to injury from things outside.   (40)

3. An ill-tempered man gets vexed over trifles, and vexed too much or too long about graver matters.   (42)

4. But is rich stupidity a better housemate than wise poverty?   (29)

5. Time is unwearied and full in its eternal flowing, and is generated by itself alone.   (18)

6. [O Time,] thou who art self-begotten, weaving the nature of everything into the rhythmic turn of the sky: around thee in perpetual dance go the light of day, the shimmering darkness of night, and the unnumbered throng of stars.   (19)

7. After the shadow falls Time grows old most rapidly.   (26)

9

Hippocratic Medical Philosophy

IN ADDITION TO and largely independent of the explicit philosophical theories—the recognized philosophers and schools of philosophy, such as those studied in the foregoing eight chapters—
there are always present in any culture various marks of implicit
philosophy. By implicit philosophy is meant that which expresses
itself not so much in definite propositions and arguments supporting them, but rather as the not fully probed assumptions, over-
tones, and outcomes of modes of living and shared aspirations.
Ancient medicine, in particular, is often thus implicitly philosophical. Medical practice may give rise, in a reflective physician, to
wonder about the essential nature of the human body, and hence
about the human mind, which appears to have been generated
out of the body's more developed activities and yet is able to win
some degree of control over it. Thus medical theory on the one
hand is rooted in human needs, sometimes needs of the greatest
urgency, while on the other hand it points toward unsolved questions about human life which in their fuller implications are
metaphysical.

The most considerable body of medical writings that has come
down from ancient Greece is that associated with the name of
Hippocrates (460-390 B.C.). On his native island of Cos Hippocrates founded what was probably the first school of medicine dedi-

cated unflinchingly to the investigation and application of scientific principles. The extant writings of that school constitute what is called the Hippocratic Corpus; although their individual authorship is undiscoverable in most cases, they are apparently typical expressions of the methods employed by that school of physicians and of their resulting speculations. At any rate, for convenience and by accepted custom, we shall use the name of Hippocrates when referring to the authors of the excerpts.

Although Hippocrates never organized the philosophical principles of his thinking, and although it is impossible to be sure how much of the Corpus was written by the master himself and how much by medical disciples, we can best think of his philosophy as resting upon a pair of complementary propositions: (a) *Health is the natural state, disease is unnatural;* and (b) *Disease, no less than health, is governed by natural causes,* which it is the task of the physician to understand. Are these two propositions contradictory? In discovering the sense in which they are consistent from Hippocrates' point of view, and are to him equally important sides of the truth about human organisms, we take an important step into an understanding of his philosophy.

To describe health as "natural" has for Hippocrates a very specific meaning. Living nature is telic, it moves toward certain discoverable biological goals. Referring to the cycle of births and deaths which marks the career of every living species Hippocrates postulates that each organism tends by nature to play its part in that cycle in a healthy manner, appropriately to the species of which it is a member, unless something hinders. When a creature is injured or falls ill, provided that its departure from normal is not unduly severe, it tends by the force of its own living nature to heal the injured part and to restore the balance that is health. Since this is so, the role of the physician as Hippocrates conceives it is not to manipulate the patient as one would handle something inanimate, but to remove, both from within and from outside the patient's body, obstructions to healthy recovery. The essential relation is not dyadic, he holds, but triadic: the physician, the patient, and the disease.

But if there is one sense in which health is the natural state, there is also a sense in which disease likewise is a part of nature. For the possibility of understanding disease lies, Hippocrates insists, in the fact that disease is not entirely haphazard, however it may appear superficially, but follows patterns of development which in general, if not always in detail, can be traced. What, then, is the physician's task with respect to it? Hippocrates defines that task in terms of arranging the bodily and environmental conditions so that the disease can go through its own peculiar cycle as expeditiously and safely as possible. Proper food and drink, calmness of mind and body, suitable exercise, and the like, are among the chief ways in which the bodily conditions can be made as favorable as possible to the speedy and firm completion of the cycle through illness and back again to health.

When illness begins it is marked by an excess of some bodily element over the rest—say an excess of heat, as in a fever, or of moisture as in dropsy. This excessive element is an intruder and a usurper: it must be either expelled or sent back to its proper place in the bodily complex. The physical body contains within itself the forces of healing, which act generally by a process called *pepsis,* which can be translated both as coction or cooking and as digestion. The physician must learn its character and role with respect to the particular patient and disease with which he is concerned. The wise physician will know when to try to aid and accelerate the peptic process and when to let it alone. The situation differs in different organisms; the physician cannot work by strict rule, but must watch for the "opportune moment" (*kairos*) when the situation is exactly right for the exercise of his art. There comes at some point the "crisis" (*krisis*), the moment at which the balance is ready to be tipped either way—so that the patient succumbs to the disproportionate mixture or so that the healthy forces begin to regain their ascendancy and the patient begins to recover. Since health was regarded as a right proportion of the elements in the organic body, and any ailment or disease as a disproportion, it was logical to regard the *krisis* as somehow marking a change, or the beginning of a change, from disproportion to proportion. Such a change involves, by Greek medical logic, a "washing away" (*katharsis, katharmos*) of the superfluous elements that caused the disproportion and the reestablishment of the new "blended maturity" (*krasis*) which is health.

But what precisely is it that by becoming excessive or defective produces variations of health? What is it that gets washed away, catharated, as a step in the curing of illness, or gets built up by proper regimen? To ask this question is to ask, in Aristotle's later terminology, about the nature of the "material cause." What are the material factors, the bodily ingredients, whose right proportion constitutes health? The Pythagorean physicians at Crotona conceived such ingredients in terms of pairs of contrary qualities, explaining health accordingly as a right proportion and blend of moisture and dryness, of cold and heat, etc., in the body. The physicians who were influenced by Empedocles, in the so-called Sicilian school of medicine, conceived their problem in terms of the four basic substances: too much earth in the human body and psyche was taken to be the cause both of constipation and of general lethargy, too much water as causing either catarrhal and other discharges or in extreme cases dropsy, too much fire as causing both bodily fever and ecstatic mental genius. Hippocrates criticized both of these medical groups for making assumptions which could not be sufficiently tested and for seeking their explanations in areas too remote from the perceptible facts of bodily life. What we actually find within the body, he said, are "flowing juices"; which he classified (on the basis of such physiological observations as it was then possible to make) as blood, yellow bile, black bile, and phlegm. The Greek word for flowing juice was *chymos,* which later got taken into the Latin language as "*humor,*" and the subsequent "doctrine of humors" in European medical theory had a long and quaint history. But the Greek word in Hippocrates' time meant simply "that which flows"; and the doctrine as he and his followers developed· it represents in essence a first step toward a science of physiological chemistry.

Although there is no means by which to identify the individual authors of the passages that follow, it is virtually certain that they were all members of the Hippocratic school of physicians, and it is not impossible that some of the writings may be the work of Hippocrates himself. In any case the basic teachings are his, or are closely similar to and developed out of the teachings which he introduced.

i. From *The Sacred Malady*

1. My topic is the so-called sacred malady [epilepsy]. In my opinion it is no more divine [in origin] or sacred [in character] than any other kind of illness. It has natural characteristics and a natural explanation; those who regard it as a divine visitation evidently do so out of ignorance and because they are struck with wonder by its strange manifestations. But if the malady is to be considered of divine origin just because it is so remarkable, then there will be not one but many sacred maladies; for I can give instances of numerous others, such as [certain kinds of] fevers, which are no less remarkable and awe-inspiring but which nobody ever considers sacred.

2. My opinion is that those who first called this particular malady sacred were like the men whom we nowadays describe as magicians, ritualists, charlatans, and exorcizists, all of whom lay claim to great piety and special wisdom. Those early would-

be healers, not knowing how to proceed, called the malady sacred in order to conceal their ignorance of it. With a persuasive line of talk they would prescribe certain purificatory rituals and this or that kind of food. Thereby if the patient recovered their reputation for cleverness was enhanced, whereas if the patient died they would blame not themselves but the gods.

3.   It seems to me that those who attempt such [magical] cures for an illness thereby implicitly admit it to be neither sacred nor of divine origin. For if they are able to cure it by purifications and similar treatments there is nothing against supposing that it can be produced in the same way; in which case its cause is not of a divine but of a human order. For it stands to reason that he who can remove an affliction by purifications and magical chants can use the same means to bring it on—an argument (logos) *which destroys the claim of divine origin.*

21.   The so-called sacred malady, then, is produced by the same type of cause as other ailments—by the things that pass into and out of our bodies, such as cold and sunlight and the inconstant restless winds. Such things are indeed divine. But therein the malady in question is no more divine than any of the others: all of them are divine and human at once. For each of them has a nature (physis) *and a power* (dynamis) *of its own, and there is none which is utterly incapable of being investigated and subjected to medical treatment.*

A physician's aim in dealing with any illness, including the one we are considering, should be to halt the conditions that promote its flourishing and to wear it down by applying remedies hostile to it. Whoever knows how, by means of regimen, to produce moisture or dryness and heat or coolness in human bodies according as the situation may require, will be able to

*cure the so-called sacred malady without resorting to purifica-
tions and magical spells—provided he can discern the "right
moment"* (kairos) *for applying specific remedies.*

ii. From *The Nature of Man*

*1. Those who are accustomed to hear speakers talk about
the nature of man independently of its relations to the medical
art will not be interested in the present account. For I am not
going to explain man as air or fire or water or earth, nor as
anything else that is not clearly descriptive of him. Such theories
I leave to those who relish them—men deficient in medical
knowledge, in my opinion. Theorists of that kind, although
they are alike in the general type of explanation they seek,
cannot agree on the right answer. Although all of them want
to find some entity by which everything in the universe can be
explained, they cannot agree on how to name that entity. One
of them calls it air, another fire, another water, and another
earth; each of them trying futilely to adduce evidence to sub-
stantiate his own account. The fact that they give different
answers, although making the same kind of inquiry, shows how
faulty their knowledge must be.*

*2. Putting aside theories of that sort, let us look at theories
held by medical physicians. Some physicians say that a man is
blood, another that he is bile, a few that he is phlegm. They
too, like the former class, add qualifications as needed. For when
they say that man is made from a single kind of element, which
they name according to their individual preference, they modify
their conception of its character* (idea) *and power* (dynamis)

according to the qualitative differences—sweet, bitter, white, black, etc.—that have to be explained by it. In my opinion such views are wrong, even though they or something very much like them are commonly held by most physicians. My own view is that if man were composed of a single kind of element he would never feel pain, since there would be no clash of differences from which pain could arise. And even if it were possible for him to receive pain, the cure would have to be of a single kind. In actuality, however, cures are of many kinds. For the body contains many ingredients, and these cause illness by heating, cooling, drying, or dampening one another contrary to nature. That is why the characteristics of illness are many and accordingly the ways of curing are many.

3.   When the body of a man dies each component must return to its own elemental nature: moist to moist, dry to dry, hot to hot, cold to cold. Such, too, is the nature of animals and of all else. All things come-to-be in that way and terminate in that way. For the nature of them is composed of such elements as those just mentioned; and each organism finally ends by passing into the elements of which it was composed.

4.   The human body contains blood, phlegm, yellow bile, and black bile: these constitute the nature of the body, and through them a man suffers pain or enjoys health. A man enjoys the most perfect health when these elements are duly proportioned to one another in power, bulk, and manner of compounding, so that they are mingled as excellently as possible. Pain is felt when one of these elements is either deficient or excessive, or when it is isolated in the body without being compounded with the others. For when a component is isolated and stands by itself it causes pain and illness, both by its ex-

cessive presence in one place and by its absence from the place it has left. Whenever more of a component flows out from the body than is necessary to get rid of superfluity, the emptying causes pain.

5. Both by convention and by nature the constituents of man remain always the same—namely, blood, phlegm, yellow bile, and black bile. By convention, because the different names are commonly employed and distinguished; by nature, because their actual characteristics are distinct, phlegm being quite unlike blood, blood unlike bile, and bile unlike phlegm. How could they be like one another when their colors appear different to the eye and their textures to the hand?

iii. From *On Ancient Medicine*

1. All who have spoken or written about medicine hitherto have set up a "special assumption" (hypo-thesis) as a basis for their investigations. Taking either one or two elements—such as heat or cold, moisture or dryness, or something else that they prefer—as their basic causal principle, they reduce to it even such humanly important concerns as disease and death, giving the same general explanation in all cases. Their method is an erroneous one, as a number of considerations make evident. The error is especially to be blamed in that it has to do with an art which is important to all men and upon the greatest occasions, so that they hold in the highest esteem those who grasp and practice the art.

That the art of medicine does exist is proved by the fact that *we recognize a distinction between inferior and outstanding practitioners. The distinction would be meaningless if there were no such thing as an art of medicine involving research and discoveries; for then all practitioners would be equally ignorant and unskilled, and treatment of the sick would be entirely a matter of chance. Such is not the case, however; for just as in all other arts the practitioners differ from one another in skill and in knowledge, so it is too in medicine.*

Accordingly I do not think that the art of medicine has any need of such unprovable assumptions as have to be introduced when one is dealing with dark mysteries concerning "what is in the sky and below the earth." In such remote matters, to be sure, an inquirer is free to make whatever assumptions he may please; and even if he has made a considerable study of the subject, there is no way in which either he or his audience can know whether the things he says are true or false, because there is no way of testing his statements by reference to anything clearly known.

2. Medicine, on the other hand, in dealing with its problems, possesses a long-established starting-point (archê) and method of procedure. Thereby it has been making many excellent discoveries for quite a while; and what remains will be discovered provided the investigator is competent and sets out from a knowledge of discoveries already known. But when anyone neglects or casts aside these requirements and seeks to make discoveries in an arbitrary way of his own, then he will only deceive himself if he claims to have discovered anything. He would be attempting the impossible, and the reason for the impossibility I shall endeavor to prove by explaining what the medical art really is. Thereby it will become clear why it is impossible to make discoveries in any other way than the one I am proposing.

It is of particular importance, I believe, that anyone who discusses the medical art should keep his discussions relevant to what concerns everyday people; for what he investigates and propounds is nothing else than the maladies that can befall anyone. And while it is not easy for ordinary folk to discover for themselves the nature of their own ailments and the reasons why they get worse or better, they are quite able to understand when someone else explains to them what has been discovered. On hearing a description of some ailment that he himself has experienced, a man has only to remember in order to understand. If, on the other hand, someone fails to affect his hearers in this way and to be understood by them, his talk is not to the point. Here, then, is a further reason why medical theory should not rely upon special assumptions.

15. As for those who depart from the method here put forward and theorize about the medical art on the basis of some special assumption or other, I am at a loss to understand what connection there is between their therapeutic practices and their special theory. For I do not think they have ever discovered an absolute hot or cold or dry or moist, since these qualities are to be found not in a pure state but always conjoined with something of another kind. In prescribing diets, I dare say, they deal with the same foods and drinks as we all use, and yet they will characterize one food as essentially hot, another as essentially cold, another as moist, another as dry. Now there is no point in simply prescribing something hot: the patient will immediately ask, "What sort of hot food?" Thereupon the physician would have either to talk nonsense or else, taking leave of his theory, to prescribe some known food. It may well be that one food is both hot and astringent, that another is hot and soothing, and that a third hot food produces belly rumblings; for there are many varieties of hot foods, often having contrary effects. Presumably it would make quite a difference whether one were to take what is hot and astringent or what is hot and soothing, as also whether one were to take something cold and astringent or something cold and soothing. Everything, so far as I know, has its specific effect—not only upon a man but even upon leather, wood, and other things less sensitive than the human body. It is not simply heat that has great power (dynamis), *but likewise such qualities as the astringent and the soothing, both when they characterize food and drink taken internally and when they characterize an ointment or a plaster applied externally.*

iv. Precepts and Aphorisms

1.   Life is short, the Art is long, opportunity is fleeting, experience precarious, judgment difficult. It is not enough for the physician to do his duty; he must also receive cooperation from the patient, from the attendants, and from external circumstances.

2.   Time is that in which there are opportune moments, and an "opportune moment" (kairos) *is that in which there is not much time. Healing goes on in time, when the moment is opportune.*

3.   The healing art involves a weaving of a knowledge of the gods into the texture of the physician's mind. The Art is held in honor by the gods, in its relations not only to bodily mishaps but to bodily conditions generally. For it is not by individual cleverness that a physician is effective. Although he has his hands on many aspects of an ailment, it may still happen that the cure comes about quite spontaneously. Of course whatever contributions the healing art is able to make should be accepted from it. But the path of wisdom in the Art lies in making final acknowledgment to Those Very Ones.

4. He who would be a healer should be guided not primarily by plausible-looking theories, but by practice combined with reason. Properly, a theory is a sort of composite memory of data that have been received by sense-perception. After the phantasms of sense have been received by us their details are sent up to the intellect, which, receiving them again and again and noting what kind they are, stores them up in itself—which is to say, remembers them. Accordingly I approve of theorizing so far as it finds its initial principle in, and draws its conclusions from, a variety of actual phenomena. For if theory has its starting-point in discoverable facts, it then partakes of the power of intellect to receive into itself particulars from various sources.

Hence we are to conceive of our nature as being set in motion and taught by various sorts of data, these working together with the intellect, as I have said, which by drawing from that source attains to truth. Where, on the other hand, the process begins not from what is clearly going on around us but from plausible counterfeit reason, it often produces a depressing and troublesome condition of mind.

5. Wisdom is admittedly of many kinds, especially as applied to life. Ordinary sorts of wisdom, by which I mean those that do not confer any real benefit upon the matters discussed,

*are evidently nothing but superfluities. In moderation they can
be tolerated, provided they do not encourage laziness and produce evil. But idleness and lack of occupation tend to slip into
evil, whereas alertness and a focussed activity of mind produce a
tensive condition which makes for the beauty of life. The former
kind of thinking, which produces no real benefits, we can ignore.
A more graceful kind is that which, whatever it may be about,
has been fashioned into an art, provided it be such an art as
will lead to wise behavior and good repute.*

6.   *In the healing art, as in wisdom generally, use is not
something that can be taught. Nature was at work before any
teaching began, and it is the part of wisdom to make adjust-
ments to the situation that nature has provided.*

7.   *In reflecting upon the matters that have been discussed
let your aim be to transfer wisdom into the healing art and the
healing art into wisdom. A physician who is a "lover of wisdom"*
(philosophos) *is equal to the gods. There is no sharp distinction
between wisdom and the healing art; for in the latter are to be
found all the qualities that constitute wisdom—disinterestedness,
conscience, modesty, reserve, sound opinion, judgment, calm,
straightforwardness, purity, a dispensing of what cleanses, freedom from superstition, and godlike superiority.*

8.   *The healing art is the noblest of all the arts; but nowadays, because of the ignorance both of those who practice it
and of those who judge them uncritically, it has fallen into very
low repute.*

*Holy things are revealed only to men who are holy. That such
things should be shown to the profane is contrary to eternal
law; they must first be initiated into the mysteries of medical
science.*

NOTES

THE PASSAGES in ancient writers from which our knowledge of Presocratic philosophy has been acquired are partly fragments, partly testimonia. The fragments are actual quotations from the Presocratic originals, so far as can be determined; the testimonia are accounts given by later ancient writers in their own words about those earlier thinkers. Occasionally it is hard to be sure whether a given passage is merely a testimonium or includes some quoted fragment, for the Greek texts had no definite way of indicating what was quoted; but usually it is possible to judge with reasonable assurance from the syntax and sometimes by comparison of passages. The Fragments in the present collection represent what appear to be, on the balance of evidence, actual quotations; the Testimonia have a supplementary value, sometimes interpreting and occasionally modifying the doctrines expressed in the Fragments.

Except for a few pages in Plato and a larger number in Aristotle, practically all the documentary evidences about the Presocratics, whether fragments or testimonia, are to be found in post-Aristotelian writings—most of them in Greek, a few in Latin. The latter, being culturally and linguistically more remote from the originals, are at best of a secondary and confirmatory value. On the other hand the Greek post-Aristotelian documents, here designated "later Greek," include a number of quotations and testimonia which, provided they are judged critically and comparatively, offer the most extensive and valuable evidence we possess regarding the Presocratic philosophies. The Hellenistic documents are of four main kinds, with of course some degree of combining and overlapping: independent treatises which make occasional and incidental references to an early philosopher; textual commentaries; compilations; and Christian writings, whether homiletic or polemical.

(1) Of the independent later philosophers the two who offer most copious evidence about the Presocratics (except for Theophrastus, to be mentioned separately) are Plutarch (46-120 A.D.) and Sextus Empiricus

(third century A.D.). Plutarch's references are to be found not so much in his well-known *Lives* as in his *Moralia*—i.e., his large collection of essays on humanistic and general subjects, available (except for one or two volumes yet to be published) in the Loeb Classical Library, generally designated "LCL." Although the essays of the *Moralia* have individual titles (sometimes rather charming ones, such as "Whether Fire or Water is the More Useful," "Whether Old Men Should Engage in Politics," "How to Listen to a Lecture," "How to Tell a Flatterer from a Friend," and so on), the references in the present book are simply to the pages of the standard edition of Plutarch by the Renaissance scholar Xylander. Since the large pages of the Xylander edition were divided into six parts marked by the first six letters of the alphabet, it has become the general practice, followed both in LCL and here, to locate the passages by page number and letter as found in that edition.

Sextus Empiricus (usually but somewhat inaccurately described as one of the late Greek sceptical philosophers) is published by LCL in four volumes. Several highly important quotations (notably the opening fragments of both Heraclitus and Parmenides) are to be found in Sextus' treatise *Against the Logicians* (Vol. II of LCL), divided into two books. In some editions these two books are published as Books VII and VIII of *Adversus Mathematicos* (which might be translated "Against the Professors," or "Against the Experts"); consequently if elsewhere a reference is made to "*Adv. Math.* VII. 132" (which contains Fr. 2 of Heraclitus) this is identical with our own reference to *Against the Logicians* I. 132.

(2)   The textual commentators who mainly concern us are Alexander of Aphrodisias (about 200 A.D.) and Simplicius (sixth century A.D.), both of whom wrote extensive commentaries on major works of Aristotle, and Proclus (410-485 A.D.) who did the same for several of Plato's dialogues. The two former writers appear in *Commentaria in Aristotelem Graeca*, and references to them will be to their writings in that edition. Simplicius' commentary on Aristotle's *Physica*, which is cited most frequently, occupies Volumes IX and X, which are paged in continuity.

(3)   Compilers are called "doxographers" when their materials consist of the opinions (*doxa*) of earlier philosophers. There were many doxographers in the centuries following Aristotle, and the most useful of their extant compilations have been published by Hermann Diels in his *Doxographi Graeci*. This invaluable reference work will be referred to as "*Dox.*"

It is now agreed by most scholars that the so-called doxographical tradition had its beginning in a lost work of Theophrastus in sixteen books, entitled *Opinions of the Physicists*. This work, which appears to have dealt comprehensively with cosmological theories prior to the writer's own day, is known to us only through quotations by later writers, notably Simplicius; Diels has arranged an ordered presentation of such quotations on pp. 475-495 of *Dox*. Theophrastus, who in 323 B.C. succeeded Aristotle as head of the Lyceum at Athens, was not only a doxographer and historian of ideas; for he produced original writings also—e.g., his *Treatise on Plants* (the first known systematic treatment of botany), *Characters* (concerning diverse types of human personality), *Metaphysics*, and *Concerning Sense-Perception*. The last named work is at once doxographical and philosophically critical, and is available to English readers in George M. Stratton's *Theophrastus and the Greek Physiological Psychology before Aristotle*.

Diogenes Laertius (third century A.D.) is at once a doxographer and a gossip. His one extant work, *Lives of the Eminent Philosophers* (two volumes in LCL) contains in nearly equal measure anecdotes about the early philosophers and the opinions which he ascribes to them. Diogenes' presentation is haphazard and uncritical; but if taken with caution it furnishes much valuable information, some of which is not available elsewhere. Because of the casual and disorderly way in which his materials are thrown together the present quotations are reordered wherever necessary for clarity.

(4)   The two Christian writers most useful in their quotations of early Greek philosophers are Clement of Alexandria (about 150-219 A.D.) and Hippolytus (died about 236 A.D.). Both of them are controversial writers with a strongly anti-pagan bias—a bias quaintly expressed in the title of Hippolytus' main work, *The Refutation of All Heresies* (abbreviated here *"Refutatio"* and elsewhere sometimes designated by its alternative title, *Philosophymena*). Hippolytus' aim, as he openly professes, is to prove that the heresies of early Christianity did not originate within Christianity itself, but were to be blamed upon the influence of various pagan philosophies by which certain Christian intellectuals had been corrupted. In carrying out his ambitious demonstration Hippolytus has frequent occasion to quote or paraphrase one or another of the Presocratic philosophers. While his paraphrases need to be judged in the light of other evidences, there is good reason to believe that his quotations are accurate (cf. the Atheneum *Heraclitus*, Appendix B, pp. 131-134); and a number of those quotations are the source of some of our most cherished Fragments.

GENERAL BIBLIOGRAPHY

MAJOR WORKS IN ENGLISH:

Bréhier, Emile, *The Hellenic Age* (Eng. tr., University of Chicago Press, 1963): Part I, The Pre-Socratics.

Burnet, John, *Early Greek Philosophy* (4th ed., 1930). Includes Burnet's translation of the Fragments. Designation: *"EGP."* Not to be confused with Burnet's *Greek Philosophy, Thales to Plato,* a book of subsidiary value.

Cleve, Felix M., *The Giants of Pre-Sophistic Philosophy,* 2 vols. (The Hague: Nijhoff, 1965).

Cornford, Francis M., "Mystery Religions and Pre-Socratic Philosophy," in *The Cambridge Ancient History ("CAH"),* Vol. IV, Chap. 15.

Fairbanks, Arthur C., *The First Philosophers of Greece* (London, 1898). The extant Fragments from Thales to Anaxagoras, in Greek and English, together with selected Testimonia in English.

Freeman, Kathleen, *Ancilla to the Pre-Socratic Philosophers* (Harvard University Press, 1948). A translation of the fragments of both major and minor philosophers as arranged in Diels' *Fragmente der Vorsokratiker.*

———, *The Pre-Socratic Philosophers: A Companion to Diels' Fragmente der Vorsokratiker* (Harvard University Press, 1947); 3rd ed., 1953 *("PSP").*

Gomperz, Theodor, *Greek Thinkers* (Eng. tr., London, 1901): Vol. I.

Guthrie, W. K. C., *A History of Greek Philosophy,* Vols. I and II (Cambridge University Press, 1962-1965). These two published volumes cover the Presocratics. Subsequent volumes will deal with later Greek philosophers.

Kirk, G. S., and J. E. Raven, *The Presocratic Philosophers* (Cambridge University Press, 1957). Selected quotations in both Greek and English of the most important Fragments and Testimonia, together with scholarly interpretations and discussions. Designation: "KR."

Nahm, Milton C., *Selections from Early Greek Philosophy* (4th edition, Appleton-Century-Crofts, 1964).

Robin, Leon, *Greek Thought* (Eng. tr., Knopf, 1928): Books I and II.

Windelband, Wilhelm, *A History of Philosophy: Greek, Roman, Medieval* (Macmillan, 1901; Harper Torchbooks, 1958): Pt. I, Chaps. 1, 2. *A History of Ancient Philosophy* (1899; Dover, 1956).

Zeller, Eduard, *A History of Greek Philosophy from the Earliest Period to the Time of Socrates* (Eng. tr. in 2 vols., London, 1881). *Outlines of the History of Greek Philosophy* (Humanities Press, 1931; Meridian Books, 1955); Introduction and First Period.

GREEK TEXTS:

Diels, Hermann (editor and translator into German), *Die Fragmente der Vorsokratiker,* revised by Walter Kranz (Zürich and Berlin, 1934, 1964). References to this revised edition are indicated by "DK." Under the name of each philosopher Diels puts the Testimonia first and labels them "A"; the Fragments follow and are labelled "B." Our references are to the "B" groups unless stated otherwise. The numbers in parentheses after the Fragments in the present volume refer to the numbers in the "B" groups in DK.

——— (editor), *Doxographi Graeci* (Berlin 1879, 1958). Designation: *"Dox."*

Commentaria in Aristotelem Graeca (Royal Prussian Academy of Letters, 1882-1907). Designation: *"Comm."*

The Loeb Classical Library (designation: "LCL"), now published by Harvard University Press, furnishes the Greek (or Latin) text with English translation of numerous ancient authors. Frequent use will be made, in particular, of Diogenes Laertius (2 vols.), Sextus Empiricus (4 vols.), and Plutarch's *Moralia* (14 vols. when completed).

DIVERSE APPROACHES:

Beare, John I., *Greek Elementary Theories of Cognition from Alcmaeon to Aristotle* (Oxford University Press, 1906; William C. Brown Reprint Library, 1964).

Cherniss, Harold, *Aristotle's Criticism of the Presocratic Philosophers* (Johns Hopkins University Press, 1935; Octagon Books, 1964).

———, "The Characteristics and Effects of Presocratic Philosophy": *Journal of the History of Ideas,* Vol. XII (1951), pp. 319-345.

Cornford, Francis M., "The Invention of Space": *Essays in Honor of Gilbert Murray* (1936).

———, *Principium Sapientiae: The Origins of Greek Philosophical Thought* (Cambridge University Press, 1945).

Heidel, W. A., "On Certain Fragments of the Presocratics": *American Academy of Arts and Sciences, Proceedings,* Vol. XLVIII (1913), pp. 681-734.

———, *"Peri Physeôs:* A Study of the Conception of Nature among the Pre-Socratics": *op. cit.,* Vol. XLV (1910), pp. 79-133.

———, "Qualitative Change in Presocratic Philosophy": *Archiv zur Geschichte der Philosophie,* Vol. XIX (1906), pp. 333-379.

Jaeger, Werner, *Paedeia: The Ideals of Greek Culture* (Eng. tr., Oxford University Press, 1945): Vol. I.

———, *The Theology of the Early Greek Philosophers* (Eng. tr., Oxford University Press, 1947).

McDiarmid, John B., "Theophrastus and the Presocratic Causes": *Harvard Studies in Classical Philosophy,* Vol. LXI (1953), pp. 85-156.

Nietzsche, Friedrich, *Philosophy in the Tragic Age of the Greeks* (Eng. tr., Regnery, 1962).

Sambursky, S., *The Physical World of the Greeks* (Eng. tr., 1956; Collier, 1962).

Sarton, George, *A History of Science: Ancient Science through the Golden Age of Greece* (Harvard University Press, 1962): Parts I, II.

Seidel, George Joseph, *Martin Heidegger and the Pre-Socratics* (University of Nebraska Press, 1964).

Snell, Bruno, *The Discovery of the Mind: Greek Origins of European Thought* (Eng. tr., Harvard University Press, 1953; Harper Torchbooks, 1960).

Stratton, George M., *Theophrastus and the Greek Physiological Psychology before Aristotle* (Macmillan, 1917; William C. Brown Reprint Library, 1964).

NOTES TO INTRODUCTION

[1] Among other instances consider the symbol of the vine (John 15: 1-5), and the idea of burial by baptism (Rom. 6:4 and Col. 2:12).

[2] Of particular interest is F. M. Cornford's discussion of the origin and significance of the ethics of observing the boundary, in his *From Religion to Philosophy*, Chaps. 1, 2.

[3] Consider especially in this connection Frs. 10 and 11 in Chap. 1, Sec. ii.

[4] Thus the French word *pouce* means both "thumb" and "inch." Webster's Dictionary (2nd ed.) reports that in certain European countries where the metric system (meters, centimeters, etc.) is employed for exact measurement there is some variation in the length of what is called (in the language of the country) a "foot."

[5] The theorem as it appears in Euclid nearly three centuries later is generalized as holding true for all triangles (not only right-angled triangles) when one side and its two adjacent angles are known.

[6] The proof of Thales' theorem is very simple. In the original square the intersecting diagonals produce four isosceles right-angled triangles; in the second square (that which is erected on a diagonal of the first square), when the diagonals and the lines connecting opposite midpoints have been drawn, there will be eight triangles, each of them identical with each of the original four.

[7] The earlier view, implying a rectilinear cosmology, is represented by Fr. 2 of Thales; the later, implying a spherical cosmology, by T 4 relating to Anaximander.

[8] Although Aristotle may be right in identifying Empedocles as the author of the philosophical doctrine of the four elements, a popular belief in the four as somehow basic ingredients in nature was much older.

[9] Diels' three-volume work is of unparalleled importance, since it provides the fullest existing collection of Presocratic fragments. Scholarly references are now almost always made to the 1934 edition of that work, drastically revised by Walter Kranz: cf. the first Diels entry in the General Bibliography, p. 279. Near the end of his life Diels declared, "I count myself fortunate that it has been my privilege to devote the best part of my powers to the Presocratics" (*Das Neue Jahrbuch für das klassische Altertum*, 1923).

CHAPTER 1

SUGGESTED READINGS:

Cornford, Francis M., *From Religion to Philosophy* (London, 1912; Harper Torchbooks, 1957).

Dodds, E. R., *The Gods of the Greeks* (University of California Press, 1951).

Farnell, L. R., *The Higher Aspects of the Greek Religion* (London, 1912).

Festugière, André-Jean, *Personal Religion among the Greeks* (University of California Press, 1954).

Greene, William C., *Moira: Fate, Good and Evil in Greek Thought* (Harvard University Press, 1944).

Guthrie, W. K. C., *The Greeks and their Gods* (Beacon Press, 1951).

————, *Orpheus and Greek Religion* (Methuen, 2nd ed., 1952).

Harrison, Jane E., *Prolegomena to the Study of Greek Religion* (Cambridge University Press, 1903; Meridian Books, 1955).

————, *Themis* (Cambridge University Press, 1912; Meridian Books, 1962).

Kerenyi, C., *The Gods of the Greeks* (Thames and Hudson, 1951; Penguin, 1958).

Nilsson, Martin P., "Early Orphism and Kindred Religious Movements": *Harvard Theological Review,* Vol. XXVIII (1935), pp. 181-230.

————, *The Mycenean-Minoan Religion and its Survival in Greek Religion* (Lund, 1950).

Macchioro, Vittorio, *From Orpheus to Paul* (Holt, 1930).

Otto, Walter F., *The Homeric Gods* (Eng. tr., Pantheon Press, 1954).

Rohde, Erwin, *Psyche: The Cult of Souls and Belief in Immortality among the Greeks* (Harcourt, Brace, 1925).

Rose, H[erbert] J., *A Handbook of Greek Mythology* (London, 1928).

Willoughby, Harold R., *Pagan Regeneration* (University of Chicago Press, 1930)

Sections i-iii

Frs. 1-4.   Of course these passages carry more meaning and interest when they are read in the rich context of the two Homeric epics. Of the many available translations, appealing differently to different readers, special mention should be made of Richmond Lattimore's freshly conceived version of *The Iliad* (University of Chicago Press, 1951). On the gods in Homer see Walter F. Otto, *op. cit.;* H. J. Rose, *Gods and Heroes of the Greeks* (Methuen, 1957).

Frs. 5, 6.   Hesiod's *Theogony* and *Works and Days* are contained in the LCL volume entitled *Hesiod, the Homeric Hymns and Homerica.* Cf. the new translation by Richmond Lattimore (University of Michigan Press, 1959).

Frs. 10, 11.   The former Fragment is from a lost play by Aeschylus, *The Danaids;* numbered Fr. 25 in the LCL edition of Aeschylus, Vol. III. The latter is from a lost play by Euripides, title unknown; quoted by Aristotle in Book VIII of *The Nicomachean Ethics:* 1155b 4. Both passages exemplify the tendency to combine ouranian and chthonic ideas in the cosmological metaphor of the marriage of sky and earth. When a widely shared metaphor persists for some time in group consciousness, and especially when it becomes associated with ritualistic observances, it tends to expand itself into a story, to make easy personifications, and thus to become a myth. Cf. Wheelwright, *Metaphor and Reality* (Indiana University Press, 1962): Chap. 7.

Frs. 12, 13.   In chthonic perspective sin tends to be conceived as pollution, vividly symbolized in the spilling of a murdered man's blood upon the land. Such sin carries its own penalty: community life is tainted and sickened, producing blight and pestilence. Release from the evil must be sought in a symbolic act of cleansing which is outwardly ritualistic and inwardly redemptive. Ritualistic lustration, ceremonies of baptism, and such casual linguistic survivals as "washing one's hands of the matter," thus appear to have had a remote chthonic origin.

Frs. 14-16.   For a brief account of Dionysus, to whom these three invocations are addressed, see Oskar Seyffert, *Dictionary of Classical Antiquities* (Meridian paperback ML 2). Fr. 14 is a translation of an ancient choral ode discovered during excavations at the ancient sacred precincts of Delphi in 1895. Cf. Theodor Gaster, *Thespis* (1950), p. 103. Frs. 15 and 16 are from Euripides' tragedy of religious violence, the title of which means "the female worshipers of Bacchus." Dionysus might be described, although inadequately, as the god of ecstatic return to nature. Hence in certain localities and in certain contexts he was identified with Bacchus (in Greek, Iacchos), the god of wine; and he was also called "Bromios," connoting the raging one.

Frs. 17, 18.   Demeter, goddess of the bounty of the earth, particularly of grain, is traditionally she who feeds man's body; here by metaphorical extension she is seen as the power and gracious intelligence that feed his soul and mind as well.

The so-called Homeric Hymn to Demeter is believed to have been written several centuries after the composition of the Homeric epics. It tells the traditional story of the goddess Demeter, whose daughter Persephone (the Proserpine of English poets) was ravished by Pluto, king of the underworld realm of the dead, and was carried away by him to his gloomy abode. Demeter, wandering in search of her daughter, came to Eleusis, where she was received hospitably by King Celeus. She rewarded him by teaching agriculture to him and his people, and by instituting the sacred ceremonies which gave eternal blessedness to the initiates.

Frs. 18-21.   Little is known about the ancient Greek mystery religions, because their secrets were carefully guarded, and such reports as have leaked out are partial and usually of a later period. Initiation into the cult was the first requisite, and it was granted only to those who showed themselves worthy and took the sacred vows, including the vow of silence about sacred matters. In Cornford's *From Religion to Philosophy* see the concluding chapter, "The Mystical Tradition." Cf. Cornford in *CAH,* Vol. XV, pp. 522-538. From a different standpoint cf. E. R. Dodds, *op. cit.:* III, "The Blessings of Madness."

Fr. 30.   The Greek word *"logos"* has rich and varying meanings, a number of which are distinguished by Guthrie, *HGP,* Vol. I, pp. 419-431. Its nearest and most usual translation is "Word," as in the opening verse of the Christian Gospel according to John. It connotes at once the moral law for mankind and the cosmic law by which events are steered. In DK it is Fr. 57 under "Epicharmus," although a doubt is there expressed as to the authorship.

Frs. 31, 32.   The religious and philosophical meaning of beginning (*archê*) and end (*teleutê* in 31, *telos* in 32) is by no means simple. In most instances *archê* carries the double meaning of a beginning and source, with temporal and causal implications, and also of explanatory principle; hence the word is usually translated "first-principle" or "starting principle" in the pages that follow. While both *telos* and *teleutê* do tend to mean "end" in the temporal sense, the former carries also some idea of inherent aim and direction, the latter an idea of fulfillment. The affinity between *archê* and *telos-teleutê* is expressed in Christian thought when God is spoken of as "the Alpha and Omega." Fr. 31 is quoted by Plato in *The Laws,* Book IV, 715E. Fr. 32 corresponds to DK Fr. 2 under "Alcmaeon."

iv. Xenophanes

SUGGESTED READINGS:

Bowra, C. M., *Problems in Greek Poetry* (Oxford University Press, 1953), Chaps. 1, 2.

Guthrie, *HGP,* Chap. 6; KR, Chap. 5; Kathleen Freeman, *PSP,* Chap. 21; Burnet, *EGP,* pp. 112-129.

Apropos of T 4, the materials taken from Diogenes Laertius are selected and reordered so as to make an intelligible arrangement; for Diogenes seems to have no idea of orderly connection. The same procedure is employed, without particular indications, in all further quotations from Diogenes.

T 5. Theophrastus, the follower of Aristotle as leader of the Peripatetic School, and himself the founder of systematic botany, wrote among other things a treatise in sixteen books entitled *Physical Opinions* or *History of Physical Opinions.* The learned commentator Simplicius (sixth century A.D.) supplies us with most of what we know about that lost work by quoting from it repeatedly in the course of commenting on Aristotle's writings.

T 8. The late Greek work entitled *History of Philosophers,* from which the present Testimonium is taken, is traditionally ascribed to Galen the physician, but there is no adequate evidence that he was really its author. The passage is preserved in Hermann Diels' *Doxographi Graeci* (hereafter *"Dox."*), p. 604.

T 9. The *Stromata* (*Miscellanies*) which in late ancient times were ascribed to Plutarch are not in his style and were almost certainly the work of another and otherwise unknown author. The passage is given in *Dox.,* p. 580.

T 10. The passage is taken from St. Hippolytus' lengthy diatribe, *The Refutation of All Heresies* (sometimes mentioned in bibliographies under its older ascribed title, *Philosophymena*); where, in the course of blaming pagan Greek writers for their allegedly bad influence upon the doctrines of the early Christian Church, he preserves many valuable quotations from them.

CHAPTER 2

SUGGESTED READINGS:

Appropriate chapters of the books listed in the General Readings (pp. 278-280), especially Guthrie, KR, Burnet, Cornford, Fuller, Robin, Windelband, Zeller.

Burch, G. B., "Anaximander the First Metaphysician": *Review of Metaphysics,* Vol. III (1949-1950), pp. 137-160.

Cornford, Francis M., "Anaximander's System": Chap. 6 of *Principium Sapientiae.*

———, "The Invention of Space": *Essays in Honor of Gilbert Murray* (1936).

Dilks, D. R., "Thales": *Classical Quarterly,* n. s., Vol. IX (1959), pp. 294-309.

Heidel, W. A., "The δίνη in Anaximander and Anaximenes": *American Philological Association, Transactions,* Vol. XL (1909), pp. 5-21.

Kahn, Charles H., *Anaximander and the Origins of Greek Cosmology* (Columbia University Press, 1960).

Kirk, G. S., "Some Problems of Anaximander": *Classical Quarterly,* n. s. Vol. V (1955), pp. 21-28.

Matson, W. I., "The Naturalism of Anaximander": *Review of Metaphysics,* Vol. VI (1952-1953), pp. 387-395.

Seligman, Paul, *The Apeiron of Anaximander* (Athlone Press, 1962).

i. Thales

Frs. 1-4. The four propositions which Aristotle attributes to Thales may with approximate accuracy be designated "Fragments," even though Aristotle's syntax does not authenticate them as verbally exact quotations. In any case the ideas are admittedly those of Thales, and the ideas are so simple and definite that there is no need to cavil over a word or two.

T 10. The two paragraphs represent two separate passages in Proclus, in both of which he draws upon Eudemus, a follower of Aristotle and author of the first systematic history of astronomy and mathematics, written about 300 B.C. In DK they are numbered A 11, 20. Another remark

which Proclus quotes from Eudemus' history credits Thales with the discovery that a line through the center of a circle divides the circle into
two equal parts. "Scientific knowledge": *theôria*.

T 11.   Simplicius, in his commentary on Aristotle's *Physica*, p. 23.

T 12.   The so-called "pseudo-Plutarch" is an anonymous doxographical writer quoted at length by Aëtius (*Dox.*, pp. 273-344) under the
name "Plutarch"; but whatever his name may have been he is clearly not
the Plutarch who wrote the *Moralia* and the *Lives*.

T 12-14.   In *Dox.*, pp. 579, 475, 301, 386.

T 15.   Simplicius, comm. on Aristotle's *De Anima*, p. 73. His reference
is to the passage in Aristotle from which T 8 is taken.

T 17-20.   In *Dox.*, pp. 276 (abridged), 376, 360, 353.

T 21, 23.   Cicero translates *archê* as *initium*, stressing the temporal aspect; Augustine more aptly as *principium*.

ii. Anaximander

Fr. 1.   Intriguing questions are raised by this unique Fragment, preserved by Simplicius in his commentary on Aristotle's *Physica*, p. 24. Cf.
note to T 6, 7.

(a) The word *apeiron* is translated by Burnet "the infinite," by Freeman "the non-limited," by others "the boundless" and even "the indefinite." Perhaps "the Qualitative Unlimited" would convey its meaning
most nearly. It might be described as a boundless reservoir of potential
qualities; Anaximander appears to have been reaching toward the idea
of potentiality, although there was as yet no word for it.

(b) Coming-to-be (*genesis*). The hyphenated coinage is necessitated
by the fact that there is no single word in English to express clearly
and accurately the idea of pure coming-into-existence—as when a light
appears out of darkness when the flint is struck. Not the word "creation,"
which connotes agency; not "becoming," which is more likely to mean
change from one state to another, rather than absolute coming-to-be. The
words "emergence" and "emerge" may please some thinkers, but they suggest to others a special philosophical theory, and they may be misleading.
The idea of stark beginning, although not the entire meaning of *genesis,*
is an essential part of it and should be clearly recognized; it does seem to
be the intended meaning here.

The opposite of coming-to-be is ceasing-to-be (*phthora*); here it seems that the English word "perish" can be employed without ambiguity.

(c) First-principle (*archê*) seems to carry the double meaning of a temporal beginning and a continuing effecting principle. The Latin word *principium* serves the same double function.

(d) Justice (*Dikê*) and the giving of satisfaction (*tisis*) express the moral or quasi-moral nature of the universe. Like a political usurper each quality that comes into existence practices injustice (*a-dikia*) by its usurpation of existence and its suppression of its opponent, as when summer heat drives out wintry cold or vice versa. Eventually in the order of time (the *taxis* of *chronos*)—or, as we more lightly say, "in the natural course of events"—the usurping quality will be overthrown and be sent down to oblivion.

T 6-8.   All are from Simplicius' commentary on the *Physica*. T 6 and 7 are on p. 24, where they surround the quotation of Fr. 1. T 8 is on p. 150, lines 22ff., where "underlying substance" represents the Greek word *hypokeimenon,* literally "the underlying."

T 9.   Simplicius on *De Caelo,* p. 202, lines 14ff. On the doctrine of innumerable worlds see Guthrie, *HGP,* pp. 106-115; KR, pp. 121-126.

T 10-17.   T 10 is in *Dox.,* p. 579; T 11, *ibid.* p. 559; T 12, p. 351; T 13, p. 494; T 14, p. 560; T 15, p. 579; T 17, p. 430.

iii. Anaximenes

Fr. 1.   As the soul (*psychê*), which is air (*aêr*), holds a man together and gives him life, so breath-wind (*pneuma*) and air hold together the universe (*kosmos*) and give it life.

T 6.   Simplicius on the *Physica,* p. 24, following T 6 and 7 in the Anaximander section.

T 9.   *Dox.,* p. 579.

T 11.   The six quotations from Aëtius are in *Dox.,* respectively on pp. 331, 377, 339, 344, 347, 352.

CHAPTER 3

SUGGESTED READINGS:

Kirk, G. S., *Heraclitus: The Cosmic Fragments* (Cambridge University Press, 1954).

Wheelwright, Philip, *Heraclitus* (Princeton University Press, 1959; in paperback, the Atheneum Publishers, 1964). The numbering of pages, Fragments, and Testimonia is the same for both editions of the book, which will here be designated the Atheneum *Heraclitus*.

An earlier book, still useful in some respects, is *The Fragments of Heraclitus of Ephesus on Nature* by G. T. W. Patrick, with a historical and critical introduction (Baltimore, 1889).

Fränkel, Hermann F., "Heraclitus on God and the Phenomenal World": *American Philological Association, Proceedings,* Vol. LXIX (1938), pp. 230-244.

———, "A Thought Pattern in Heraclitus": *American Journal of Philology,* Vol. LIX (1938).

Kirk, G. S., "Natural Change in Heraclitus": *Mind,* Vol. LX (1951).

Merlan, Philip, "Ambiguity in Heraclitus": *Actes du XIème congrès international de philosophie,* Vol. XII (1953).

Minar, F. L., "The Logos of Heraclitus": *Classical Philology,* Vol. XXXIV (1939).

Mondolfo, Rodolfo, "Evidence of Plato and Aristotle relating to the *Ekpyrosis* of Heraclitus": *Phronesis,* Vol. III (1958).

Rabinowitz, W. G., and W. I. Matson, "Heraclitus as Cosmologist": *Review of Metaphysics,* Vol. X (1956).

Vlastos, Gregory, "On Heraclitus": *American Journal of Philology,* Vol. LXXVI (1955).

Guthrie, *HGP,* Vol. I, Chap. 7; KR, Chap. 6; Burnet, *EGP,* Chap. 8; Jaeger, *Theology of the Early Greek Philosophers,* pp. 109-127.

A fuller commentary on the Heraclitean Fragments may be found in the editor's book *Heraclitus* mentioned above. Since copyright limitations prevent the repetition of the commentary here, the present set of notes is limited to certain basic explanations supplemented by some interpretations and questions which have suggested themselves subsequently to the publication of that volume. The numbering of the Fragments, and with some minor changes their translations, are the same here as in the Athe-neum *Heraclitus.*

Frs. 1, 2.   The *Logos* may be translated the Word, provided it be un-derstood as having a religious and trans-human source. The Word is also Heraclitus' word in the sense that he is its chosen spokesman; he is in the basic sense a "prophet" (*prophêtês*), "one who speaks on behalf of." The problem is discussed on pp. 21-28 of the Atheneum *Heraclitus.* Cf. Fr. 118.

Fr. 18.   The Lord of Delphi is Apollo.

Fr. 24.   The word for "time" is not the usual *chronos,* but *aeôn,* signifying a cosmological period of time, probably the long period be-tween two world conflagrations (cf. note on T 16). But to say this in the translation of the Fragment would destroy its epigrammatic brevity and flavor, so essentially a part of Heraclitus' thought.

Fr. 29.   Two interpretations are possible. Scholars who think that Heraclitus held the doctrine of cosmic cycles take the last clause as describing two temporarily distinct movements; those who think he did not hold such a doctrine interpret the kindling and extinguishing as going on simultaneously, at all times but perhaps to changing degrees. Note that the same question of interpretation may arise with regard to the next five Fragments, 30-34. The question is discussed in the Athe-neum *Heraclitus,* pp. 44-56.

Fr. 41.   The anonymous Aristotelian writer who quotes this Fragment (in *De Mundo* 401a, 11 of the Aristotelian corpus) makes it evident that by "blow" Heraclitus means the divine force of inner instinct.

Fr. 42.   The word for "meaning" here is *logos;* the Greek word is clearly being employed in a more casual sense than in Frs. 1, 2, 64, and 118.

Fr. 46.   Of the two versions Burnet argues cogently that the former is the more authentic (*EGP,* p. 138, n. 2). Even so, the imagery of light is entirely in keeping with Heraclitus' thought, and he may well have made the remark in both forms.

Fr. 50.   The sacred drink (*kykeôn,* from a verb signifying "stir up and mix") was concocted out of wine, cheese, and barley-meal. Ob-viously such a beverage could preserve its character only if stirred; the analogy suggests that souls likewise lose their character through slug-gishness.

Fr. 56.   In traditional speech "the sacred disease" meant epilepsy.

Fr. 65.   The Greek verb *haptetai* in the middle voice can mean: (1) kindle for one's own purposes, (2) kindle oneself, i.e., burst into flame, (3) attach oneself to. Heraclitus makes full and expressive use of the double ambiguity.

Fr. 66.   Of course if the remark were taken literally it would be a baffling paradox; for if immortal beings were to become mortal it would mean that they had not been truly immortal in the first place, and vice versa. But the difficulty is easily resolved; because from Homer down the word "immortals" means the gods, usually the Olympian gods. But Heraclitus denies that gods or anyone or anything else (except ongoing change in general) can be truly immortal; at most some things may last for a relatively long time.

Fr. 69.   "Guardian divinity": *daemôn*.

Fr. 74.   The pleasant anecdote is told by Aristotle (*Parts of Animals,* I. 5: 645a, 17). "Gods": the plural of *theos*. There is a good deal of overlapping between the idea of *daemones* and that of *theoi*.

Fr. 81.   There is a pun, lost in translation, between the datives "with rational awareness" and "in common": see Glossary, *xynos*. For Heraclitus an expressive pun like this is philosophically significant (cf. Fr. 115), and no doubt the present one leaves its traces in his mind in other uses of "common", as in Frs. 2, 80, and 109; perhaps also in Fr. 15, where, if Plutarch quotes correctly, the later word *koinos* is used for the idea.

Fr. 86.   Cf. G. E. Kirk, "Heraclitus and Death in Battle": *American Journal of Philology,* Vol. LXX (1949), pp. 385-411.

Fr. 111.   Presumably the "straight way" carries also the meaning of *right* way; which makes the paradox possible.

Fr. 115.   A pun here. The word *bios* means life, while the same word with a shift of accent means a bow.

Fr. 121.   In the Greek text as it has survived there is no clue to the missing word. In the Atheneum *Heraclitus,* pp. 106 and 155, several proposed solutions are considered and it is concluded that Heraclitus' intended meaning was something like "a neutral base"—probably a waxen base into which concentrated fragrances were pressed in the making of cosmetics. Cf. Plato's description of some such process in *Timaeus* 50c.

T 15.   Quoted by Simplicius in his commentary on Aristotle's *Physica,* pp. 23-24.

T 16. Conflagration: *ekpyrôsis*. Since the word appears to have been of later and probably of Stoic coinage, some scholars argue that the idea of world conflagration was a Stoic invention also. The argument may surely be challenged, since whatever language may have been employed it is easy enough for anyone, certainly for someone with the fertile imagination of Heraclitus, to envisage the idea of world cycles and of periodic destruction by fire. A good statement of objections to attributing the doctrine of *Ekpyrôsis* to Heraclitus is offered by Kirk, *Heraclitus: The Cosmic Fragments,* pp. 335-338. The opposing view is presented in Chapter 3 of the Atheneum *Heraclitus.* On the idea of cosmic cycles in general see Mircea Eliade, *The Myth of the Eternal Return* (Eng. tr. in the Bollingen Series, 1954), particularly Chapter 2, "The Regeneration of Time."

T 16, 17, 18 are respectively on pp. 283, 303, and 548 of *Dox.;* two from Aëtius, the third from Chrysippus.

T 19. There is more reason in this curious remark, that Heraclitus did not identify fire with pyramids, than may be evident at first glance. Simplicius here (p. 621 of his commentary on the *De Caelo*) is speaking about a passage in Aristotle (*De Caelo* 304a 8ff.) where, without mentioning Heraclitus, Aristotle criticizes the theory that fire is composed of pyramids. Simplicius comments that the reference is not to Heraclitus himself, for whom fire was ultimate reality and not reducible to anything else, but presumably to certain of his followers.

But why, a modern reader may want to ask, should anyone have held the theory that fire is composed of pyramids? Well, in the first place, the pyramid in question is not the familiar architectural structure with a square base, but a figure consisting of a triangular base and three equal triangular sides, in other words a regular tetrahedron. Now a tetrahedron is the simplest figure that can be constructed in three-dimensional space; moreover, of the regular solid figures the tetrahedron is the only one to have acute angles. (The square has right angles, the other regular polyhedrons have obtuse angles.) These two characteristics of the triangular pyramid—simplicity of structure and sharpness of angles—evidently led some of the neo-Heracliteans to think of that figure as having an essential affinity with fire. Fire, they seem to have argued, is the first-principle of everything and therefore somehow of special simplicity, and its "sharpness" is evident to anyone who has been burnt.

T 27-31 from Aëtius are in *Dox.,* respectively on pp. 338, 322, 331, 351, and 359.

CHAPTER 4

On the Eleatics in general there are two books in English of considerable value, although advanced in character and more fully available to readers with some knowledge of Greek: J. H. M. C. Loenen, *Parmenides, Melissus, Gorgias* (Assam, Netherlands, 1958); J. E. Raven, *Pythagoreans and Eleatics* (Cambridge University Press, 1948). Studies of the individual Eleatic philosophers are listed below by sections.

i. Parmenides

SUGGESTED READINGS:

Bowra, C. M., "The Proem of Parmenides,": Chap. 3 of *Problems of Greek Poetry* (Oxford University Press, 1953).

Havelock, Eric A., "Parmenides and Odysseus": *Harvard Studies in Classical Philology,* Vol. LXIII (1958), pp. 133ff.

Jaeger, Werner, "Parmenides' Mystery of Being": Chap. 6 of *Theology in the Early Greek Philosophers.*

Loenen, *op. cit.,* Part I.

Raven, *op. cit.,* Chap. 3.

Tarán, Leonardo, *Parmenides: A Text with Translation, Commentary and Critical Essays* (Princeton University Press, 1965). The only full volume in English that is devoted to Parmenides.

Vlastos, Gregory, "Parmenides' Theory of Knowledge": *American Philological Association, Transactions,* Vol. LXXVII (1946).

Fr. 1. It is unwise to try to interpret the symbolism of the journey too minutely; commentators who have done so have disagreed in their conclusions. Nevertheless it is well to be observant, in order that the imagery and its likely associations may work suggestively upon the mind. Especially pertinent to this Fragment are the writings by Bowra and Havelock mentioned above; also pp. 7-31 of Tarán and pp. 92-98 of Jaeger.

The goddess is called *daemôn* in the opening sentence and *thea* later on.

The "maidens who led the way" are more specifically called "hand-maidens of the sun" in the second sentence below. The plural of *kourê*, poetic form of the more familiar word *korê*, is used in both instances. As it is a function of the handmaidens of Helios to guide his chariot across the sky by day and along the highway through the underworld by night, so in the present account these same semi-divinities are guiding Parmenides' chariot along the resounding road toward the gates of dawn.

The bolts of the gates "both punish and reward," according as Justice (*Dikê*) shuts or opens them in requital of the soul's deserts.

Some have translated the Goddess's opening words as "Welcome, young man" or "Welcome, O youth," and thence have concluded that Parmenides was young when he experienced the vision. But *kouros* in the vocative, when spoken by a goddess, could have been addressed to a mortal of any age; it is the language of divinity addressing a favored mortal. We do not know at what period of Parmenides' life the vision occurred.

Right and Justice: see *Themis* and *Dikê* in the Glossary.

All but the last sentence is quoted from Sextus Empiricus, *Against the Logicians,* I. 111. Simplicius (Comm. on *De Caelo,* pp. 557-558) quotes the last two sentences together; and since their connection appears quite natural it is generally supposed that Sextus dropped the last sentence out.

Fr. 2. In Sextus Empiricus' quotation this passage follows the next to last sentence of Fr. 1. Parts of the new passage are quoted by Plato, *Sophist* 237A, Aristotle *Metaphysica* 1089a 4, and Simplicius, Comm. on the *Physica,* p. 650; but only Sextus quotes the whole of it.

Fr. 3. Some have thought that the last clause may have been aimed at Heraclitus' remark in his Fr. 31. Since Heraclitus speaks in prose and Parmenides in verse there are verbal differences, but both the main idea and the word for "scattering" are virtually the same.

Fr. 5. The word *hodos* is generally translated as "road" or "path"; in those cases where the metaphoric image seems very faint, as "way." The Greek *esti* and *ouk esti* are most nearly rendered by simply "Is" and "Is Not"; sometimes, however, for the sake of intelligible syntax the word "It" has to be supplied.

Fr. 6. From Simplicius' commentary on the *Physica,* p. 117. Tarán, *op. cit.* (pp. 61-62) inclines to the view that Parmenides' attack is aimed against Heraclitus, and that the plural words are employed to express contempt. He admits the possibility, however, that others besides Heraclitus may have been intended. Despite the legend that Heraclitus spent his last years living as a hermit, it may be that his startling paradoxes and odd reputation led various young men of Elea and elsewhere to follow his lead. Plato's reference in the *Theaetetus* to "the friends of motion" lends some semblance to the possibility.

Fr. 7.   When Simplicius in his commentary on the *Physica* (pp. 145-146) quotes this passage he adds, as continuous with it, the first two sentences of Fr. 9. See the note on that Fragment.

The present Fragment, needless to say, represents the fullest statement of Parmenides' Way of Truth that is extant. As in so many other cases we owe much to Simplicius for having preserved it. The division into five sections marked by capital letters is an editorial device for ease of reference. The corresponding lines (in DK and Tarán) are: A, lines 1-18; B, 19-25; C, 26-33; D, 34-41; E, 42-49.

B. Here the text of Simplicius is followed as edited by Diels (Simplicius, *loc. cit.*) and as carried over by him into his own earlier edition of *Die Fragmente der Vorsokratiker*. Burnet and Tarán accept the same reading. But Kranz in reediting Diels (in DK) has changed the 19th line of the passage, making the second question of Section B read, "How could it be destroyed?" But there is a sufficient logic in the passage without making so drastic an emendation.

C. Necessity (*Anangkê*) and Natural Law (*Themis*) can best be regarded as connotatively different words for what is virtually a unified idea. See Glossary for both words. Correspondingly, "in the bonds of limit" and "perfectly complete" are twin characteristics of Being; Parmenides seems to be saying that if it lacked them its lack would be unlimited and it would not then be truly Being.

D. Fate (*Moira*): see Glossary. For the purposes of the argument its meaning is not very different from that of *Anangkê* and *Themis* above, although its connotations differ widely.

Fr. 8.   For the first time in this set of Fragments the quotation marks are omitted. It may well be that the Goddess is still speaking, but there is no evidence within the Fragment itself.

Fr. 9.   The Fragment is a translation of the passage quoted by Simplicius on pp. 38-39 of his commentary on the *Physica*. On pp. 30-31 he had already quoted the same passage but with the last two lines omitted. Later, on p. 146, he quotes the first three lines of it as following immediately after Fr. 7; for which reason DK, followed by Tarán, treats Frs. 7 and 9 as forming one continuous Fragment. In view of Simplicius' varied way of handling the material there seems to be some doubt as to just how Frs. 7 and 9 were related in Parmenides' poem.

On the transition from the way of truth to the way of opinion, see KR, pp. 278-283; Tarán, Chap. 2; and for a more controversial view, Burnet *EGP*, pp. 182-187.

Fr. 10. Light, night: *phaos, nyx.* It would seem, on the testimony of Theophrastus in T 16, that light is not distinguished from fire and that night is essentially associated with earth, the former pair serving as effecting cause, the latter pair as material cause.

Fr. 13. As for the omission of quotation marks in this and later Fragments, see the note on Fr. 8.

T 16, 17. Both testimonia are from Theophrastus, quoted respectively by Alexander of Aphrodisias and by Simplicius. The former gives the title of the source work as *Concerning Physical Matters,* the latter as *History of Physics;* they may be different parts of the lost multi-volume work called *Physical Opinions.*

T 19. The quotation from Aëtius is in *Dox.,* p. 335. The word *stephanê* means usually a crown, a diadem. Its connotation is "something bright which encircles the head"; hence, by extension, a circle of fire of cosmic proportions. Cf. T 22, where Cicero uses the same Greek word.

ii. Zeno

SUGGESTED READINGS:

Bergson, Henri: *Time and Free Will* (Eng. tr., 1910), pp. 104-115; *Matter and Memory* (same, 1911), pp. 250-259; *Creative Evolution* (same, 1911), pp. 304-313.

Black, Max, "Achilles and the Tortoise": *Analysis,* Vol. XI (1950-1951), pp. 91-101. Criticisms of Black's proposed solution are published in Vols. XII, XIII, and XV of *Analysis.*

Blake, R. M., "The Paradox of Temporal Process": *Journal of Philosophy,* Vol. XXIII (1926), pp. 645-654.

Cajori, F., "The History of Zeno's Arguments on Motion": *American Mathematical Monthly,* Vol. XXII (1915), pp. 1-6; 39-47; 77-82; 109-115; 143-149; 179-186; 253-258; 292-297.

King, Hugh B., "Aristotle and the Paradoxes of Zeno": *Journal of Philosophy,* Vol. XLVI (1949), pp. 657-670.

Lee, H. D. P., *Zeno of Elea* (Cambridge University Press, 1936).

Peirce, Charles S., *Collected Papers:* Vol. II, Sec. 666; Vol. VI, Sec. 177.

Russell, Bertrand: *Our Knowledge of the External World* (London and

Chicago, 1914), pp. 165-179; *Mysticism and Logic* (London and New York, 1921), pp. 83-90; *A History of Western Philosophy* (Simon and Schuster, 1945), pp. 800-808, criticism of Bergson's solution.

Ushenko, Andrew, "Zeno's Paradoxes": *Mind,* Vol. LV (1946), pp. 151-165.

Whitehead, Alfred North: *Process and Reality* (1929), pp. 101-108; *Science and the Modern World* (1926), pp. 157-160.

Frs. 1, 2.   Preserved by Simplicius on pp. 139-140 of his commentary on the *Physica.* Fr. 1 begins at p. 140, line 29; Fr. 2-A at p. 139, line 11; Fr. 2-B at p. 141, line 1.

Fr. 3.   Quoted by Epiphanius, *Against Heresies (Dox.,* p. 590). Although DK does not include the Fragment, Epiphanius says definitely "Zeno . . . speaks as follows," and there is no clear reason to disbelieve him. Cf. DK 4, from Diogenes Laertius.

Fr. 4.   Aristotle *Physica* 210b 23. Cf. T 3. Aristotle's fuller solution, as paraphrased by Ross, is as follows: "Granted that that which is must be in something. Yet it need not be in a place; there are, as we have seen, other senses of 'in'. It may be in something as health is in warm living tissues as a state embodied in them, or as warmth itself may be in a body as a concomitant attribute. No infinite series is involved. If the place of a body were in another place just as the body is in the first place, an infinite series would result. But if the first place is in something else in a different sense of 'in', an infinite series is not involved." W. D. Ross, *Aristotle's Physics . . . with Introduction and Commentary* (Oxford University Press, 1936, 1955), p. 571.

iii. Melissus

The ten extant Fragments are preserved by Simplicius: eight of them in his commentary on the *Physica,* and two in that on the *De Caelo.*

T 2.   More than one of Aristotle's remarks about Melissus give the impression that he thought poorly of him, we do not know why. It seems doubtful that Melissus committed so crude a fallacy as this.

T 5.   Elsewhere Aristotle argues against an infinite universe on the ground that it could not have a center.

T 7.   Standing outside of the Greek language it is perhaps easier for us to see the ambiguity of *archê* than it was for the Greek thinkers, who took the conjunction of starting principle and governing principle as a matter of course.

CHAPTER 5

i. Empedocles

SUGGESTED READINGS:

Furley, D. J., "Empedocles and the Clepsydra": *Journal of Hellenic Studies*, Vol. LXXVII (1957), pp. 31-34.

Jaeger, Werner, *Theology of the Early Greek Philosophers* (1947), Chap. 8.

Kahn, C. H., "Religion and Natural Philosophy in Empedocles' Doctrine of the Soul": *Archiv zur Geschichte der Philosophie,* Vol. LXXIII (1960), pp. 3-35.

Long, H. S., "The Unity of Empedocles' Thought": *American Journal of Philology,* Vol. LXX (1949), pp. 142-158.

Pertinent chapters in KR, Burnet, Zeller, etc.

Reiche, Harald A. T., *Empedocles' Mixture, Eudoxian Astronomy and Aristotle's Connate Pneuma* (Amsterdam: Hakkert, 1960).

Frs. 6-9.   Empedocles accepts Parmenides' principle that there cannot be any coming-to-be or passing-away of what is real; therefore the changes that are observed to take place have to be explained in terms of changing relations among unchanging realities.

Frs. 12-15.   Different ways of stating or suggesting the four elements. Fire is symbolized both by shining Zeus (lord of the sparkling Grecian sky, and the sky itself) and by Hephaestus (god of fire and of the arts which need fire for their exercise); air by Hera (mythologically Zeus' wife); earth by Aidoneus (another name for Hades, both ruler of the underworld and the underworld itself); water by Nestis (a deity of the sea).

Frs. 16, 17.   Love: *Philotês*. Strife: *Neikos*. They are the rival cosmic powers, whose continual warfare, now the one winning mastery and now the other, keeps the world in ever-moving process. Cf. Fr. 31, where Aphrodite, goddess of love, symbolizes the universal power of Love itself.

Fr. 53.   The previously mentioned article by D. J. Furley is helpful to an understanding of this Fragment. "The clepsydra was a hollow vessel, covered at the top except for a narrow vent or tube which could be plugged with the thumb; the bottom was perforated to form a strainer. It was used for transferring liquids from one vessel to another. What

Empedocles describes is the normal use of the clepsydra, except that normally it would be dipped into the liquid with the vent unplugged." What, then, is the analogy between this process and human breathing? According to Professor Furley, "Empedocles' theory was that breathing in through the nose was simultaneous with breathing out through the pores, and vice versa, and that this is made possible by a sort of oscillation of the blood" (*loc. cit.*). As air enters the nose and lungs in breathing, it pushes away blood, which in turn pushes air through the pores of the skin; then as we expel our breath the reverse occurs. Cf. Plato *Timaeus* 79c.

Frs. 56-59. On Empedocles' theory of vision see John I. Beere, *op. cit.* (General Bibliography), pp. 14-23. Cf. T 36.

Fr. 59. The principle that "like perceives like"—i.e., that perception involves some kind of affinity between the sense-faculty and the object that is perceived—is complemented, not contradicted, by the principle that unlikeness and contrast must be involved in the perceptual act.

Fr. 76. Kalliopeia, or Calliopê, ("she of the fair voice") was the Muse of epic poetry.

Fr. 80. The similarity between this and Fr. 26 is obvious; but DK has established the practice of grouping the one with Empedocles' more expository writings, the other with his more rhapsodical.

Fr. 85. The passage must be understood in the light of the theory of Transmigration, and is thus a warning against animal sacrifice. The beast that is slain at the altar may be one's own deceased parent or child in a different bodily form.

Frs. 88-89. Although the divinity mentioned in Fr. 88 is presented as feminine by Plutarch (*Moralia* 998c) and Porphyry, and the divinity in Fr. 89 as masculine by Clement of Alexandria (*Stromata* III. 14), there is no reason to suppose that the difference is significant. The nature of divine forces can hardly be determined with precision!

T 16. It is clear from Aristotle's discussion in *Physica* II. 5 that he accredits Empedocles with the view that chance is an irreducible aspect of physical occurrence, not to be explained away. Cf. Fr. 62.

T 20. The idea that a distant object can only be seen if the light from it traverses the intervening space, although nowadays a commonplace, was by no means evident until someone, perhaps Empedocles, first formulated it.

T 29, 45. Simplicius quotes these two passages as fragments from Theophrastus, *Physical Opinions*.

T 31ff.   The testimonia of Aëtius are in *Dox.*, on the following pages:
T 31, p. 336; T 32, p. 287; T 33, p. 303; T 34, p. 334; T 35, p. 315;
T 37, p. 440; T 38, p. 425; T 39, p. 437; T 41, p. 389; T 42, p. 303;
T 44, p. 430; T 46, p. 369; T 47, p. 354; T 49, p. 357; T 50, p. 368.

T 36.   Greek text and English translation of the longer passage from
which this is taken are in G. M. Stratton, *op. cit.*, pp. 70-91.

T 43.   The human soul consists of various tensive relations—between
earthy and skyey influences, between discord and harmony, quickness and
sluggishness, etc.—and the varied traits of human character depend on
the proportions in which the tensively related "seeds" are mingled.

ii. Anaxagoras

SUGGESTED READINGS:

Cleve, Felix M., *The Philosophy of Anaxagoras* (Columbia University
Press, 1949).

Cornford, F. M., "Anaxagoras' Theory of Matter": *Classical Quarterly*,
Vol. XXIV (1930), pp. 83-95.

Gershenson, Daniel E., and Daniel A. Greenberg, *Anaxagoras and the
Birth of Physics* (Blaisdell, 1964).

Leon, Philip, "The Homoiomeries of Anaxagoras": *Classical Quarterly*,
Vol. XXI (1927), pp. 133ff.

Mathewson, R., "Aristotle and Anaxagoras: An Examination of F. M.
Cornford's Interpretation": *Classical Quarterly*, Vol. LII, n. s. 8
(1958), pp. 67-81.

Peck, A. L., "Anaxagoras and the Parts": *Classical Quarterly*, Vol. XX
(1926), pp. 57ff.

————, "Anaxagoras: Predication as a Problem in Physics": *Classical
Quarterly*, Vol. XXV (1931), pp. 27ff., 112ff.

Raven, J. E., "The Basis of Anaxagoras' Cosmology": *Classical Quarterly*, Vol. XLVIII, n. s. 4 (1954), pp. 123ff.

Reeser, M. E., "The Meaning of Anaxagoras": *Classical Philology*, Vol.
LV (1960), pp. 1ff.

Taylor, A. E., "On the Date of the Trial of Anaxagoras": *Classical Quarterly*, Vol. XI (1917), pp. 81ff.

Vlastos, Gregory, "The Physical Theory of Anaxagoras": *Philosophical
Review*, Vol. LIX (1950), pp. 31ff.

Fr. 3.   "A real thing" translates *chrêma;* the plural of which is translated in the next clause as "things that really are."

Fr. 5.   "Seeds": plural of *sperma.* "Of all realities": genitive plural of *chrêma.* "Composite things" translates the passive participle of *synkrinô,* of which the first-given dictionary meaning is: "separate from other matter and compounded anew." Thus the Fragment seems to draw a distinction between "realities" (*chrêmata*) and "composite things." "The seeds of all realities and all kinds of characteristics" is a literal rendering, but the meaning appears to be that the seeds *have* such characteristics; for the logical point is that the characteristics must always be in the seeds (i.e., always exist in germ, which is to say potentially) if they are ever to show themselves forth in composite things. "Ways of affecting our sensitivities": plural of *hêdonê.*

Fr. 9.   Insight into the nature of the infinitessimal, originating with Zeno or the Pythagoreans before him, here produces the realization that a large object cannot be said to contain more infinitessimal parts than a small one.

Frs. 15-20.   "Mind": *Nous.* Frs. 15, 17, 18, 19 are quoted by Simplicius (commentary on the *Physica,* p. 164 to top of 165) as belonging to one continuous passage; the division here is for greater clarity of analysis.

Fr. 18.   Pure mind produces a rotary motion. The physical rotation, which is postulated in Anaxagoras' cosmogonic theory, has its psychical counterpart in the disposition of a mind, when perfectly calm and not distracted, to think and act in the serene and balanced manner which is symbolized by the ideal center of a circle or wheel that rotates with perfect regularity.

T 8.   The word *"homoeomerês"* is now generally believed to have been coined by Aristotle. It does not appear in any of the surviving Fragments, but of course such negative evidence is not conclusive. The meaning of the word, whether first employed by Anaxagoras or by his followers or by Aristotle, is clear enough. It indicates anything of which the part is of the same character as the whole, no matter how small you divide it.

T 31.   From Theophrastus' *Physical Opinions:* quoted by Simplicius, *Commentaria,* Vol. IX, p. 47.

T 33-40.   The testimonia of Aëtius are in *Dox.* on the following pages: T 33, pp. 279-280; T 34, p. 326; T 35, p. 326, bottom; T 37, p. 351; T 38, p. 385; T 39, p. 337; T 40, p. 397.

CHAPTER 6

SUGGESTED READINGS:

Bailey, Cyril, *The Greek Atomists and Epicurus* (Oxford University Press, 1928).
Burnet, John, *EGP,* Chapter 9, "Leukippos of Miletos."
Heidel, William A., "Antecedents of Corpuscular Theories": *Harvard Studies in Classical Philology,* Vol. XXII (1911), pp. 111-172.
Vlastos, Gregory, "Ethics and Physics in Democritus": *Philosophical Review,* Vol. LIV (1945), pp. 578ff.; Vol. LV (1946), pp. 53ff.

i. Leucippus

Fr. 1. Although the single surviving Fragment of Leucippus is confined to a general statement of determinism without any mention of atomism, this deprivation is a historical accident. From many evidences it is clear that he preceded Democritus in enunciating the basic principles of the atomic theory. Burnet, *loc. cit.,* even goes so far as to treat him as the author of the entire theory and to downgrade Democritus correspondingly, but that is to go farther than the evidence warrants.

T 2. "Surface-rhythm": *rhythmos.* Evidently differences of magnitude are either ignored in the present passage or are subsumed under this category. In the next sentence Aristotle gives his own word for the idea: "shape," *schêma.*

"Inter-contact": *dia-thigê.* Aristotle's word: "arrangement," *taxis.*

"Inclination": *tropê.* Aristotle's word: "direction of turning," *thesis.*

T 5. Of the three possible birthplaces mentioned by Diogenes, Gomperz argues that Miletus is the most probable, on the ground that legendary connections with Elea and Abdera could easily have arisen from Leucippus' known relations with Zeno and Democritus respectively.

In the next paragraph what are we to make of the statement that "atoms which are like one another form particular unions"? Since it is postulated that the only differences are pure geometrical ones, the statement must refer to similarities of shape. Yet one would suppose that complementary shapes rather than similar ones would provide atoms with the means of hooking together. Does the statement reveal some lingering influence of the qualitative doctrine of "like to like"?

ii. Democritus

Fr. 6. The Greek word *skotios,* "obscure," was used, at least in ancient Crete, to describe boys before the age of puberty and initiation, in that the distinguishing character of manhood had not yet come out clearly. Thus the word carries the connotation of an immature way of thinking.

Fr. 7. The word "convention," *nomos,* is here drawn out of its usual socio-ethical context and is applied as a derogatory epithet to all acceptance of qualities other than purely geometrical ones. Sextus Empiricus (who quotes Frs. 6 and 7 in Book I, Secs. 135 and 138 of *Against the Logicians*) explains the use of the word by saying: "Perceptible objects [i.e., objects in their precise character as directly sense-perceived] are conventionally assumed and believed to be real, although in truth they are not."

Fr. 8. This charming bit of dialogue, preserved in Galen's treatise *On Empirical Medicine,* shows a side of Democritus that is too often overlooked in the usual expositions of him.

T 18. It may be surmised from this brief remark by Aristotle that Democritus may have tried to prove the existence of air from the fact that objects appear blurred at a distance.

T 31. Sextus here (*Against the Logicians* II. 6) perceives the element of abstract identity between the otherwise sharply opposed positions of Democritus and Plato: in that both of them, for different reasons and with different aims, refuse to put their trust in the warm bright world of experience, which Sextus is attempting to reaffirm; and that both of them will trust only in what they separately regard as intrinsically intelligible.

T 32, 33. Both Aëtius quotations are in *Dox.,* p. 285. Vibration: *palmos.*

T 36. The familiar Greek idea of effluences, and of imprinting the air by compressing it, must here be interpreted in terms of atomic configurations.

CHAPTER 7

SUGGESTED READINGS:

Burch, G. A., "The Counter-Earth": *Osiris,* Vol. IX (1954), pp. 267-294.

Burnet, John, *EGP,* Chapter 2.

Bywater, Ingram, "On the Fragments attributed to Philolaos the Pythagorean": *Journal of Philology,* Vol. I (1868), pp. 20-53.

Cameron, Alister, *The Pythagorean Background of the Theory of Recollection* (Menasha, Wisconsin, 1938).

Cornford, Francis M., "Mysticism and Science in the Pythagorean Tradition": *Classical Quarterly,* Vol. XVI (1922), pp. 137-150; Vol. XVII (1923), pp. 1-12.

Fritz, Kurt von, "The Discovery of Incommensurability by Hippasus of Metapontum": *Annals of Mathematics,* Vol. XLVI (1945), pp. 242-264.

————, *Pythagorean Politics in Southern Italy* (Columbia University Press, 1940).

Gomperz, Theodor, *op. cit.,* Chaps. 3-5.

Heath, Thomas L., *op. cit.,* Chap. 8.

KR, Chaps. 9, 13.

Heidel, W. A., "Pythagoras and Greek Mathematics": *American Journal of Philology,* Vol. LI (1940), pp. 1-33.

Long, H. S., *A Study of the Doctrine of Metempsychosis in Greece from Pythagoras to the Present* (Princeton University Press, 1948).

Minar, E., *Early Pythagorean Politics in Practice and Theory* (New London, Conn.: College Bookshop, 1942).

Morrison, J. S., "Pythagoras of Samos": n. s. Vol. VI (1956), pp. 135-156.

Philip, J. A., "Aristotle's Monograph *On the Pythagoreans*": *American Philological Association, Transactions,* Vol. XCIV (1963), pp. 185-198.

————, "The Biographical Tradition—Pythagoras": *ibid.,* Vol. XC (1959), pp. 185-194.

Raven, J. E., *Pythagoreans and Eleatics* (Cambridge University Press, 1948), Chaps. 1, 4.

Robin, Leon, *op. cit.,* Chap. 2: "Science as the Instrument of Moral Purification."

Santillana, G. de, and W. Pitts, "Philolaos in Limbo, or: What Happened to the Pythagoreans?": *Isis,* Vol. XLII (1951), pp. 112-120.

Sarton, George, *op. cit.,* Chap. 7.

Stapleton, H. E., "Ancient and Modern Aspects of Pythagoreanism": *Osiris,* Vol. XIII (1958), pp. 12-53.

Waerden, B. L. van der, *Science Awakened* (Oxford University Press, 1961), Chap. 4: "The Age of Thales and Pythagoras."

i. Aspects of the Doctrine

T 2. Simmias, according to Plato's statement in the *Phaedo,* was or had been a pupil of the Pythagorean Philolaus; here he speaks of a doctrinal inconsistency, which may have been raised by Philolaus or may have been raised by Plato against him. The Pythagoreans believed the soul to be immortal; they also held, or some of them did, that the soul is a blending (*krasis*) and attunement (*harmonia*) between opposed physical qualities. Are these two conceptions of the soul consistent? "Tensive relation" translates the passive participle of *ekteinô.* More literally: "that the body is in a state of tension and is held together by the hot and the cold," etc.

T 6. The statement that the even is limited and the odd unlimited will make sense if it is remembered that the two predicates carry the added connotations of "definite" and "indefinite" respectively. See T 11 and its note. The statement that unity consists of both even and odd is explained, after a fashion, by T 34.

Alcmaeon of Crotona was a physician at the medical school of Crotona. Although not a member of the Pythagorean brotherhood he was on friendly terms with it, dedicating his book to three of its members. Cf. KR, pp. 232-235.

T 7. "Visible heaven": *ouranos.* In some contexts (e.g., T 11) it is translated "heavenly vault." Earlier in the *Metaphysics* Aristotle asks critically: "But how can qualities such as white, sweet, hot, and so on ever possibly be numbers?" (1029b 15).

T 8. The Greek text as it stands, after saying that the limited and the unlimited are not merely attributes or properties of something else, concludes the sentence by saying that the unlimited and the One are the *ousia,* the real subject of whatever is predicated. In order to make sense of the passage it seems necessary to assume that this last statement refers to the limited also. What the passage might then be saying is that both the One and the primal duality of limited-vs.-unlimited are the implicit subject (*ousia*) of every real proposition, and therefore the implicit substance (*ousia*) underlying every situation.

In Aristotle's own philosophy the two meanings of *ousia*—what may be described approximately as the grammatical and the metaphysical— are treated as inseparable aspects of a single large conception. In its grammatical aspect *ousia* is the natural subject of a sentence; in its metaphysical aspect it is a substance or thing which undergoes changes of properties but remains "substantially" the same. An inference from the first to the second meaning seemed more natural and plausible to the ancient Greeks than it does to us.

T 9.   The distinction between a "mathematical" (*mathêmatikos*) number and an "arithmetical" (*arithmêtikos*) number plays an essential part in Aristotle's criticism of Pythagorean number-theory. The former is conceived as consisting of spatially extended units, the latter as consisting of abstractly arithmetical units—i.e., units which can be postulated for the sake of counting. The distinction is employed when, a little later, Aristotle criticizes the Pythagorean theory as follows:

"It makes the impossible supposition that physical bodies are composed of numbers which are 'mathematical' [instead of perceiving that they are arithmetical]. For to speak of indivisible magnitudes is logically false: no matter how far we push the notion of very small magnitudes, we never get down to absolute units; and conversely if we postulate indivisible units they cannot be magnitudes" (1083b 12).

When number is conceived arithmetically it is conceived as consisting of postulated units; and the Pythagoreans err by identifying number in this conceptual sense with actually existing things. That is what they do when they speak of propositions about numbers as if they were actual descriptions of bodies, Aristotle declares.

T 11.   In order to see the point of the second paragraph, (1) refer to the diagrams and explanation on p. 204 and (2) keep in mind that limited and unlimited connote respectively *definite* and *indefinite*. Now when the gnomon builds up a number series by starting from an initial One, it does so by adding successive *odd* numbers (3, 5, 7, etc.) and it thereby produces perfect squares (4, 9, 16, etc.) which are "definite-limited" in that they maintain always the same form. But when the gnomon starts out from an initial Two, it proceeds by adding successive *even* numbers (4, 6, 8, etc.) and it thereby produces a series of "oblong" numbers (6, 12, 20, etc.). Arithmetically an oblong number is a number of the form $n(n + 1)$—i.e., the product of any number multiplied by its immediate successor. Since the series of oblong numbers approaches the condition of the square without ever reaching it, the Pythagoreans described the series, and hence the even numbers producing it, as *apeiron* (indefinite and unlimited). By contrast, the series of squares is definite ("limited") since the form of the square is always the same; consequently the odd numbers which successively produce the series of squares are also considered definite-limited. By Pythagorean logic, odd numbers are therefore masculine, even numbers are feminine.

T 15-16.   On the theory of the counter-earth see G. A. Burch, "The Counter Earth": *Osiris,* Vol. IX (1954), pp. 267-294. Since the central fire and the counter-earth are never seen, the Pythagoreans had to suppose that our earth must revolve and rotate at the same speed, so as to keep its inhabited face (the only inhabited face then known) always turned away from the center. But such behavior would not be unique, for the moon observably behaves in the same manner with respect to the earth. Indeed, is it not possible that lunar observations helped to suggest the theory in the first place?

T 24.   Iamblichus was a late Pythagorean philosopher, who died soon after 330 A.D. The incidents which he narrates in his *Life of Pythagoras* need to be taken with caution, for he makes no effort to distinguish fact from legend. But there is no reason to doubt his account of Pythagorean educational methods and daily ways of living.

T 25ff.   Vol. XII of the Oxford University Press edition of Aristotle in English translation is entitled "Selected Fragments" (1952), and pp. 134-146 contain Sir David Ross's collection of fragments which either quote from or refer to Aristotle's lost work *On the Pythagoreans.* T 25 is taken from Fr. 3 of that collection; T 26 from Fr. 1; T 31 from Fr. 11; T 34 from Fr. 9; T 37 from Fr. 16.

T 35.   DK, A (Testimonia), 13.

ii. The Pythagorean Symbola

The interpretations that follow are based, so far as possible, on explanations offered by later Greek writers in the Pythagorean tradition (like Iamblichus) or friendly to it (like Porphyry).

S 1-3.   There is no difficulty about these, since the symbolic meaning of balance, of privacy, and of taking up a burden have become commonplace.

S 4.   The bushel measure, of grain or the like, represents one's possessions. Don't cling to them.

S 5.   The crown has been interpreted as representing established political authority, and also as referring to the leader of a religious banquet, who was crowned with laurel leaves.

S 6.   Two proposed meanings, an ethical and a metaphysical: (i) Don't get into altercations with wrathful men; (ii) Don't falsify the unity of Being by conceptually chopping it into parts.

S 7.   The Pythagoreans obeyed this prohibition literally, as various legends attest, and even to the extent of refusing to walk where beans were growing. Whatever the meaning may have been in early Pythagorean times, it was too sacred to be divulged. Later speculations as to the meaning of the taboo are so diverse and conflicting that they have no value as evidence.

S 8.   Cf. Jesus' words in *Matthew* 5: 13.

S 9.   Don't sully the sources of spiritual regeneration.

S 10.   Don't perform vulgar actions in the presence of what is holy.

S 11.   Don't sully a man's past reputation.

S 12.   Swallows symbolized idle chatter.

S 13.   Since Dionysus was, in part, a calf-god or bull-god, it may be that to step over the tether referred to transgressing Dionysian religious ordinances.

S 14, 15, 16.   In addition to their plain meanings these precepts were intended to convey the idea that on the threshold of dying (i.e., of entering into a new life) one should not cling to the present life.

S 17.   Don't seek death (the cypress tree) permaturely nor seek to know its mysteries (the closed chest).

S 18.   Don't confine your mind and spirit to narrow boundaries.

S 19.   Harmony within the individual singer is not enough; we should become attuned also with the larger harmonies of the cosmos—with the Music of the Spheres.

S 20.   Do not make a public display of your religion.

S 21.   When you worship the gods let it be with joyful freedom and by your own decision. The handle of the cup is that part of it where one can keep firmest control.

S 22.   Engage in religious worship only when you have brought your thoughts and emotions into order.

S 23. The symbolic importance of the cock in religious and intellectual history appears to have been derived from three familiar characteristics: (i) his commanding way with the hens, making him a symbol
of generative potency and hence (by usual mytho-religious logic) of spiritual regeneration; (ii) his daily act of ushering forth the dawn by his
crowing; (iii) his red crown, suggesting both royalty and the potencies
associated with blood.

S 24, 25. Both fire and wind can represent the quickening, regener-
ative potencies of the spirit.

iii. The Golden Verses

Although the Golden Verses were not written until somewhat later
than the period under review, they represent the main ethical teachings
of earlier and later Pythagoreanism alike.

Vs. 2. The following form of the Pythagorean oath has been preserved: "I swear by Him who has revealed the Tetractys to men's souls—
by Him in whom is the source and root of eternal nature." What the
content of the oath was we do not know, except that it contained a
promise not to reveal the holy secrets of the Brotherhood.

Hierocles, a later Pythagorean who composed a long commentary on
the Golden Verses, writes: "The mortal oath, which is employed by men,
is to be reverenced as the image of the Oath itself. To reverence the
Oath is to do all in one's power to understand the governing laws of
the universe and to endeavor to preserve harmony and order throughout."

Vss. 1, 3, 4. The Pythagoreans held that emanating from ultimate
Godhead, which is ultimate Reality, there are three types of trans-human
being: gods, "heroes," and daemons. The gods are described in the
Verses by the traditional Homeric epithet "immortal," although Hierocles
declares them to be the highest of *created* beings. They are highest, he
explains, in that they are the powers who preserve and sustain the universe, although they did not create it.

Some Pythagorean accounts set the terrestrial daemons higher than
the heroes, but the order of the Golden Verses is followed here. The
daemons are spirits of light who stir men's souls to thoughts and acts
of goodness; they are described as terrestrial in that they are connected
with human deeds and earthly affairs, as the gods are not. The heroes
are a higher order of being than the English word "hero" implies. A

man who is of heroic stature in human life was believed by the Pythagoreans to be but an image of the true Heroes, who are superhuman and disembodied. Hierocles describes them as masters of wisdom and models of truth and excellence.

Vss. 61, 62.   "The daemon to be invoked is one's own essential self, for to see and know it is to be freed from all evils." (Hierocles)

Vs. 66.   "Purifications are divided into two parts, the one concerned with the physical body, the other with the luminous body. Purification of the former kind is accomplished by diet and by the entire management and usage of the mortal body; purification of the latter kind involves mathematical science, medical science, and religious ceremony." (Hierocles)

iv. Philolaus

Fr. 1.   "Fitted together and harmonized" translates the passive of the verb *harmazo,* which carries both connotations. The coupling of the English words "unlimited" and "limiting" corresponds to the coupling of passive and active forms in the Greek.

Fr. 2.   In other words, if all things were limiting, there would be nothing to connect one with another, and hence nothing would be intelligible; whereas if all things were unlimited, there would be no discrimination of this from that, and so again nothing would be intelligible. Either concept alone is impossible, and consequently both concepts are indispensable. In Fr. 3 Iamblichus confirms the second half of the argument.

Fr. 12.   "The ship's hull" would seem to be a metaphor to express the concept of "that which contains the four elements." Cf. "the hearth" in Fr. 8. Beneath the difference of imagistic vehicles there is an underlying congruence of meaning.

Frs. 14, 15.   Both Fragments are preserved only in Latin; DK in listing them casts doubt on their genuineness. But although they are known only in translation, the ideas are Pythagorean. The first part of each quotation has the force of an epigram: (14) *Anima inditur corpori per numerum;* (15) *Diligitur corpus ab anima, quia sine eo non potest uti sensibus.*

CHAPTER 8

SUGGESTED READINGS:

Burnet, John, *Early Greek Philosophy, Thales to Plato,* Chap. 7. Burnet's more frequently cited *EGP* does not cover the Sophists.

Davison, J. A., "Protagoras, Democritus, and Anaxagoras": *Classical Quarterly,* Vol. XLVII (1953), pp. 33-45.

Freeman, Kathleen, *The Pre-Socratic Philosophers,* pp. 343-367.

Gomperz, Theodor, *op. cit.,* Book III, Chaps. 5-6.

Grote, George, *A History of Greece* (1846-1856), Vol. VIII.

Jaeger, Werner, *Paedeia,* Vol. I, pp. 286-331.

————, *Theology in the Early Greek Philosophers,* Chap. 10.

Kerferd, G. B., "Protagoras' Doctrine of Justice and Virtue in the *Protagoras* of Plato": *Journal of Hellenic Studies,* Vol. LXXIII(1953), pp. 42-45.

Levi, Adolfo, "Studies in Protagoras": *Philosophy,* Vol. XV (1940), pp. 147-179.

Loenen, Dirk, *Protagoras and the Greek Community* (Amsterdam, 1941).

Schiller, F. C. S., "The Humanism of Protagoras": *Mind,* n. s. Vol. XX (1911), pp. 181-196.

Segal, Charles P., "Gorgias and the Psychology of the Logos": *Harvard Studies in Classical Philology,* Vol. LXVI (1962), pp. 99-155.

Sidgwick, H., "The Sophists": *Journal of Philology,* Vol. IV (1872), pp. 228-307; Vol. V (1873), pp. 66-80.

Stallknecht, Newton P., "Protagoras and his Circle": *Journal of Philosophy,* Vol. XXXV (1938), pp. 39-45.

Untersteiner, Mario, *The Sophists,* translated by Kathleen Freeman (Oxford: Blackwell, 1954).

i. Protagoras

Fr. 1. This most famous of Protagoras' sayings is quoted once by Plato, twice by Sextus Empiricus. Plato (*Theaetetus* 152A) puts the statement into indirect discourse (subject accusative and verb infinitive); Sextus does the same in his essay on Pyrrhus (I. 216), but in *Against the Logicians* (I. 389) he sets it down as a direct quotation in the indicative. The translation in the present Fragment 1 steers as close to the Greek as possible. An alternative translation, freer and perhaps more suggestive, might be: "Man is the measure of all things—of whatever is and of the fact that it is; of whatever is not and of the fact that it is not."

Frs. 2, 3.   Although DK lists these two passages as testimonia (A 14) rather than quotations, there appears to be reasonable ground for taking them as offering Protagoras' own words, or something very close to them. Sextus Empiricus, after announcing that he will "commensurately unfold" Protagoras' views in order to show how they differ from the scepticism of Pyrrho, introduces both fragments by "he says" (*Outlines of Pyrrhonism* I. 217-218).

Fr. 4.   "Natural endowment": *physis.* "Self-discipline": *askêsis.*

Fr. 6.   What happened to Protagoras after making such unpopular remarks about the gods is told by Diogenes Laertius in T 10 and by Philostratus in T 11.

T 10.   Diogenes leaves the story of Protagoras and Euathlus half untold. The complete argument, as told by Apuleius, is in T 13.

T 11.   Philostratus' book *Lives of the Sophists,* written shortly after 300 A.D., is not as useful for our purposes as it sounds. The accounts of Gorgias and Protagoras (that is the order in which Philostratus puts them) are brief, and are reproduced here in full; most of the book deals with sophists of later generations, generally unknown except for what Philostratus tells about them. The "long myth" is evidently the tale of Prometheus and Epimetheus in Plato's *Protagoras,* 320Dff.

T 13.   Apuleius' *Florida* in English is contained in *The Works of Apuleius* (London, 1876). Apuleius goes on to comment: "When those sophists wrangle among themselves, don't they seem to you like burrs rolled together by the wind, mutually sticking one another with their prickles? Let us leave to the crafty and avaricious the tale of Protagoras' fee, and pass on." Cf. Aulus Gellius *Noctes Atticae* (LCL) V. 10.

ii. Gorgias

Fr. 6.   The word *"kosmos"* in this context is impossible to translate adequately. It connotes both order and jewelled ornament. Gorgias is thus enabled to say succinctly that courage is at once a city's principle of order and its gem-like excellence.

Frs. 7-10.   These four passages are taken from Gorgias' connected rhetorical essay usually called *The Encomium of Helen.* As readers of the *Iliad* know, Queen Helen's desertion of her royal husband Menelaus and her flight to Troy with young Prince Paris were the legendary cause of the Trojan War. Helen had long been regarded as an archetype of glamorous but wicked beauty, responsible for the dreadful ten years' war and the deaths of many heroes. Gorgias, in the essay from which these excerpts are taken, employs his argumentative skill to challenge the traditional judgment and to absolve the errant lady from blame.

Fr. 11.   Although DK lists this among the doubtful fragments, there seems to be no good reason for doing so. The Vatican manuscript from which DK quotes the passage introduces it with the plain words, "Gorgias the sophist says"; and the light wit is surely in character. Miss Freeman, in the *Ancilla,* despite her general adherence to DK, wisely accepts and includes it.

T 3.   Eristical argument has as its aim the refutation of an opponent, and is not possible without the existence, actual or assumed, of an opponent. In a way, therefore, it is a special form of rhetoric, which is the employment of language in order to establish a position and sway opinions. It was customary, however, to distinguish them as two different types of method.

T 5.   In ancient legend Philomela had been transformed into a swallow. Theater, for the Greeks, involved the use of masks; and Gorgias' quick wit in an unpleasant situation treated the swallow as virtually the mask of Philomela; hence his sardonic remark was effectively theatrical (*tragikos*). After the present passage Aristotle adds his own dry comment: "It was no disgrace for a bird to have done it, but for a maiden it was." And a little later (*Rhetorikê* 1419b 2): "Some jests are becoming to a gentlemen, others are not; take care to choose such as are becoming to yourself!"

T 7.   See note on Protagoras T 11.

CHAPTER 9

SUGGESTED READINGS :

The extant writings of Hippocrates, the Greek text with an English translation by W. H. S. Jones, is published in the Loeb Classical Library in four volumes. Vol. IV contains also the Fragments of Heraclitus, in DK's arrangement and with Jones' translation.

A good selection, comprising the writings of likeliest general interest, in English only, is published as *The Medical Works of Hippocrates,* translated by John Chadwick and W. N. Mann (Oxford: Blackwell Scientific Publications; and Springfield, Illinois: Charles C. Thomas, 1950).

Edelstein, Ludwig, "Greek Medicine in its Relation to Religion and Magic": *Institute of the History of Medicine,* Vol. V (1937), pp. 201ff.

Gillespie, C. M., "On εἶδος and ἰδέα in Hippocrates": *Classical Quarterly,* Vol. VI (1912), pp. 179-203.

Heidel, William A., *Hippocratic Medicine, its Spirit and Method* (Columbia University Press, 1941).

Jones, W. H. S., *Philosophy and Ancient Medicine* (Johns Hopkins Press, 1946). Greek text and a translation (revised subsequently to the publication of the LCL volume) of *On Ancient Medicine;* preceded by a historical sketch of early Greek medicine.

Longrigg, James, "Philosophy and Medicine": *Harvard Studies in Classical Philology,* Vol. LXVII (1963), pp. 147-175.

Moon, Robert O., *Hippocrates and his Sources in Relation to the Philosophy of their Time* (Longmans, 1923).

Naylor, John, "Luke the Physician and Ancient Medicine": *Hibbert Journal,* Vol. VIII (1909), pp. 28-46.

Temkin, Owsei, "Greek Medicine as Science and Craft": *Isis,* Vol. XLIV (1953), pp. 213-225.

i. The Sacred Malady

"The sacred malady" was the name traditionally given to epilepsy. Heraclitus (Fr. 56) has that identification in mind when he remarks ironically that the real "sacred disease," which lies beyond the skill of any physician to cure, is bigotry.

Naylor, *op. cit.,* characterizes *The Sacred Malady* as "a masterpiece of scientific sanity; broad in outlook, keen and ironical in argument, and humane in spirit."

iii. On Ancient Medicine

The Greek word *"hypothesis"* does not mean hypothesis in the sense of a tentative explanation to be tested by further observation and experiment. Etymologically it means "set down under"; thus it denotes a prejudiced assumption. Isaac Newton, writing in Latin, later employed the word in the ancient sense when he made his celebrated statement, *"Hypotheses non fingo,"* "I do not make—"; which would have been an absurd statement for a scientist to make if the word had been used in the modern sense.

iv. Precepts and Aphorisms

Aphorism 1:   "The Art" refers, of course, to the art of medicine.

Aphorism 8:   The second paragraph imitates the language and tone of the mystery religions.

APPENDIX: THE PHYSICIAN'S OATH

I swear by Apollo the Physician, by Asclepius, by the powers of Health and Healing, and by all the gods and goddesses, making them my examiners, that I will keep this Oath and this Covenant, both in letter and in spirit, to the best of my ability and judgment.

I will respect my teacher in the Art [of medicine] no less than I do my parents; sharing my life with him, supporting him with money when he needs it, and regarding his sons as my brothers, teaching them the Art, if they wish to learn it, without asking a fee or anything else in return. But while I may hand on the precepts and the oral and written teachings to my sons and to the sons of my teacher, as well as to apprenticed students who have taken the Oath, I will not do so to anyone else.

I will prescribe dietary regimen for the benefit of the sick, to the best of my ability and judgment, and never with a view to injuring or wronging them.

I will not administer a poison to anyone if I am asked to do so, nor will I suggest such a thing.

Similarly, I will not give an abortive remedy to a woman.

I will pursue my life and my practice in a pure and holy manner.

I will not cut into my patients, not even if they are suffering from the stone, but will turn over such cases to those who are skilled in handling them.

On entering any house I will go for the purpose of helping the sick, and will abstain from all intentional wrong-doing and harm. Nor will I indulge there in carnal intercourse with either women or men, whether they be free persons or slaves.

Whatever I see or hear that ought not to be divulged, whether it comes to me in my professional or in my private capacity, I will not tell to anyone, but will keep silent about it.

If, then, I am faithful to this Oath and do not violate it, may I enjoy, both in my life and in my art, good repute among men for all time; but if I break the Oath and swear falsely, may the opposite befall me.

Although this famous Oath has traditionally been called "the Hippocratic Oath," there is no real evidence as to its source. The traditional name proves nothing, since in ancient times an anonymous document was frequently connected with a well-known name. Ludwig Edelstein in his study, *The Hippocratic Oath* (Johns Hopkins Press, 1943), has adduced strong reasons, from a study of the document itself, for holding it to be more Pythagorean than Hippocratic in character. The relation between the fourth and fifth paragraphs (expressed by "similarly," *homoiôs*) becomes more intelligible on the Pythagorean hypothesis. On Professor Edelstein's interpretation the fourth paragraph refers to a kind of situation that must have arisen frequently in ancient Greece, when effective medical knowledge was comparatively sparse—a situation in which a suffering patient, seeing no hope of a cure, sought relief through death and asked his physician for an effective poison. In general there was no moral disapproval in Greece either of suicide or of abortion. There is no evidence whatever, outside of the present Oath, that Hippocrates or his disciples entertained such disapproval. But the Pythagoreans did disapprove, mainly because of their belief in reincarnation. To destroy life either at its beginning by abortion or at its end by suicide, they believed, impedes the soul's pilgrimage through many lives toward self-perfection. In addition, the stress on brotherhood among initiates and the importance of silence are typical Pythagorean teachings. While such evidences are by no means conclusive, and the authorship of the Oath cannot be definitely assigned, there is good reason at least, in view of these and other considerations adduced by Edelstein, to regard the Pythagorean hypothesis as deserving of consideration.

GLOSSARY
of Latinized Greek Words

WORDS ARE LISTED alphabetically according to their Latin-English transliterations, not in all cases according to the Greek initial letters. As hitherto, a circumflex is placed over *e* and *o* in the transliterated words when the Greek vowel is long— i.e., *êta* or *ômega* as distinguished from *epsilon* and *omikron*.

Whereas full Latinization would require changing the Greek *-os* and *-ôn* (as masculine endings), *ai* (when a diphthong), *u*, and *k* to the Latin forms *-us, -o, ae, y,* and *c* respectively, such changes are made sparingly here, in order to preserve where possible the tone of the Greek. While the familiar Latin spelling is used for such words as *Bacchus, Dionysus,* and *aethêr,* the Greek spelling is more generally preserved, as in *kairos* and *kalos.*

aeôn: αἰών: a period of time, an *age,* an *era.* Cosmologically it signifies the vast period of time between two world dissolutions.

aêr: ἀήρ: the *lower air* that surrounds the earth; the *atmosphere.* To be distinguished from *aether.*

aesthêsis: αἴσθησις: *perception* by the senses; *sense-impression.* Its adjective is *aesthêtikos.*

aethêr: αἰθήρ: the pure *upper air;* the sparkling blue *sky.*

Aisa: Αἶσα: a synonym of *Moira.*

aitia, aition: αἴτια, αἴτιον: cause. The original meaning was "guilty of," "responsible for." Although the idea of guilt is no longer present in the word in later presocratic times, a generalized telic idea of responsibility lingers on. Just how far *aitia* emphasizes an effecting cause, and how far a telic pull, must be judged from the particular instance.

anathymiasis: ἀναθυμίασις. No single English word conveys the

317

full idea. The word denotes the cosmological "upward" process, the three phases of which are melting (earth turning into water), evaporation (water into air), and conflagration (air into fire). Cf. *ekpyrôsis*.

anangkê: ἀνάγκη: *necessity,* often with the connotation of violence and metallic hardness. Since the *g* before *k* is pronounced like *ng*, the resultant metallic sound is iconically functional. Philosophically the word refers to whatever opposes human purpose and is ungovernable by it. Cf. *tychê*.

anemos: ἄνεμος: *wind, breeze; breath.* Related to Latin *anima*.

apeiron: ἄπειρον: the *boundless,* the *infinite.* Except perhaps in Zeno and the atomists it has some qualitative reference: it is the *qualitatively unlimited.* Sometimes it blends this meaning with that of *indefinite, indeterminate.*

Aphroditê: 'Αφροδίτη. By derivation, "born of the foam"; hence the myth that she was born from the sea. She was the goddess of sexual love—principally of its delights, less frequently of its productive consequences.

Apollo: 'Απόλλων. He was variously god of the sun, of soothsaying, of archery, of music and song, and of medicine. The sun's rays are indicated by his bright flowing hair and by his arrows. Although originally independent of Delphi he became associated with it, and a temple was erected there in his name. By Socrates' time it had become customary (as Plato records in the *Apologia*) to make pilgrimages to it in order to seek advice and information from Apollo's oracle.

archê: ἀρχή. Since the word combines the ideas of *beginning* and *principle*—i.e., of temporal and logical priority, of source and explanation—it is here usually translated *first-principle.*

Arês: Ἄρης. The god of war—both of discord and of martial bravery. Roughly equivalent to the Roman god Mars.

aretê: ἀρετή: *specific excellence,* the proper *virtue* of a person or thing as determined by its nature.

Atê: Ἄτη. As a common noun it refers to a blinding of the judgment by passion, infatuation, or stubbornness, also to the rash actions that result. Personified Atê is a dreadful goddess who leads men to self-destruction and who has power even over her father Zeus.

atomos, atomon: ἄτομος, ἄτομον. Feminine and neuter forms of an adjective signifying "uncut"; hence, that which is *uncuttable, indivisible.* Democritus employs both forms; with the former the noun *ousia* is probably implicit.

Bacchus: Ἴακχος. His name having derived from a verb meaning "to shout," he was god of festal song, hence of wine and good cheer.

bios: βίος, βιός: *life* and *bow* respectively.

Bromius: Βρόμιος: one of the epithets of Dionysus. As an adjective it connotes emotional vehemence.

catharsis; clepsydra; cosmos: see the corresponding word spelled with *k-.*

chrêmata: χρήματα (plural): *goods, merchandise, paraphernalia, inanimate things.*

chthôn: χθών: *earth.* In religious perspective it connotes the maternal and depth properties of earth, as containing the womb of life, from which all living organisms have sprung and to which they must return.

chymos: χυμός: *juice.* In Hippocratic medicine it means a *humor*—i.e., one of the four basic liquid elements in the human body.

daemôn: δαίμων: *spirit, demigod.* Can be either masculine or feminine. Like the Latin word *genius* it may also have a

more personal reference, signifying one's guardian spirit.
In general *daemones* are spiritual powers superior to men
but inferior to the gods.

Dêmêtêr: Δημήτηρ. Goddess of agriculture, whose best known
religious symbol was the sheaf of grain. Cf. the Roman
goddess Ceres.

diakrisis: διάκρισις: *separation.* The logical contrary of *synkrisis.*

dialektikê: διαλεκτική: *dialectic,* the art of reasoning by discussion (the noun *technê* being understood). Plato distinguishes dialectic as discussion in pursuit of truth from
eristic (*eristikê*) which is disputation for the sake of winning an argument .

dikê: δίκη: *right; law; justice.* Sometimes personified as a
goddess.

Dionysus: Διόνυσος. The god of vibrant nature and of the
quickening pulse of animal life. The cult of Dionysus
spread from Thrace to Greece, where Dionysus was sometimes merged with Bacchus, sometimes with Orpheus.

doxa: δόξα: opinion. *Doxographi:* those late Greek writers,
such as Aëtius, whose writings were entirely or mostly
compilations of earlier men's opinions.

dynamis: δύναμις: *power; potentiality.*

eidos: εἶδος: *form.* Concretely it may signify actual shape;
abstractly, conceptual intelligibility. In Chapter 7 at the
end of T 11 both meanings are involved; for the failure of
the series of oblongs to preserve a single geometrical shape
is taken to mean that the series is "feminine"—i.e., conceptually indeterminate and unlimited.

ekpyrôsis: ἐκπύρωσις: *conflagration.* Particularly the cosmological process, occurring at vast intervals of time, wherein
all things dissolve into flame.

ekteinô: ἐκτείνω (verb): *stretch out; be in tension.*

epicheirêma: ἐπιχείρημα. In Thucydides and Xenophon it means a military undertaking; in Zeno, a form of argument which proceeds by reducing an opponent's thesis to absurdity.

Erebus: Ἔρεβος. A place of nether darkness, and the deity of that place.

Erinys, plural *Erinyes:* Ἐρινύς, Ἐρινύες. They are avenging deities, but also restorers of order. In Heraclitus, Fr. 122, both aspects are implied.

esti: ἐστί: [it] *is.* Its predicative use ("is so-and-so") and its existential use ("exists") are not clearly distinguished in most of the early instances where the word occurs.

genesis: γένεσις. Two meanings merge: *relative becoming,* as when something that was warm becomes cool; and *absolute becoming,* as when something that did not formerly exist begins to exist. Since the latter meaning is dominant in most of the instances considered, the word is here usually translated "coming-to-be." *Genetai* (γένεται), third person singular of the verb, carries the same ambiguity.

gnômôn: γνώμων: the *gnomon* or *index* of the sundial; also the carpenter's L-shaped *ruler.* The latter, with certain connotations drawn from the former, was held in special esteem by the Pythagoreans, as the instrument by which square and oblong numbers can be built up geometrically: cf. note to T 11, Chap. 7.

gnôsis: γνῶσις: knowledge.

Haidês: Ἀΐδης: the *hidden place* under the earth; *Hades;* sometimes the god of that place.

harmonia: ἁρμονία. Derived from ἁρμόζω ("fit together") the word's original meaning was *adjustment.* Gradually it came to connote the pleasing adjustment of musical combinations—something between our notion of harmony and melody. Also, human and cosmological *concord.*

Hermês: Ἑρμῆς: Hermes, messenger of the gods, roughly equivalent to Latin Mercury. As Hermes Psychopompos he was the guide of newly deceased spirits to Hades.

hybris: ὕβρις: *overbearing pride, arrogance*—as distinguished from aristocratic pride. It was conceived as the kind of pride that leads to disaster, whether by nature or by divine agency or both.

hyle: ὕλη: *matter.* Originally it meant wood, hence (in Homer) timber for the building of ships, hence any stuff or material from which something can be made.

hypokeimenon: ὑποκείμενον: that which underlies; *underlying substance.*

hypothesis: ὑπόθεσις: *presupposition, postulate.* (Not "hypothesis" in the modern sense.)

idea: ἰδέα: (1) a *species,* or *kind,* together with its special characteristics; (2) virtually synonymous with *eidos.*

kairos: καιρός: *opportune moment,* the right or *propitious moment.* Human time, as distinguished from the abstract concept of time, is not homogeneous but is marked by moments of greater or less significance, both experientially and practically.

kalos: καλός: *beautiful, excellent.* A word of highest praise.

katharsis, katharmos: κάθαρσις, καθαρμός: *cleansing, purification.* In medicine (the latter form of the word being preferred by Hippocratic writers, since the former had a religious import) it refers to a discharge of superfluous substances or "humors" (*chymoi*) from the body. In religious context, *purification from guilt, atonement.* Later developing meanings of the word, under the influence of Aristotle's *Poetics,* are discussed in the article "Catharsis" in the *Encyclopedia for Poetry and Poetics* (Princeton, 1965).

kinêsis: κίνησις: *motion, change.* Not exclusively spatial, it includes also qualitative change and the biological activity of growth and decay.

klepsydra: κλεψύδρα. "A water-clock, or earthenware vessel filled with a certain measure of water and having a hole in the bottom of a size to ensure the water running away within a definite limit of time."—Oskar Seyffert, *Dictionary of Classical Antiquities.*

koinos: κοινός: *common, shared.* Cf. *xynos.*

korê, kourê: κόρη, κούρη: *maiden.* Sometimes maiden-goddess, especially Persephone.

kosmos: κόσμος. Two meanings: (1) *order,* especially the ordered *universe;* (2) *jewelled ornament,* a woman's adornment.

krasis: κρᾶσις: a *blending.* In Hippocratic medicine it applies to the new blending of elements that marks the restoration of health.

kykeôn: κυκεών: a sacrificial mixed drink for religious ceremonies, consisting of barley-meal, grated cheese, and wine.

Kypris: Κύπρις: a name for Aphrodite, to whom there was a temple on the island of Cyprus.

logos: λόγος: *word, proposition; meaning.* In religious context it may refer to the divine Word, conferring both wisdom and spiritual direction. He whose speech (*logos*) speaks forth the divine *Logos* is a *prophêtês* (q.v.).

mathêma: μάθημα: *learning, what is learnt.*

mathêmatikos: μαθηματικός. Derived from the preceding word; whence it means (1) *disposed to learn;* then (2) a *scientist,* a *scholar.* (3) In Pythagorean theory the *mathematikos* number is conceived geometrically, as distinguished from the *arithmetikos* number.

methexis: μέθεξις: *participation*. Employed by Plato for the relation of particular objects to the appropriate *eidos* or *idea*.

metron: μέτρον: (1) a *measuring instrument;* (2) *proper measure, proportion*.

mimêsis: μίμησις: *imitation, representation*. Like *methexis*, whose meaning it complements, it is employed by Plato with reference to the relation between universals and subsumed particulars.

Moira: Μοῖρα. Originally it meant (1) *part,* as opposed to the whole; then (2) one's part in life, hence *fate, destiny*. (3) Personified, Moira is the goddess of destiny.

neikos: νεῖκος: *strife*.

noêma: νόημα: a *thought*.

nomos: νόμος: *custom, convention;* a received body of opinions as imposing an unwritten law.

nous: νοῦς: *mind*. When the actual operation of mind is meant, the cognate form *noêsis* is employed.

nyx: νύξ: *night*. When personified, Nyx is the goddess of night, and according to Hesiod was the daughter of Chaos.

Olympus: Ὄλυμπος or Οὔλυμπος. A mountain near the Macedonian border, whose peak juts above the cloudy *aer* into the bright and pure *aether;* in early mythic tales it was the dwelling-place of the ouranian deities, who then gradually came to be regarded as inhabiting the sky.

omphalos: ὀμφαλός. In anatomical context it refers to the navel; in geographical and religious contexts it refers to the great Omphalos at Delphi, which was believed to mark the central point of the earth. The connection between the two meanings is shown by the Latin translation, *umbilicus*. As the new-born babe is attached to its mother by an umbilical cord at the navel, so the race of

men was believed to be attached, through the earth's navel
(physically indicated by a supposedly bottomless pit from
which mephitic gases were emitted), to the undesignated
maternal-like forces below.

on: ὄν. The simplest noun-form made from the verb "to be"
(εἶναι), hence in meaning it is the most abstract of all
words. Cf. *esti*.

ouranos: οὐρανός: the *vault of heaven,* the *visible universe,*
the *sky,* in a more comprehensive sense than *aether.* Personified, Ouranos is the grandfather of Zeus.

ousia: οὐσία. Another derivative from the verb "to be," but
with more specificity of reference than *on*. It is the *essence*
of whatever is in question, whether in its individuality or
with respect to its definition and class-affiliation. In some
instances it can be translated *substance* (cf. *hypokeimenon*); in a few it is roughly synonymous with *hylê*.

paideia: παιδεία. By derivation it means the training of a
child (*paid-*), but it comes to mean something close to
what we might describe as a *cultural education,* conceived
as the education of a youth toward responsible and accomplished manhood.

palmos: παλμός: *vibration, pulsation.*

pathos: πάθος: *feeling, emotion.* More broadly it may refer
to whatever befalls one in so far as he receives it passively,
but usually with some implication of emotional effect. It
may even mean *pain,* a pain in which the emotions are
involved—as in the traditional adage, *pathei mathos* (πάθει
μάθος), "[man is] taught by suffering."

pepsis: πέψις. In Hippocratic medicine it means *digestion.*
This is part of a broader meaning which includes the
ripening of fruit, the cooking of food, and the fermenta-
tion and ageing of wine. It is the process whereby a new
blending (*krasis*) results.

phaos: φάος: *light.*

philia: φιλία: *friendship, love.* Variant form in Empedocles: *philotes* (φιλότης).

phthora: φθορά: *destruction; annihilation, ceasing-to-be.* In general it refers to destruction by natural means, with no agency implied. Metaphysically, a ceasing-to-be in the absolute sense, of passing from being into nothingness. E.g., when a light is extinguished, the light that was has ceased to exist; when a man dies, the living man has ceased to exist.

physis: φύσις. Derived from the verb *phyo* (φύω), "grow," it means the *nature* of anything but usually with a quasibiological connotation of growth, or potential growth. The adjective that is derived from it, *physikos* (φυσικός), when employed as a noun means an inquirer into nature —at once a natural scientist and a naturalistic philosopher.

pneuma: πνεῦμα: (1) *wind, breeze,* air in motion; (2) the *spirit* of man; (3) occasionally (but mainly in later times) a spiritual force affecting man from without.

polemos: πόλεμος: *battle, war.*

polis: πόλις: *city-state.* I.e., a Greek city having political autonomy.

prophêtês: προφήτης. Because of the double meaning of *pro-* in Greek as in Latin compounds, the word can mean either he who *fore*tells the future or he who speaks *on behalf* of a higher authority. The two meaings are frequently blended.

pseudo-: ψευδο-: *false; falsely ascribed to.* A name such as "pseudo-Aristotle" or "pseudo-Plutarch" is attached to documents that have traditionally but wrongly been attributed to the writer mentioned.

psyche: ψυχή: *soul.*

rhêtorikê: ῥητορική. The feminine form of the adjective (with *technê* understood) is employed as a noun, to mean the *art of oratory.* Since planned composition was an essential part of Greek oratory, the word is often translated *"rhetoric."*

rhiza: ῥίζα: *root.* In Empedoclean philosophy the related plural *rhizomata* (ῥιζώματα) is employed as a cosmological metaphor to mean the *roots of existence.*

rhythmos: ῥυθμός (Ionian form, ῥυσμός): (1) a regular *vibratory motion;* (2) *symmetry;* (3) a *state* or *condition* of a thing. The atomists' use of the word combines meanings (1) and (3).

schêma: σχῆμα: *shape, form.*

sêma: σῆμα: (1) a *sign;* (2) a *grave.* The two meanings are connected through the ancient custom of using a sign to mark the grave of a dead person.

sêmaino: σημαίνω (verb): *show by sign, indicate, mean.*

skotios: σκότιος: *dark.*

sôma: σῶμα: the human *body.*

sophia: σοφία: *wisdom.*

sophistês: σοφιστής. By derviation it would mean something like an expert in wisdom—a self-contradictory idea, as Socrates never tired of pointing out.

sperma: σπέρμα: *seed.*

stephanê: στεφάνη: a *crown.* Literally, anything that encircles (στεφ-) the head. Hence applied also to a wreath or chaplet of leaves or flowers, and to a constellation of stars.

stoicheion: στοιχεῖον: an *elementary part* of anything.

strômata: στρώματα (plural of στρῶμα). From its homely semantic role of denoting mattresses and bedclothes the plural form came to be used as the title of certain writings of a doxographical character. An approximate translation then is *miscellanies.*

symbolon: σύμβολον. An early meaning of the word was *pledge* or *token*—as when two contracting parties would break a coin or a ring or a bone between them, so that the shape of the break would identify the pieces to be joined. Hence the word came to mean *symbol,* mainly in the sense of an outward sign for a hidden meaning or abstract conception.

synkrinô: συγκρίνω (verb): *put together, compound.* Sometimes it carries the idea also of a previous separation from other matter. The corresponding noun is *synkrisis* (σύγκρισις). Cf. *diakrisis.*

taxis: τάξις. Concretely it may mean the battle array of an army; abstractly, an *ordered arrangement,* sometimes implying a linear arrangement.

technê: τέχνη. Combines the meanings of an *art* and a *technique,* involving both a knowledge of the relevant principles and an ability to achieve the appropriate results.

teleutê: τελευτή: (1) *accomplishment;* (2) *termination, death.*

telos: τέλος: the *end* toward which an action or a process moves, whether by nature or by purposed artifice.

tetraktys: τετρακτύς. In Pythagorean theory, the triangular figure based on the number 4. Cf. p. 204.

thanatos: θάνατος: *death.* The negative adjective *athanatos* (ἀθάνατος), "immortal," was a common epithet for the Olympian gods.

themis: θέμις: *established right*—i.e., what is established by custom rather than by statute. When personified Themis is the goddess of law and order.

theôria: θεωρία: *rational contemplation.*

theos: θεός: *god.* Employed both in the comprehensive sense,

where in English we would employ a capital, and as referring to one god among others. The feminine *thea* (θεά)
means *goddess*.

thesis: θέσις: (1) *position, situation;* (2) *thesis* of an argument
—i.e., a proposition to be proved.

thespis: θέσπις (adj.): *inspired,* i.e., filled with divine spirit
and power.

tisis: τίσις: *recompense, revenge.*

tropê: τροπή: a *turning around;* hence a *trope*—i.e., any twist-
ing of the meaning of a word or phrase so as to produce an
unusual meaning, as in metaphor.

tyrannos: τύραννος: (1) *king, lord, sovereign;* (2) *usurper.*
Those who won absolute power in a *polis* by overthrow-
ing its previously existing government were called *tyran-
noi,* irrespective of whether beneficent or evil.

tychê: τύχη: *luck, chance.* That which, in a situation that has
some bearing upon human beings, occurs unpurposed and
unforeseen.

xynos: ξυνός: *common, shared.* An older synonym of *koinos.*
Since the dative is *xynôi* (ξυνῷ) it enables Heraclitus to
make his pun between this dative form and the expression *xyn nôi* (ξὺν νῷ), "with mind," "rationally." Cf. the
note to Chapter 3, Fr. 81.

Zeus: Ζεύς. In classical times he was the father of the Olympian gods; Homer calls him "father of gods and men."
The connotative meaning of the word is "bright sky" (as
distinguished from that of *Ouranos,* "vast, all-embracing
sky"). But Zeus is also the lord of rain and storms: by the
spermatic power of his rain he impregnates the earth. In
prayer (in localities where there was a Zeus cult) he would
be addressed in the vocative as "Father Zeus," *Zeu pater*
(Ζεῦ πατήρ), which is etymologically parallel to the Latin
Ju-piter.

INDEX